D0482611

RC
669
.C288
1993

Blascovich, James
J., ed.
CARDIOVASCULAR
REACTIVITY TO
PSYCHOLOGICAL STRESS

03999

LIBRARY
Argosy University
San Francisco Bay Area
1005 Atlantic Ave.
Alameda, CA 94501

L

18

CARDIOVASCULAR REACTIVITY
to Psychological Stress & Disease

CARDIOVASCULAR REACTIVITY
to Psychological Stress & Disease

EDITED BY
Jim Blascovich
AND
Edward S. Katkin

LIBRARY
Argosy University
San Francisco Bay Area
1005 Atlantic Ave.
Alameda, CA 94501

AMERICAN PSYCHOLOGICAL ASSOCIATION
Washington, DC

03999

Copyright © 1993 by the American Psychological Association. All
rights reserved. Except as permitted under the United States
Copyright Act of 1976, no part of this publication may be reproduced
or distributed in any form or by any means, or stored in a database
or retrieval system, without the prior written permission of the
publisher.

Published by the
American Psychological Association
750 First Street, NE
Washington, DC 20002

Copies may be ordered from
APA Order Department
P.O. Box 2710
Hyattsville, MD 20784

Typeset in Century Book by Techna Type, Inc., York, PA

Printer: Braun-Brumfield, Inc., Ann Arbor, MI
Cover and Jacket Designer: Donya Melanson Associates, Boston, MA
Technical/Production Editor: Mark A. Meschter

Library of Congress Cataloging-in-Publication Data

Cardiovascular reactivity to psychological stress and disease / edited
    by James J. Blascovich and Edward S. Katkin.
        p.   cm.
    Includes bibliographical references and index.
    ISBN 1-55798-192-2 (acid-free paper)
    1. Cardiovascular system—Diseases—Psychosomatic aspects—
Congresses.   2. Stress (Psychology)—Congresses.   3. Cardiovascular
system—Diseases—Risk factors—Congresses.   4. Coronary Disease—
complications—congresses.   I. Blascovich, James J.   II. Katkin,
Edward S.
    [DNLM: 1. Cardiovascular System—physiology—congresses.
2. Hypertension—complications—congresses.   3. Psychological—
complications—congresses.   WG 300 C267875 1993]
RC669.C288   1993
616.108—dc20
DLC
for Library of Congress   92-48401
                                               CIP

Printed in the United States of America
First Edition

APA Science Volumes

A PA expects to publish volumes on the following conference topics:

The Contributions of Psychology to Mathematics and Science Education
Emotion and Culture
Maintaining and Promoting Integrity in Behavioral Science Research
Sleep Onset: Normal and Abnormal Processes
Stereotypes: Brain–Behavior Relationships
Temperament: Individual Differences in Biology and Behavior
Women's Psychological and Physical Health

As part of its continuing and expanding commitment to enhance the dissemination of scientific psychological knowledge, the Science Directorate of the APA established a Scientific Conferences Program. A series of volumes resulting from these conferences is jointly produced by the Science Directorate and the Office of Communications. A call for proposals is issued several times annually by the Science Directorate, which, collaboratively with the APA Board of Scientific Affairs, evaluates the proposals and selects several conferences for funding. This important effort has resulted in an exceptional series of meetings and scholarly volumes, each of which individually has contributed to the dissemination of research and dialogue in these topical areas.

The APA Science Directorate's conferences funding program has supported 24 conferences since its inception in 1988. To date, 17 volumes resulting from conferences have been published.

William C. Howell, PhD
Executive Director

Virginia E. Holt
Scientific Conferences Manager

Contents

Contributors

Norman B. Anderson, Department of Psychiatry, Duke University Medical Center and Geriatric Research, Education, and Clinical Center, Veterans Affairs Medical Center, Durham, NC

Jim Blascovich, Department of Psychology and the Center for the Study of Behavioral and Social Aspects of Health, State University of New York at Buffalo

John W. Burns, Department of Psychology, Chicago Medical School

John J. Furedy, Department of Psychology, University of Toronto

Thomas W. Kamarck, Behavioral Physiology Laboratory, University of Pittsburgh

Jay R. Kaplan, Department of Comparative Medicine and the Comparative Medicine Clinical Research Center, Bowman Gray School of Medicine

Alfred S. Kasprowicz, Behavioral Physiology Laboratory, University of Pittsburgh

Edward S. Katkin, Department of Psychology, State University of New York at Stony Brook

David S. Kayden, Nuclear Cardiology, North Shore University Hospital, Manhasset, NY

Robert M. Kelsey, Department of Psychology, University of North Texas

Stephen B. Manuck, Department of Psychology and Western Psychiatric Institute, University of Pittsburgh

Maya McNeilly, Department of Psychiatry, Duke University Medical Center and Geriatric Research, Education, and Clinical Center, Veterans Affairs Medical Center, Durham, NC

Hector Myers, Biobehavioral Laboratory, Department of Psychiatry, University of California at Los Angeles

Patrice G. Saab, Department of Psychology, University of Miami

Neil Schneiderman, Department of Psychology, University of Miami

Andrew Sherwood, Department of Psychiatry, University of North Carolina at Chapel Hill

William Strawn, Department of Comparative Medicine and the Comparative Medicine Clinical Research Center, Bowman Gray School of Medicine

Shari R. Waldstein, Behavioral Physiology Laboratory, University of Pittsburgh

J. Koudy Williams, Department of Comparative Medicine and the Comparative Medicine Clinical Research Center, Bowman Gray School of Medicine

Preface

The purpose of this book is to evaluate the evidence concerning the so-called cardiovascular reactivity hypothesis. In its simplest form,[1] this hypothesis states that excess cardiovascular reactivity to psychological stress may constitute a risk factor for cardiovascular disease. Such a simple presentation of the hypothesis obviously demands further definition. What, precisely, do we mean when we speak of cardiovascular reactivity? What is properly considered "excess" reactivity? What is psychological stress, and is there a reliable relationship between stress and cardiovascular reactivity? Finally, a myriad of questions may be asked about the pathophysiological mechanisms that mediate the relationship between excess cardiovascular reactivity and its presumed endpoint, cardiovascular disease.

The 10 chapters that follow represent the contributions of leading scholars in the field, all of whom met to present and evaluate the evidence at a conference held in Buffalo, New York, in the spring of 1991. From a historical point of view, this conference may be seen as the third such conference of leading experts in cardiovascular psychophysiology and behavioral medicine to be held in the past 20 years. The first conference,[2] which was held in Chapel Hill, North Carolina, in 1972, focused almost exclusively on basic problems in cardiovascular psychophysiology and devoted considerable attention to formulating methodological definitions for the emerging field. The second conference[3] was held in Pittsburgh in 1984 and focused primarily on stress, cardiovascular reactivity, and disease. The Pittsburgh conference or-

---

[1]Krantz, D. S., & Manuck, S. B. (1984). Acute psychophysiologic reactivity and risk of cardiovascular disease: A review and methodologic critique. *Psychological Bulletin, 96*, 435–464.
[2]Obrist, P. A., Black, A. H., Brener, J., & DiCara, L. V. (Eds.). (1974). *Cardiovascular psychophysiology: Current issues in response mechanisms, biofeedback and methodology.* Chicago: Aldine.
[3]Matthews, K. A., Weiss, S. M., Detre, T., Dembroski, T. M., Falkner, B., Manuck, S. B., & Williams, R. (Eds.). (1986). *Handbook of stress, reactivity and cardiovascular disease.* New York: Wiley.

ganizers stipulated that their aim was to clarify the state of the art with respect to four basic issues: (a) the state of basic science in the evaluation of stress and cardiovascular disease, (b) the relationship of stress-induced hyperreactivity to cardiovascular disease, (c) the establishment of standards of measurement of cardiovascular reactivity, and (d) the establishment of a consensus on the critical variables to be subjected to research scrutiny.

The Buffalo conference of 1991 shared goals with both of the earlier conferences. On the basis of the great success and heuristic impact of the two previous conferences, however, we believed that it was time to determine whether the past 20 years of more refined studies have fulfilled the promise of linking cardiovascular reactivity to disease states. In short, we set out to discover if we have any more certainty now than we had 20 years ago about the utility of the cardiovascular reactivity hypothesis as a predictor of cardiovascular disease. Three broad aims were established to guide the participants in the conference and, ultimately, to help organize this book: (a) to reexamine the conceptual, theoretical, and methodological basis for linking cardiovascular reactivity to disease; (b) to assess the current status of scientific research linking reactivity to disease; and (c) to propose an agenda for future research.

To achieve these aims, a number of conceptual and methodological questions were addressed. Some were answered clearly, some were left unresolved, and some were set aside for future research. First, we must define *excess reactivity*. For instance, can we define *hyperreactivity* as a statistically reliable deviation from baseline, or is it essential that reactivity be defined as a clinically significant departure from baseline? If the latter is implied, then do we have appropriate criteria for determining clinically significant responses?

A second, equally important question is as follows: What is the relationship between laboratory assessments of cardiovascular reactivity and reactivity in vivo? The answer to this question, of course, will vary as a function of the definition of *reactivity* that is used by an investigator. A subsidiary question to explore is whether there is adequate technological sophistication to allow reliable measurement of reactivity in the field.

To what extent are the results of laboratory investigations of reactivity task specific? And to the extent that they are, how valid are the laboratory tasks as analogues of in vivo life stress? This question also focuses attention on the issue of habituation of reactivity to repeated stress. For instance, it may be found that some stressors, presumed to have good construct validity as representative of in vivo stress, elicit substantial cardiovascular reactivity in the laboratory. Yet, it may be that repeated exposure to this class of stressors in the field results in habituation of the reactivity, thereby reducing the potency of this stress both as an elicitor of reactivity and as a risk factor for disease. To what extent have laboratory studies examined habituation and the related issue of the potential for habituation effects in the natural environment where people may be chronically subjected to certain specific stressors?

Another fundamental question to be addressed concerns the underlying mechanisms by which reactivity becomes a risk factor. What is the current status of evidence for the "hyperperfusion" model that was the cornerstone of Obrist's[4] seminal research program? Does increased reactivity cause arterial damage because of stress and/or turbulence in the coronary arteries? If so, then what is the nature of the evidence that such arterial stress can be psychologically induced? Associated with the focus on pathophysiological mechanisms is the question of the relative importance of central nervous system integration of autonomic responses in the development of disease. That is, how much of our research attention should be focused on peripheral reflex autoregulation (as implied by the hyperperfusion model), and how much should be addressed to understanding centrally mediated increases in sympathetic tone elicited by individual traits?

Is cardiovascular reactivity a unidimensional or a multidimensional variable? How much can we say with confidence about the role of hemodynamic patterning in response to stress, and is there any evidence that different patterns of reactivity pose different levels of risk for different components of cardiovascular disease?

With respect to mediating pathophysiological models, do appropriate methods exist to assess the neurohumoral and hemodynamic variables that come into play when cardiovascular reactivity is psychologically induced? An essential component of any evaluation of the utility of methods must also include attention to the reliability of those methods over time.

---

[4]Obrist, P. A. (1981). *Cardiovascular psychophysiology: A perspective.* New York: Plenum.

The available methods have increased significantly since the first conference on cardiovascular psychophysiology in 1972. We must now ask which methods are most appropriate for evaluating the risk factor inherent in cardiovascular reactivity. Do we have appropriate methods for noninvasive assessments of inotropic as well as chronotropic parameters of myocardial performance? What about vascular reactivity and its interaction, if any, with myocardial performance? Are our currently used methods, including impedance cardiography and nuclear ventriculography, adequate for assessing complex aspects of myocardial performance?

Finally, we must address the question of what, if anything, remains of the utility of the personality trait–disease link. During the past decade there has been a general trend toward discounting the importance of the so-called global type A personality factor as a predictor of heart disease. Instead, most investigators in this area are searching for the "toxic" component of personality traits, focusing to a large extent on hostility, anger, and their associated states. To some extent, most such studies have used cardiovascular reactivity as a mediating link between personality and disease, assuming that individual differences in one trait or another may reliably predict differing degrees of cardiovascular reactivity to specific elicitors. To that extent, these investigators have contributed to the continuing, and expanding, interest in cardiovascular reactivity as a risk factor. Furthermore, they have leaned on measures of reactivity as validators of the utility of the presumed toxic personality trait.

If nothing else, the examination of correlations between personality traits and disease incidence may be quite heuristic as a way of defining a subpopulation of subjects at high risk for disease. This subpopulation may then be an ideal group for further experimental investigation of the link between stress and cardiovascular reactivity. Of course, it may be observed that the continued use of cardiovascular reactivity as a validation of the utility of certain personality-based risk factors will be a dead end unless we can be certain that cardiovascular reactivity is indeed a risk factor itself. The exciting research reports contained in this book make a substantial case for the validity of that hypothesis.

In addition to our indebtedness to the authors of the chapters in this book, many other individuals deserve thanks for the implementation of the conference and the production of this book. The attendees at the Buffalo, New York, conference are to be acknowledged for their active participation in the conference and for their useful input to the many contributors to this book. Christa Greenberg, who provided clerical services throughout as well as coordinating the meeting logistics, especially deserves our thanks.

We are indebted for funding to the Science Directorate of the American Psychological Association. Additional funding was provided by the Conferences in the Disciplines Program at the State University of New York at Buffalo, the Center for the Study of Behavioral and Social Aspects of Health at the State University of New York at Buffalo, and the Vice Provost for Research at the State University of New York at Stony Brook.

Jim Blascovich
Edward S. Katkin

PART ONE

Reactivity and Coronary Heart Disease

Psychosocial Influences on Atherosclerosis: Evidence for Effects and Mechanisms in Nonhuman Primates

Jay R. Kaplan, Stephen B. Manuck, J. Koudy Williams, and William Strawn

Psychosocial factors are often implicated in the pathogenesis of human atherosclerosis and coronary heart disease (CHD) (Dembroski, MacDougall, Costa, & Grandits, 1989; Friedman et al., 1984; Manuck, Kaplan, & Matthews, 1986; Olsson & Rehnqvist, 1982). Surveys and experimental manipulations of animal models have provided comparable data and indicate that environmental perturbations and individual behavioral characteristics potentiate atherogenesis and, occasionally, manifestations of CHD (Ely, 1981; Henry et al., 1971; Henry & Stephens, 1977; Kaplan, Manuck, Clarkson, & Prichard, 1985; Lang, 1967; Ratcliffe & Cronin, 1958; Ratcliffe, Luginbuhl, Schnarr, & Chacko, 1969; Ratcliffe, Yerasimides, & Elliot, 1960). There is, however, a relative paucity of publications demonstrating clear links between behavioral factors and pathophysiological

This research was supported, in part, by National Institutes of Health grants HL14164, HL26561, HL40962, and HL45666; RJR Industries, Inc.; and Astra-Hässle AB. We thank Karen Potvin Klein for her editorial contributions.

mechanisms or events. In this chapter, we summarize the results of several studies that evaluated the behavioral, physiological, and morphological responses of monkeys to benign and socially challenging environments. These results support three conclusions: (a) Psychosocial factors influence atherosclerosis and impair vascular responsiveness in monkeys, two processes that contribute to the development and expression of CHD in humans; (b) clear analogies exist between the psychosocial factors that potentiate atherogenesis and vascular dysfunction in monkeys and those that are believed to influence the development of CHD in humans; and (c) recurrent activation of the sympathetic nervous system is likely the common pathway mediating the influence of various psychosocial factors on vascular abnormalities and CHD in monkeys and, hence, possibly also in humans.

Background to the Studies

Atherosclerosis

Our investigations focused on atherosclerosis, which refers to both the development of fibrofatty plaques (atheromas) within the inner lining or intima of arteries and a stiffening (sclerosis) of the artery wall (Blankenhorn & Kramsch, 1989). As atherosclerosis progresses, plaques frequently change in composition as well as size and are often characterized by calcification and, later, by ulceration and hemorrhage. Moreover, the affected arteries develop abnormalities in vasomotor responses to hemodynamic and metabolic stimuli. In the coronary arteries of humans, the enlargement and complication of atherosclerotic plaques and concomitant functional aberrations often culminate in CHD and heart attack; similar obstructions and abnormalities in the head and neck may result in stroke, whereas blockages in the legs result in intermittent claudication.

Characteristics of the Animal Model

Studies of atherosclerosis and CHD in humans are inherently limited in at least three ways: (a) cost, (b) the fact that atherogenesis proceeds for decades before signs of disease emerge, and (c) the impossibility of applying invasive techniques to asymptomatic individuals. An obvious alternative research strategy is the use of an appropriate animal model. We have found the cynomolgus macaque (*Macaca fascicularis*) to be suitable for this purpose. These animals, when fed a diet suitably high in saturated fat and cholesterol (i.e., similar to the diet consumed by many humans), develop atherosclerosis relatively rapidly (Kaplan et al., 1985). Moreover, the pathological characteristics of their vasomotor abnormalities and atherosclerotic lesions resemble those of humans. These macaques, like humans, also have a relatively high frequency of myocardial infarction (Bond, Bullock, Bellinger, & Hamm, 1980; Williams, Vita, Selwyn, Manuck, & Kaplan, 1991). Similar to humans, premenopausal female macaques are relatively protected from atherosclerosis compared with similarly treated males (Kaplan et al., 1985).

Importantly, these group-living animals are characterized, in the wild, by complex patterns of social interaction and generation-spanning networks of affiliation, alliance, and mutual support (aspects of behavior frequently thought to play a role in the psychosocial "defense" against atherosclerosis and CHD in humans; Fleagle, 1988; Sade, 1972; Stout, Morrow, Brandt, & Wolf, 1964). The typical patterns of monkey social behavior are, in general, reminiscent of those observed in humans. Even the monkeys' outward expression of social behavior (both agonistic and affiliative) depends on postures and facial expressions that are demonstrably homologous with those of humans (Eibl-Eibesfeldt, 1970; Kaplan et al., 1985; Sade, 1973). Of particular interest to our research, the characteristic natural behavior of monkeys readily accommodates to experimental manipulation. Within their social groups, for example, cynomolgus macaques form hierarchies of social status in which some animals (*dominants*) habitually and predictably defeat others (*subordinates*) in competitive interactions (Sade, 1967). In our studies, we used the predilection of monkeys to form status hierarchies as a means of objectively categorizing individual animals as either customarily aggressive (dominants) or passive (subordinates) in their responses to exogenous challenge and stimulation. Another experimentally useful attribute of male cynomolgus macaques is their predisposition to respond aggressively to new animals attempting to join their social groupings; such newcomers, in the wild and in captivity, are treated as intruders and a threat to the prevailing social structure (Bernstein, Gordon, & Rose, 1974). The disruptive influence of strangers on social relationships within groups provides the basis for an ecologically valid behavioral challenge and one that was used in many of our studies, namely, the periodic reorganization of social group memberships.

The first studies that were done in our laboratory were designed to demonstrate that behavioral factors could influence atherosclerosis. These studies were "naturalistic" in that the experimental paradigms exploited the animals' naturally occurring behaviors and patterns of response. It was only after completion of these first studies that we designed manipulations to test explicitly hypotheses regarding the mechanisms by which psychosocial factors might potentiate atherogenesis. All of these studies were done using adult male monkeys.[1]

Naturalistic Manipulations

Exacerbation of Atherosclerosis Related to Social Status and Social Disruption

Our first study contained 30 animals; of these, 15 monkeys were each assigned to one of three 5-member social groups (Kaplan et al., 1983). These animals were designated "unstable" and were regularly redistributed among the three groups at 1–3-month intervals on a schedule that ensured that each monkey would be housed with 3 or 4 new animals at every reorganization. An additional 15 animals were designated "stable" and assigned to 5-member social groups of unchanging composition. Animals in the unstable and stable groups were treated identically in all other ways. All animals consumed an atherogenic diet, which was designed to mimic that typically consumed by North Americans. The monkeys were also evaluated routinely for those clinical characteristics that are often associated with atherosclerosis and coronary heart disease (total plasma cholesterol [TPC], high-density lipoprotein cholesterol [HDLC],

---

[1]Our laboratory has done a similar series of investigations using female macaques. We found in these studies that behavioral factors did influence atherogenesis; the results, however, differed from those observed among males in that the effects in females were complicated by interactions with ovarian function. The outcomes of studies that involved female monkeys have been previously described (Kaplan, Clarkson, Adams, Manuck, & Shively, 1991).

blood pressure, body size, carbohydrate metabolism). Finally, routine behavioral observations were made of all animals, which allowed us to evaluate the rate and pattern of affiliative and agonistic interaction as well as the social status of each monkey.

The study lasted 22 months, during which time dominant and subordinate animals in the unstable social condition engaged in more extreme forms of aggression or submission and displayed a different pattern of affiliation than did their counterparts in the stable groupings (indicating the stressful nature of the manipulation). At the end of the study, the coronary arteries were removed, and the extent of coronary artery atherosclerosis was measured in each animal (in square millimeters, as the average lesion size in 15 sections taken perpendicularly to the long axis of the arteries). Coronary artery atherosclerosis was analyzed according to the social status (dominant vs. subordinate) and social condition (stable vs. unstable) of each animal (Figure 1). This analysis revealed that dominant monkeys in unstable social groupings had more extensive atherosclerosis than did monkeys in the three other groupings ($p < .05$). Thus, dominant monkeys were predisposed to develop exacerbated coronary atherosclerosis but only under conditions of social instability.

Importantly, the results of this study were independent of concomitant variability in TPC, HDLC, and blood pressure, but the effects were not wholly dependent on the consumption of an atherogenic diet. We then repeated the initial study with 30 other monkeys but substituted a diet based on the recommendations of the American Heart Association (AHA) in place of the high-fat diet that was used in the first study (Kaplan et al., 1983). As a result, TPC averaged 160 mg/dl in this second study compared with an average 470 mg/dl in the first. Thus, atherosclerosis in this study was minimal compared with that observed in the first study. Nonetheless, monkeys assigned to the unstable condition developed significantly more coronary artery atherosclerosis than did animals housed in stable social groups ($Mdns = 0.021$ vs. 0.004 mm^2, $p < .01$). Although dominance relationships fluctuated somewhat in response to the successive group reorganizations (compared with the initial study), those unstable animals that retained dominant status over the course of the study developed more extensive coronary atherosclerosis than did all other

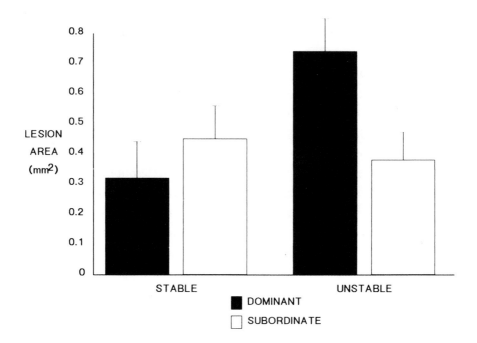

FIGURE 1. Coronary artery artherosclerosis lesion area ($M \pm SE$) averaged across 15 sections in dominant and subordinate adult male monkeys living in stable and unstable social groupings. Dominant animals were significantly more affected than subordinates ($p < .05$) but only in unstable groups; dominant and subordinate monkeys living in stable groups could not be distinguished. From "Social Status, Environment and Atherosclerosis in Cynomolgus Monkeys" by J. R. Kaplan, S. B. Manuck, T. B. Clarkson, F. M. Lusso, and D. M. Taub, 1982, *Arteriosclerosis, 2,* 359–368; copyright 1982 by the American Heart Association; adapted by permission.

study animals ($p < .05$). Hence, social disruption can accelerate atherogenesis even in otherwise well-protected (i.e., normolipemic) animals and does so most appreciably among the more aggressive, dominant monkeys.

Together, the results of these studies demonstrate that a behavioral characteristic, dominant social status, can interact with a stressful social environment to exacerbate coronary artery atherosclerosis in monkeys. The outcome of these first two studies is thus consistent with current hypotheses concerning the role of individual behavioral characteristics (such as type A traits or a high index of hostility/anger) in the development of coronary disease in humans (Manuck et al., 1986). Our data, however, not only suggest that a high degree of antagonism and competitiveness (as observed among dominant monkeys and type A humans) predispose individuals to atherosclerosis and CHD but also suggest that the pathogenicity of these characteristics may require an appropriately challenging or stressful environment to be fully expressed.

Psychosocial Stress and Vascular Responsivity

Coronary artery atherosclerosis was the dependent measure in the two studies just described. The lesions of atherosclerosis, although important in the etiology of CHD, provide little information regarding the functional state of the arteries. Functional abnormalities in coronary arteries are indicative of a predisposition to vasospasm and ischemia, both of which are important aspects of CHD (Maseri, L'Abbate et al., 1978; Maseri, Severi et al., 1978). Endothelium-dependent dilator compounds (such as acetylcholine) can be used in conjunction with cineangiography to evaluate the functional state of the coronary arteries; vessels that constrict or fail to dilate in response to infusion of acetylcholine, for example, can be described as relatively abnormal (Ludmer et al., 1986).

We recently used acetylcholine infusion and cineangiography to evaluate vascular responsivity in the coronary arteries of 27 monkeys that had established atherosclerosis as a result of consuming a high-fat, high-cholesterol diet for 14 months (Williams et al., 1991). After the dietary induction of atherosclerosis, 9 of the animals were housed in unstable (i.e., stressed) social groups and consumed a moderately atherogenic diet. Eight animals were housed in unstable social groups but were fed a diet consistent with the current recommendations of the AHA (i.e., low in saturated fat and cholesterol). The final 10 monkeys were housed in stable social groups and consumed the AHA diet. These 27 animals were part of a larger trial designed to determine whether the presence or absence of social instability could either inhibit or potentiate the regression of atherosclerotic lesions among monkeys consuming a diet based on the recommendations of the AHA. Not surprisingly, the monkeys living in unstable groups and continuing to consume an atherogenic diet had the most extensive coronary lesions. The animals that were fed the AHA diet had smaller lesions, which did not differ between monkeys in the stable and unstable conditions.

We evaluated vascular responses to acetylcholine in coronary arteries of animals in the three treatment groups as well as in a group of 4 control animals (i.e., animals known to have no atherosclerosis; Figure 2). There were no significant differences in arterial response between the control monkeys and those that were housed in stable social groups and that consumed the AHA diet, nor were there differences between monkeys that were housed in the unstable groups, regardless of the diet consumed.

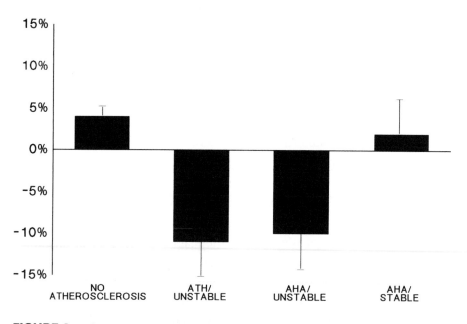

FIGURE 2. Coronary vascular responses ($M \pm SE$) measured as the percentage of change in diameter from control during intracoronary infusion of acetylcholine in monkeys that consumed monkey chow (no atherosclerosis, $n = 6$), that consumed the atherogenic diet (ATH) and were housed in unstable social conditions ($n = 9$), or that consumed the cholesterol-lowering diet (AHA) and were housed in either unstable ($n = 8$) or stable ($n = 10$) social conditions. From "Psychosocial Factors Impair Vascular Responses of Coronary Arteries" by J. K. Williams, J. A. Vita, A. P. Selwyn, S. B. Manuck, and J. R. Kaplan, 1991, Circulation, 84, 2146–2153; copyright 1991 by the American Heart Association; adapted by permission.

The stable and unstable monkeys that consumed the AHA diet did, however, differ significantly in their responses to acetylcholine.

These data indicate that the stress of chronic social instability can induce functional arterial changes that underlie certain clinical expressions of coronary heart disease. Furthermore, three kinds of evidence suggest that this effect is not mediated by differences in lesion extent: (a) Stressed animals that differed greatly in lesion extent (atherogenic–unstable vs. AHA–unstable) exhibited the same relative deficit in dilation, (b) stressed and nonstressed animals that ate the AHA diet and that had lesions of the same size differed significantly in vascular response, and (c) monkeys that consumed the AHA diet and that lived in stable groups (small lesions) displayed the same degree of dilation as did control monkeys (no lesions). Thus, socially disrupted animals (i.e., those living in unstable social groups) were generally characterized by functional abnormalities in the coronary arteries. Unfortunately, the small number of animals that were used in this study precluded a further subdivision of the monkeys for analysis of potential social status effects.

Mechanisms Mediating Behavioral Influences on Atherosclerosis and CHD

Our first three studies provided no evidence regarding the mechanism(s) responsible for either the exacerbation of atherosclerosis among dominant animals housed in a perturbed social environment or the abnormalities in vasomotion occurring among animals living in unstable social groups. The usual risk factors, most notably TPC and HDLC, did not vary as a result of the social manipulation and thus can be eliminated as potential mechanisms for the observed behavioral effects. Similarly, these and other "traditional" risk factors fail to account for the prospective relationships between behavioral characteristics and CHD in studies of humans. A number of investigators have suggested that behaviorally induced, centrally mediated neuroendocrine responses to stress play a role in atherogenesis, if experienced frequently enough or over intervals of sufficient duration (Ablad et al., 1988; Corse, Manuck, Cantwell, Giordani, & Matthews, 1982; Krantz et al., 1981; Schneiderman, 1987). The suggestion by Henry and Stephens (1977) and Ely and Henry (1978) that dominant animals undergo recurrent sympathoadrenal activation when exposed to repeated challenges to their social status may be of particular relevance to the just-described data. Repeated sympathoadrenal arousal could promote arterial injury via hemodynamic (turbulence, shear stress) or metabolic (platelet aggregation, lipolysis) changes associated with the release of catecholamines (Manuck, Muldoon, Kaplan, Adams, & Polefrone, 1989). If such arousal were more generally experienced, the arteries of all animals exposed to a psychosocial perturbation might be affected (as observed with respect to vasomotor abnormalities).

Additional data collected from a subset of 26 male monkeys in the first (i.e., high-fat) study support the speculation that a heightened sympathetic responsivity to behavioral stimuli increases the risk for coronary disease (Manuck, Kaplan, & Clarkson, 1983a). Specifically, we evaluated individual differences in cardiac reactivity to stress in these monkeys on a single occasion just before necropsy. We based our "reactivity" assessments on radiotelemetered heart rate. First, we recorded the baseline heart rates of the monkeys while the animals were in their social groups and during a period of relative quiet, when there were no humans in sight. Heart rate responses to stress then were obtained at the same time on a subsequent day during a standardized challenge in which an experimenter displayed a large monkey catch-glove in a prominent and threatening manner to the target animals. This maneuver was conducted in a stylized manner to mimic encounters that typically precede capture and physical handling of animals.

The standardized stimulus provoked relatively large mean heart rate acceleration across all monkeys (91 beats per minute [bpm]). There was, nonetheless, considerable interindividual variability in baseline-adjusted responsivity. For example, the monkeys in the upper and lower thirds of the overall disposition of heart rate reactions differed by more than 35 bpm in their mean stress-period heart rates ("high" reactors = 236 bpm; "low" reactors = 199 bpm; $p < .001$); the high and low reactors did not differ in their corresponding baseline means (126 vs. 123 bpm, respectively; ns). Interestingly, the heart rates of high and low reactors differed significantly not only in response to deliberate challenge but also on exposure to a more benign manipulation that involved the experimenter's mere appearance in the area where monkeys were housed (M for high reactors = 170; M for low reactors = 118 bpm; $p < .001$) Most notably, the high heart rate reactors had intimal lesions twice as extensive as those seen among their low-reactive counterparts ($p < .04$; Figure 3). High heart rate reactors also had heavier, thicker hearts than did low reactors, which suggests a possible association between the propensity to exhibit heightened heart rate responses to behavioral stimuli and alterations in cardiac morphology (Manuck et al., 1983a).

These heart rate findings, subsequently replicated in female monkeys (Manuck, Kaplan, Adams, & Clarkson, 1989), provide initial support for the hypothesis that an exaggerated cardiac responsivity to behavioral challenge is atherogenic (Manuck, Kaplan, Muldoon, Adams, & Clarkson, 1991). The data do not, however, offer an explanation for the principal psychosocial finding in our first two studies, that is, that atherosclerosis is exacerbated in dominant monkeys living in unstable social groups. This is because these dominant animals were not disproportionately represented among the high heart rate reactors. Furthermore, these data do not bear directly on our observations regarding vasomotor abnormalities (which afflicted stressed monkeys in general). In an attempt to reconcile

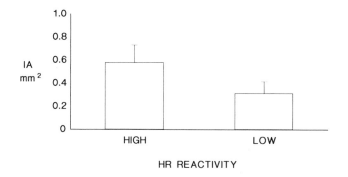

FIGURE 3.   Coronary artery atherosclerosis intimal area (IA; $M \pm SE$) averaged across 15 sections among high and low heart rate (HR) reactors. From "Behaviorally Induced Heart Rate Reactivity and Atherosclerosis in Cynomolgus Monkeys" by S. B. Manuck, J. R. Kaplan, and T. B. Clarkson, 1983, *Psychosomatic Medicine, 45,* 95–108; copyright 1983 by Williams & Wilkins; adapted by permission.

these sets of observations, we proposed that some individuals (e.g., high reactors) may be susceptible to the development of coronary disease because of an intrinsic sympathoadrenal hyperresponsivity to behavioral stimuli; others (e.g., aggressive/dominant individuals in unstable social environments) may be at increased risk because of frequent elicitation of such responses in stressful environments (Manuck, Kaplan, Adams, & Clarkson, 1988; Manuck, Kaplan, & Clarkson, 1983b).[2] The results of our vasomotor study also established the possibility that a particularly stressful environment may overwhelm individual differences, perhaps by potentiating frequent sympathetic arousal and, hence, pathogenesis among all exposed individuals.

Mechanistic Studies

Inhibition of Behaviorally Induced Atherosclerosis in Male Cynomolgus Monkeys

Based on the results of our initial studies, we hypothesized that frequent exposure to psychosocial challenge promotes atherogenesis through associated sympathoadrenal activation (Kaplan, Manuck, Clarkson, Lusso, & Taub, 1982). It follows that administration of a β-adrenergic blocking agent in such circumstances should inhibit the development of atherosclerosis, particularly in behaviorally predisposed (i.e., socially dominant) individuals. We tested this hypothesis in a study that involved 30 male cynomolgus monkeys that were fed a moderately atherogenic diet and housed for 2 years in repeatedly reorganized social groupings (Kaplan, Manuck, Adams, Weingand, & Clarkson, 1987). Half of the monkeys were administered propranolol HCl in their diet (at a human equivalent of 400 mg/day) throughout the study, and the social status of each monkey was assessed on a recurrent basis. Measurements of blood pressure, heart rate, serum lipid concentrations, and social behavior were made repeatedly over the course of the investigation. At the end of the experiment, atherosclerosis extent (in square millimeters) was again evaluated as an average of 15 cross sections of coronary artery from each monkey.

---

[2]Specifically, we have shown that dominant monkeys in unstable social groups demonstrate greater excursions of heart rate than do subordinates in the same setting (Manuck et al., 1991).

Chronic administration of propranolol achieved a significant (20%) reduction in heart rate, along with a comparable lowering of blood pressure, compared with untreated controls. Interestingly, propranolol had no effect on the social behavior of the treated monkeys, nor did the drug affect dominance relationships (Kaplan & Manuck, 1989). Thus, the behavioral attributes associated with a predisposition to atherosclerosis in previous studies (i.e., those comprising dominant social status) were fully expressed in the treated monkeys as well as untreated monkeys. Furthermore, although propranolol on occasion has a deleterious influence on HDLC concentrations in humans, no such effect was observed among the propranolol-treated monkeys in this study.

An evaluation of the coronary arteries revealed that, among untreated monkeys, the more aggressive, or dominant, animals had (as in the parallel condition of our first study) significantly more atherosclerosis than did their subordinate counterparts. In contrast, the atherosclerosis of dominant monkeys that were treated with propranolol did not differ from that of either treated or untreated subordinate monkeys. These results are summarized in Figure 4 and indicate that the exacerbated atherosclerosis that is typically observed among dominant monkeys living in disrupted social groups (Figures 1 and 4) is inhibited by treatment with a β-adrenergic blocking agent. This hypothesis suggests, in turn, that treatment with β-adrenergic blocking agents may confer a degree of protection against coronary artery atherosclerosis among humans that are behaviorally predisposed to CHD (Kaplan et al., 1987).

Notably, the psychosocial and pharmacological effects on coronary atherogenesis shown in Figure 4 were not associated with concomitant variability in serum lipid concentrations, which were equivalent across experimental groupings; nor, as noted earlier, was there any evidence that propranolol selectively affected the behavior, and thereby the atherosclerosis, of dominant monkeys. However, we previously demonstrated that heart rate changes substantially, though transiently, during periods of social reorganization and that these changes are more pronounced in dominant monkeys than in subordinate monkeys (Manuck et al., 1991). To the degree that such substantial alterations in heart rate are indicative of sympathetic arousal, propranolol may have exerted an antiatherogenic

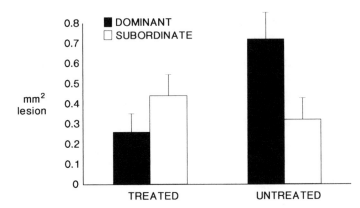

FIGURE 4. Coronary artery atherosclerosis lesion area ($M \pm SE$) averaged across 15 sections among dominant and subordinate monkeys living in unstable social groups and either treated or not treated with propranolol; $n = 6$ for each of the four subgroups. From "Inhibition of Coronary Atherosclerosis by Propranolol in Behaviorally Predisposed Monkeys Fed an Atherogenic Diet" by J. R. Kaplan, S. B. Manuck, M. R. Adams, K. W. Weingand, and T. B. Clarkson, 1987, *Circulation, 76,* 1364–1372; copyright 1987 by the American Heart Association; adapted by permission.

influence in this study by attenuating sympathetic activation in those monkeys that were behaviorally challenged most appreciably by exposure to periodic social reorganization, that is, the dominant monkeys.

Inhibition of Endothelial Injury by Beta Blockade in Stressed Monkeys

Although the previous investigation provided indirect evidence of sympathoadrenal involvement in coronary atherogenesis, the mechanistic link between sympathetic activation and the initiation of atherosclerosis remained unclear. In our next study, we tested the hypothesis that, among other effects, behaviorally evoked sympathetic activation potentiates injury of the arterial endothelium, the protective inner lining of the artery wall (Strawn et al., 1991). Endothelial injury is believed to be the first stage of atherosclerosis because an injured endothelium cannot prevent the movement of lipoproteins from the circulation to the artery wall (Ross, 1986; Schwartz, Gajdusek, & Sheldon, 1981). Moreover, lipid influx to the artery at the site of injury is often accompanied by platelet aggregation and the release of growth factors that further stimulate atherogenesis (Davies, 1986; Schwartz, Campbell, & Campbell, 1986).

The number of monkeys used in this study was relatively small ($n = 20$). We therefore elected to use a stressor that we knew, from previous experience, would uniformly provoke a profound behavioral and sympathetic response, irrespective of individual differences in social status or heart rate reactivity. Also, the animals consumed a diet that resulted in relatively nonatherogenic serum cholesterol concentrations (189 mg/dl). The psychosocial manipulation involved exposure of each of the 20 experimental monkeys, individually, as an intruder to a social group of 4 nonexperimental "host" animals for a period of 3 days. Although all experimental animals were stressed, sympathetic arousal was prevented in half of the individuals by pretreatment with the β-adrenergic blocking agent metoprolol.

As expected, exposure to the psychosocial manipulation caused substantial elevations in heart rate but only among untreated monkeys; animals that were given metoprolol experienced a decline in heart rate. Endothelial injury was evaluated by examining the aortas of all animals for evidence of cellular incorporation of immunoglobulin G (indicative of irreversible injury) and increases in endothelial cell replication (a sign that cells have died and are being replaced); endothelial cell replication was also evaluated in the coronary arteries. In the aorta (Table 1), both indices demonstrated greater endothelial injury in the untreated monkeys compared with treated monkeys but only at branching sites (i.e., locations

TABLE 1

Endothelial Injury (Percentage of Injured Cells) as Measured by Immunoglobulin (IgG) Incorporation and Cell Replication in Branching and Nonbranching Thoracic Aorta Sites of Metoprolol-Treated and Untreated Cynomolgus Macaques Exposed to Social Stress

Measure	Untreated		Treated	
	Branching	Nonbranching	Branching	Nonbranching
IgG incorporation	1.70	0.06	0.70*	0.20
Cell replication	0.42	0.05	0.12*	0.05

*$p < .05$ compared with untreated monkeys.

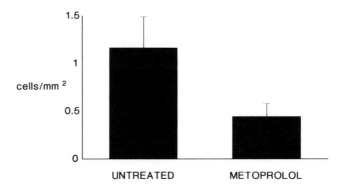

FIGURE 5. Number of endothelial cells per square millimeter ($M \pm SE$) with evidence of replication in the coronary arteries in metaprolol-treated and untreated monkeys. From "Endothelial Dysfunction in Response to Psychosocial Stress in Monkeys" by W. R. Strawn, G. Bondjers, J. R. Kaplan, S. B. Manuck, D. C. Schwenke, G. K. Hansson, C. A. Shively, and T. B. Clarkson, 1991, *Circulation Research, 68,* 1270–1279; copyright 1991 by the American Heart Association; reprinted by permission.

of greatest hemodynamic stress). Similarly, the endothelial cell replication rate was greater in the coronary arteries of untreated animals (Figure 5).

The major result of this study, then, was that acutely stressed monkeys had greater endothelial injury than did comparably treated animals that were administered a beta blocker. Notably, there was a marked elevation of heart rate during the experimental period (in relation to baseline measurements) among untreated monkeys and a concomitant attenuation of heart rate among animals that were treated with metoprolol. This pattern of heart rate changes indicates that the introduction of monkeys to a strange social environment provoked a significant and persistent cardiac response that was probably mediated sympathetically. We concluded from these results that behavioral factors, through sympathetic mediation, can injure the arterial endothelium and thereby initiate atherogenesis even in the absence of hypercholesterolemia.

Discussion

The results presented in the previous sections demonstrate that individual behavioral characteristics and the social environment influence the development of atherosclerotic lesions and vasomotor abnormalities. We obtained these results using an animal model that resembles humans in the characteristics of its atherosclerotic lesions and in aspects of its social behavior (Kaplan et al., 1985). Significantly, the observed behavioral influences on the vasculature occurred at virtually all stages of pathogenesis (endothelial injury; fatty streaks; and established, diet-induced lesions) and affected arterial function as well as structure.

Experimental induction of cardiovascular pathology by behavioral factors, as observed in our investigations, has been reported by a number of other investigators, although using different animal models and experimental paradigms (Henry et al., 1971; Kaplan et al., 1985; Lang, 1967; Ratcliffe et al., 1969). Of equal importance to the demonstration that behavioral factors influence cardiovascular pathological events or disease, however, is an elucidation of the mechanism(s) mediating these effects. Evidence from our own studies supports the hypothesis that recurrent sympathetic activation in response to behavioral stimulation may promote lesion development and/or the clinical sequelae of atherosclerosis. Additional evidence that directly relates behaviorally induced sympathetic arousal to atherogenesis is provided by studies of rats and rabbits. Rats stressed by exposure to tailshock, for example, respond with transient elevations in blood pressure and have endothelial damage similar to that which characterizes early atherogenesis; in contrast, nonstressed controls display no changes in blood pressure and no endothelial injury (Gordon, Guyton, & Karnovsky, 1981). Physical restraint also triggers a large sympathetic nervous system response in rats and causes endothelial injury; importantly, treatment with propranolol during physical restraint prevents sympathetic arousal and inhibits endothelial injury (Hirsch, Maksem, & Gagen, 1984).

Other investigators, using rabbits, have used chloralose anesthesia rather than a behavioral manipulation to obtain a persistent and reproducible sympathetic activation. Infusion of this agent produces a stable and consistent increase in heart rate, blood pressure, and plasma norepinephrine concentration (Ablad et al., 1988; Pettersson & Ablad, 1988; Pettersson, Bejne, Bjork, Strawn, & Bondjers, 1990). Pathological evaluation following infusion reveals that chloralose-treated rabbits have significantly more aortic endothelial damage than do conscious, unanesthetized controls. Importantly, this damage can be prevented by pretreatment with the β-adrenergic blocker metoprolol. These data complement our observation that psychosocially induced sympathetic arousal caused endothelial injury in monkeys, an effect that was similarly blocked by metoprolol. Together, the studies that used rabbits, rats, and monkeys have provided compelling evidence that sympathetic arousal, irrespective of its manner of induction (behavioral or pharmacological) is atherogenic.

The hypothesis that repeated activation of the sympathetic nervous system in response to stressful stimuli promotes atherogenesis and CHD is also supported, albeit indirectly, by four observations in humans: (a) Individuals who are behaviorally predisposed to coronary disease (e.g., those with type A characteristics) have exaggerated cardiovascular and catecholamine responses when they are exposed to frustrating laboratory tasks or other behavioral challenges (Houston, 1986; Wright, Contrada, & Glass, 1985); (b) CHD patients undergo larger pressor reactions to behavioral stressors than do patients without CHD or nonpatient controls (Corse et al., 1982; Dembroski, MacDougall, & Lushene, 1979; Krantz et al., 1981); (c) large blood pressure reactions to the cold pressor test predicted the 23-year incidence of CHD in one prospective study of initially healthy individuals (Keys et al., 1971); and (d) there is a positive association, in dialysis patients, between plasma catecholamine concentrations and the severity of atherosclerotic disease (Hauss, Bauch, & Schulte, 1980).

Finally, the results regarding the experimental induction of atherogenesis via sympathetic activation and its inhibition by β-adrenergic blockade suggest speculations that might be applied in the interpretation of epidemiological studies of humans. For example, beta blockers reduce mortality in post–myocardial infarction patients, an effect that may be mediated, in part, by inhibited lesion progression resulting from attenuated sympathetic stimulation of the heart and consequent reductions in heart rate and in adverse blood-flow patterns in coronary arteries (Fitzgerald, 1987). Inhibited lesion progression may also help explain the reduction in CHD mortality observed among hypertensive individuals treated with a β-adrenergic blocking agent (and who thus experience relative sympathetic inhibition) compared with patients treated with other antihypertensive agents, such as diuretics (Wikstrand et al., 1988). In such studies it follows, perhaps, that β-adrenergic blockade would be most protective for those individuals typically exhibiting the greatest sympathetic arousal—those exposed to especially stressful circumstances or having an inherent sympathetic hyperresponsivity to stress (Rosenman, 1982; Taggart, 1982).

Conclusions

Experimental investigations demonstrate that individual behavioral characteristics (e.g., dominant social status) and aspects of the social environment (e.g., stability of group memberships) influence the development of atherosclerosis and CHD in cynomolgus monkeys. Furthermore, pathogenesis is mediated in this context, perhaps substantially, by the physiological concomitants of sympathetic nervous system activation. We speculate that, because atherogenesis proceeds similarly in cynomolgus monkeys and humans and because these monkeys share many social propensities with humans, the relationship between behavioral factors and atherosclerosis observed in monkeys may extend to humans. This speculation is supported by the observation that CHD in humans has been related to competitiveness and hostility, characteristics that are associated with exacerbated atherosclerosis in cynomolgus monkeys. In addition, the observation that sympathetic arousal potentiates experimental atherosclerosis suggests that β-adrenergic blockade or any other treatment resulting in sympathetic attenuation should be antiatherogenic, particularly for humans who are exposed to stressful circumstances or characterized by sympathetic hyperresponsivity to stress.

It should be noted that the findings presented in this chapter still leave many unanswered questions regarding the behavioral influences on atherogenesis. It is unclear, for example, whether the behavioral considerations and mediating mechanisms identified as atherogenic in cynomolgus monkeys are the only ones relevant for humans. In humans, CHD has also been associated with other factors such as lack of "social support" (Cohen & Matthews, 1987; Cohen & Wills, 1985; Davidson & Shumaker, 1987). Moreover, activation of the hypothalamic pituitary adrenocortical system has been suggested as a mechanism mediating behavioral influences on lesion development (Henry et al., 1971; Henry & Stephens, 1977). Finally, serotonergic mechanisms have recently been identified as contributing to or modulating sympathetic arousal and aggressivity (Saxena & Villalon, 1990). Precise identification of the behavioral potentiators as well as mediating mechanisms for CHD and atherosclerosis is important because this information will determine the most appropriate behavioral and pharmacological interventions to be used against heart disease.

References

Ablad, B., Bjorkman, J. A., Gustaffson, D., Hansson, G., Ostlund-Lindquist, A. M., & Pettersson, K. (1988). The role of sympathetic activation in atherogenesis: Effects of beta-blockade. *American Heart Journal, 116,* 322–327.

Bernstein, I. S., Gordon, T. P., & Rose, R. M. (1974). Aggression and social controls in rhesus monkey (*Macaca mulatta*) groups revealed in group formation studies. *Folia Primatologica, 21,* 81–107.

Blankenhorn, D. H., & Kramsch, D. M. (1989). Reversal of atherosis and sclerosis: The two components of atherosclerosis. *Circulation, 79,* 1–7.

Bond, M. D., Bullock, B. C., Bellinger, D. A., & Hamm, T. E. (1980). Myocardial infarction in a large colony of nonhuman primates with coronary artery atherosclerosis. *American Journal of Pathology, 101,* 675–692.

Cohen, S., & Matthews, K. A. (1987). Social support, type A behavior, and coronary artery disease. *Psychosomatic Medicine, 49,* 325–330.

Cohen, S., & Wills, T. A. (1985). Stress, social support, and the buffering hypothesis. *Psychological Bulletin, 98,* 310–357.

Corse, C. D., Manuck, S. B., Cantwell, J. D., Giordani, B., & Matthews, K. A. (1982). Coronary-prone behavior pattern and cardiovascular response in persons with and without coronary heart disease. *Psychosomatic Medicine, 44,* 449–459.

Davidson, D. M., & Shumaker, S. A. (1987). Social support and cardiovascular disease. *Arteriosclerosis, 7,* 101–104.

Davies, P. F. (1986). Vascular cell interactions with special reference to the pathogenesis of atherosclerosis. *Laboratory Investigation, 55,* 5–24.

Dembroski, T. M., MacDougall, J. M., Costa, P. T., Jr., & Grandits, G. A. (1989). Components of hostility as predictors of sudden death and myocardial infarction in the multiple risk factor intervention trial. *Psychosomatic Medicine, 51,* 514–522.

Dembroski, T. M., MacDougall, J. M., & Lushene, R. (1979). Interpersonal interaction and cardiovascular response in type A subjects and coronary patients. *Journal of Human Stress, 5,* 28–36.

Eibl-Eibesfeldt, I. (1970). *Ethology, the biology of behavior.* New York: Holt, Rinehart & Winston.

Ely, D. L. (1981). Hypertension, social rank, and aortic arteriosclerosis in CBA/J mice. *Physiology and Behavior, 26,* 655–661.

Ely, D. L., & Henry, J. P. (1978). Neuroendocrine response patterns in dominant and subordinate mice. *Hormones and Behavior, 10,* 156–169.

Fitzgerald, J. D. (1987). By what means might beta blockers prolong life after acute myocardial infarction? *European Heart Journal, 8,* 945–951.

Fleagle, J. G. (1988). *Primate adaptation and evolution.* New York: Academic Press.

Friedman, M., Thoresen, C. E., Gill, J. J., Powell, L. H., Ulmer, D., Thompson, L., Price, V. A., Rabin, D. D., Breall, W. S., Dixon, T., Levy, R., & Bourg, E. (1984). Alteration of type A behavior and reduction in cardiac recurrences in postmyocardial infarction patients. *American Heart Journal, 108,* 237–248.

Gordon, D., Guyton, J. R., & Karnovsky, M. J. (1981). Intimal alterations in rat aorta induced by stressful stimuli. *Laboratory Investigation, 45,* 14–27.

Hauss, W. H., Bauch, H. J., & Schulte, H. (1980). Adrenaline and noradrenaline as possible chemical mediators in the pathogenesis of arteriosclerosis. *Annals of the New York Academy of Sciences, 598,* 91–101.

Henry, J. P., Ely, D. L., Stephens, P. M., Ratcliffe, H. L., Santisteban, G. A., & Shapiro, A. P. (1971). The roles of psychosocial factors in the development of arteriosclerosis in CBA mice: Observations on the heart, kidney, and aorta. *Atherosclerosis, 14,* 203–218.

Henry, J. P., & Stephens, P. M. (1977). *Stress, health and the social environment: A sociobiological approach to medicine.* New York: Springer-Verlag.

Hirsch, E. Z., Maksem, J. A., & Gagen, D. (1984). Effects of stress and propranolol on the aortic intima of rats [Abstract]. *Arteriosclerosis, 4,* 526.

Houston, B. K. (1986). Psychological variables and cardiovascular and neuroendocrine reactivity. In K. A. Matthews, S. M. Weiss, T. Detre, T. M. Dembroski, B. Falkner, S. B. Manuck, & R. B. Williams (Eds.), *Handbook of stress, reactivity, and cardiovascular disease* (pp. 207–230). New York: Wiley.

Kaplan, J. R., Clarkson, T. B., Adams, M. R., Manuck, S. B., & Shively, C. A. (1991). Social behavior and gender in biomedical investigations using monkeys: Studies in atherogenesis. *Laboratory Animal Science, 41,* 334–343.

Kaplan, J. R., & Manuck, S. B. (1989). The effect of propranolol on social interactions among adult male cynomolgus monkeys (*Macaca fascicularis*) housed in disrupted social groupings. *Psychosomatic Medicine, 51,* 449–462.

Kaplan, J. R., Manuck, S. B., Adams, M. R., Weingand, K. W., & Clarkson, T. B. (1987). Inhibition of coronary atherosclerosis by propranolol in behaviorally predisposed monkeys fed an atherogenic diet. *Circulation, 76*, 1364–1372.

Kaplan, J. R., Manuck, S. B., Clarkson, T. B., Lusso, F. M., & Taub, D. M. (1982). Social status, environment and atherosclerosis in cynomolgus monkeys. *Arteriosclerosis, 2*, 359–368.

Kaplan, J. R., Manuck, S. B., Clarkson, T. B., Lusso, F. M., Taub, D. M., & Miller, E. W. (1983). Social stress and atherosclerosis in normocholesterolemic monkeys. *Science, 220*, 733–735.

Kaplan, J. R., Manuck, S. B., Clarkson, T. B., & Prichard, R. W. (1985). Animal models of behavioral influences on atherogenesis. In E. S. Katkin & S. B. Manuck (Eds.), *Advances in behavioral medicine* (Vol. 1, pp. 115–163). Greenwich, CT: JAI Press.

Keys, A., Taylor, H. L., Blackburn, H., Brozek, J., Anderson, J. T., & Simonson, E. (1971). Mortality and coronary heart disease among men studied for 23 years. *Archives of Internal Medicine, 128*, 201–214.

Krantz, D. S., Schaeffer, M. A., Davia, J. E., Dembroski, T. M., MacDougall, J. M., & Shaffer, R. T. (1981). Extent of coronary atherosclerosis, type A behavior, and cardiovascular response to social interaction. *Psychophysiology, 18*, 654–664.

Lang, C. M. (1967). Effects of psychic stress on atherosclerosis in the squirrel monkey (*Saimiri sciureus*). *Proceedings of the Society for Experimental Biology and Medicine, 126*, 30–34.

Ludmer, P. L., Selwyn, A. P., Shook, T. L., Wayne, R. R., Mudge, G. H., Alexander, R. W., & Ganz, P. (1986). Paradoxical vasoconstriction induced by acetylcholine in atherosclerotic coronary arteries. *New England Journal of Medicine, 315*, 1046–1051.

Manuck, S. B., Kaplan, J. R., Adams, M. R., & Clarkson, T. B. (1988). Effects of stress and the sympathetic nervous system on coronary artery atherosclerosis in the cynomolgus macaque. *American Heart Journal, 116*, 328–333.

Manuck, S. B., Kaplan, J. R., Adams, M. R., & Clarkson, T. B. (1989). Behaviorally elicited heart rate reactivity and atherosclerosis in female cynomolgus monkeys (*Macaca fascicularis*). *Psychosomatic Medicine, 51*, 306–318.

Manuck, S. B., Kaplan, J. R., & Clarkson, T. B. (1983a). Behaviorally induced heart rate reactivity and atherosclerosis in cynomolgus monkeys. *Psychosomatic Medicine, 45*, 95–108.

Manuck, S. B., Kaplan, J. R., & Clarkson, T. B. (1983b). Social instability and coronary artery atherosclerosis in cynomolgus monkeys. *Neuroscience and Biobehavioral Reviews, 7*, 485–491.

Manuck, S. B., Kaplan, J. R., & Matthews, K. A. (1986). Behavioral antecedents of coronary heart disease and atherosclerosis. *Arteriosclerosis, 6*, 2–14.

Manuck, S. B., Kaplan, J. R., Muldoon, M. F., Adams, M. R., & Clarkson, T. B. (1991). The behavioral exacerbation of atherosclerosis and its inhibition by propranolol. In P. M. McCabe, N. Schneiderman, T. M. Field, & J. S. Skylar (Eds.), *Stress, coping and disease* (pp. 51–72). Hillsdale, NJ: Erlbaum.

Manuck, S. B., Muldoon, M. F., Kaplan, J. R., Adams, M. R., & Polefrone, J. M. (1989). Coronary artery atherosclerosis and cardiac response to stress in cynomolgus monkeys. In A. W. Siegman & T. M. Dembroski (Eds.), *In search of coronary prone behavior: Beyond type A* (pp. 207–227). Hillsdale, NJ: Erlbaum.

Maseri, A. L'Abbate, A., Baroldi, G., Chierchia, S., Marzilli, M., Ballestra, A. M., Severi, S., Parodi, O., Biagini, A., Distante, A., & Pesola, A. (1978). Coronary vasospasm as a possible cause of myocardial infarction: A conclusion derived from the study of "preinfarction" angina. *New England Journal of Medicine, 299*, 1271–1277.

Maseri, A., Severi, S., De Nes, M., L'Abbate, A., Chierchia, S., Marzilli, M., Ballestra, A. M., Parodi, O., Biagini, A., & Distante, A. (1978). "Variant" angina: One aspect of a continuous spectrum of vasospastic myocardial ischemia: Pathogenetic mechanisms, estimated incidence and clinical and coronary arteriographic findings in 138 patients. *American Journal of Cardiology, 42*, 1019–1035.

Olsson, G., & Rehnqvist, N. (1982). Sudden death precipitated by psychological stress. *Acta Medica Scandinavica, 212*, 437–441.

Pettersson, K., & Ablad, B. (1988). Metoprolol inhibits platelet deposition at arterial bifurcations in rabbits with sympathetic activation [Abstract]. *Journal of the Federation of American Societies for Experimental Biology, 2*, A1580.

Pettersson, K., Bejne, B., Bjork, H., Strawn, W. B., & Bondjers, G. (1990). Experimental sympathetic activation causes endothelial injury in the rabbit thoracic aorta via B_1-adrenoceptor activation. *Circulation Research, 67*, 1027–1034.

Ratcliffe, H. L., & Cronin, M. T. I. (1958). Changing frequency of arteriosclerosis in mammals and birds at the Philadelphia Zoological Garden: Review of autopsy records. *Circulation, 18*, 41–52.

Ratcliffe, H. L., Luginbuhl, H., Schnarr, W. R., & Chacko, K. (1969). Coronary arteriosclerosis in swine: Evidence of a relation to behavior. *Journal of Comparative and Physiological Psychology, 68*, 385–392.

Ratcliffe, H. L., Yerasimides, T. G., & Elliot, G. A. (1960). Changes in the character and location of arterial lesions in mammals and birds in the Philadelphia Zoological Garden. *Circulation, 21*, 730–738.

Rosenman, R. H. (1982). Coronary-prone behavior pattern and coronary heart disease: Implications for the use of beta-blockers on primary prevention. In R. H. Rosenman (Ed.), *Psychosomatic risk factors and coronary heart disease: Indications for specific preventive therapy* (pp. 9–14). Bern, Switzerland: Hans Huber.

Ross, R. (1986). The pathogenesis of atherosclerosis: An update. *New England Journal of Medicine, 314*, 488–500.

Sade, D. S. (1967). Determinant of dominance in a group of free ranging rhesus monkeys. In S. Altmann (Ed.), *Social communication among primates* (pp. 99–114). Chicago: University of Chicago Press.

Sade, D. S. (1972). A longitudinal study of social behavior of rhesus monkeys. In R. Tuttle (Ed.), *The functional and evolutionary biology of primates*. Chicago: Aldine-Atherton.

Sade, D. S. (1973). An ethogram for rhesus monkeys: I. Antithetical contrasts in posture and movement. *American Journal of Physiological Anthropology, 38*, 537–542.

Saxena, P. R., & Villalon, C. M. (1990). Cardiovascular effects of serotonin agonists and antagonists. *Journal of Cardiovascular Pharmacology, 15*, S17–S34.

Schneiderman, N. (1987). Psychophysiologic factors in atherogenesis and coronary artery disease. *Circulation, 76*(Suppl. I), I-41–I-47.

Schwartz, S. M., Campbell, G. R., & Campbell, J. H. (1986). Replication of smooth muscle cells in vascular disease. *Circulation Research, 58*, 427–444.

Schwartz, S., Gajdusek, C., & Sheldon, S. (1981). Vascular wall growth control: The role of endothelium. *Arteriosclerosis, 107*, 107–126.

Strawn, W. B., Bondjers, G., Kaplan, J. R., Manuck, S. B., Schwenke, D. C., Hansson, G. K., Shively, C. A., & Clarkson, T. B. (1991). Endothelial dysfunction in response to psychosocial stress in monkeys. *Circulation Research, 68*, 1270–1279.

Stout, C., Morrow, J., Brandt, E. N., & Wolf, S. (1964). Unusually low incidence of death from myocardial infarction: A study of an Italian American community in Pennsylvania. *Journal of the American Medical Association, 188*, 845–849.

Taggart, P. (1982). Beta-blockade as prevention and/or therapy in coronary-prone behavior. In R. H. Rosenman (Ed.), *Psychosomatic risk factors and coronary heart disease: Indications for specific preventive therapy* (pp. 58–64). Bern, Switzerland: Hans Huber.

Wikstrand, J., Warnold, I., Olsson, G., Tuomilehto, J., Elmfeldt, D., & Berglund, G. (1988). Primary prevention with metoprolol in patients with hypertension: Mortality results from the MAPHY Study. *Journal of the American Medical Association, 259*, 1976–1982.

Williams, J. K., Vita, J. A., Selwyn, A. P., Manuck, S. B., & Kaplan, J. R. (1991). Psychosocial factors impair vascular responses of coronary arteries. *Circulation, 84*, 2146–2153.

Wright, R. A., Contrada, R. J., & Glass, D. C. (1985). Psychophysiologic correlates of type A behavior. In E. S. Katkin & S. B. Manuck (Eds.), *Advances in behavioral medicine* (Vol. 1, pp. 39–88). Greenwich, CT: JAI Press.

CHAPTER 2

Psychological Stress Testing for Coronary Heart Disease

Jim Blascovich and Edward S. Katkin

The study of cardiovascular reactivity to psychological stress is motivated, in part, by its potential etiological significance for the relationship between individual differences in the experience of stress and cardiovascular disease, particularly coronary heart disease (CHD) and hypertension (cf. Matthews et al., 1986). Other contributors to this book review evidence that suggests the stability of individuals' cardiovascular responses across psychologically stressful situations (see Chapters 6 and 7), whereas still other contributors review evidence that demonstrates a relationship between cardiovascular reactivity to psychological stress and both CHD and hypertension (see Chapters 4 and 5).

The assumptions that there are stable individual differences in cardiovascular reactivity to psychological stress and that there is a causal relationship between such reactivity and disease have guided research across various empirical approaches. Within an epidemiological framework, cardiovascular reactivity to psychological stress should predict CHD and/or hypertension in the long run. Within an experimental/theoretical framework, manipulations of cardiovascular reactivity to psychological stress should result in biological variations of etiological significance with respect to cardiovascular disease. Within a clinical framework, cardiovascular reactivity to psychological stress (i.e., psychological stress testing) should be diagnostic of disease at least in a population at risk because of age.

It is safe to say that with few exceptions (see later discussion) nearly all empirical research to date has fallen within the epidemiological and experimental/theoretical approaches. Although several researchers have suggested that psychological stress testing may prove clinically useful for diagnosing individuals who have CHD, and at least a few have suggested clinical psychological stress testing protocols (Ernst, 1986; Janota, Lexa, Maleckova, & Fabian, 1987), few studies have examined directly the utility of psychological stress testing in this regard.

There are at least two reasons for the paucity of actual psychological stress testing research. First, there is a problem of access for research psychologists to appropriate patient populations and facilities for psychological stress testing study. Access to patients and clinical electrocardiogram (EKG) facilities are controlled in large part by physicians who are often skeptical of the value of behavioral studies and, hence, are not receptive to such research. Research psychologists, for their part, are often located in nonmedical settings and are not familiar with clinical protocols, staff, patient safety, and so on and, hence, are often hesitant to be proactive in securing the necessary resources for clinical psychological stress testing research. Second, there are apparent ethical issues. Should individuals at risk for cardiovascular diseases such as CHD undergo a psychologically stressful procedure that is unhealthy (as cardiovascular reactivity researchers hypothesize)? The answer to this ethical problem question can be resolved in the positive, but many researchers are hesitant to confront the issue in the first place.

Prior Psychological Stress Testing Research

To the best of our knowledge, only five studies have been reported in the literature that can be interpreted as evaluating psychological stress testing as a clinical diagnostic procedure for CHD. Although the scope of each of these studies is limited and although not one of these studies is without theoretical and methodological problems, they represent an important foray into the area of psychological stress testing and in the aggregate suggest some utility for psychological stress testing procedures.

Keys and Taylor (1971) reported the first and perhaps only truly prospective study in which hemodynamic reactivity to psychological stress was assessed and later related to the development of CHD. Keys and Taylor reported that diastolic blood pressure (DBP) responses to a cold pressor test were significantly related to the development of coronary artery disease 23 years later, a relationship that was relatively robust compared with more traditional indicators. Although Keys and Taylor used a mixed physical/psychological stressor (i.e., ice-cold water), they opened the door to psychological stress testing research.

Several years later, Schiffer, Hartley, Schulman, and Abelmann (1976) devised a more pure psychological stressor, the *quiz EKG*, as a potential test for diagnosing coronary artery disease. They used this stressor in a retrospective study of insurance executives who had been assigned to three groups (control, angina, and angina plus hypertension). Schiffer et al.'s results indicated that the group with both angina and hypertension had significantly higher heart rate (HR) and blood pressure reactivity to the quiz EKG than did the group with angina only, and the latter group had significantly higher HR and blood pressure reactivity than did the control group. In addition, the two angina groups evidenced significantly greater EKG ST-segment depressions than did the control group. Furthermore, among a subset of insurance executives that were given both the psychological stress test and an exercise stress test, there was a reliable correlation in ST-segment depression recording during exercise stress testing and psychological stress testing ($r = 0.63$, $p < .01$). Thus, Schiffer et al.'s psychological stress testing procedure furthered the promise of Keys and Taylor's (1971) research but with a more pure psychological stress testing procedure.

However, the clinical utility of psychological stress testing was questioned by a group of researchers after performing their own study (DeBusk, Taylor, & Agras, 1979). These researchers compared a treadmill exercise stress testing with psychological stress testing. The psychological stress testing was a multiple task that included an open-ended interview, a videotape of stressful scenes, and a puzzle task. Like Schiffer et al. (1976), DeBusk et al. conducted a retrospective study. The psychological tasks and the exercise test were administered to myocardial infarction (MI) patients 7 weeks after MI. Although the psychological stress tasks induced significant increases in HR and blood pressure reactivity, these increases were relatively small. Importantly for the researchers, only the exercise stress test induced ST-segment depressions.

DeBusk et al. (1979) concluded that exercise stress testing was superior to psychological stress testing because ischemic abnormalities (i.e., ST-segment depressions) did not appear during the patients' experience of the psychological stressors. This conclusion assumes that ischemic abnormalities, in particular ST-segment depressions, are invariant markers of CHD. Furthermore, because they did not assess coronary occlusion, they were unable to report any relationships between HR or blood pressure reactivity and the extent of disease.

Specchia et al. (1984) also compared exercise stress testing and psychological stress testing. Mental arithmetic (serial subtraction) constituted the psychological stress testing. Although this study was not truly prospective, the researchers were unaware of the extent of participants' coronary artery disease because patients performed the stress tests 24–72 hr before undergoing coronary angiography. Specchia et al. reported that 22 of 122 patients exhibited significant ST-segment abnormalities during the mental arithmetic task. These patients were coded as positive for psychological stress testing. Twenty of these 22 patients also performed an exercise stress test, and all 20 were coded positive for exercise stress testing. Of the remaining patients, 70 were coded positive for exercise stress testing but negative for psychological stress testing, and 30 patients were coded negative on both tests. As a consequence, no patients were positive on the psychological stress testing who were not also positive on the exercise stress testing, but the converse was not true.

Specchia et al. (1984) reported that, although all patients showed increased HR and blood pressure reactivity during psychological stress testing, cardiovascular reactivity was greater in the doubly positive group. In addition, the duration of exercise for this group was shorter than for the other two groups. Angiographic evidence indicated that both groups with positive exercise stress tests had higher proportions of two-or-more-vessels coronary artery disease. Although these investigators concluded that mental stress testing could induce ischemic EKG abnormalities, like DeBusk et al. (1979), they apparently assumed that such abnormalities are invariant markers of coronary artery disease and, consequently, did not report relationships between their measures of cardiovascular reactivity and the extent of coronary artery disease.

Deanfield et al. (1984) compared the effects of psychological stress testing (mental arithmetic) and exercise stress testing on ST-segment depressions, regional myocardial perfusion, and ischemia. Subjects for this study were 16 patients with stable angina pectoris. Exercise stress induced ST-segment depressions and regional perfusion abnormalities in all 16 and angina in 15. Psychological stress induced regional perfusion abnormalities in 12, ST-segment depressions in 6, and angina in 4. Deanfield et al. did not find any significant differences in their measures of cardiovascular reactivity (i.e., HR and blood pressure increases) as a function of perfusion changes.

These five prior investigations paint a suggestive but inconclusive picture. As a group, these prior studies suggest that exercise stress testing is more sensitive to such ischemic EKG abnormalities as ST-segment depression than is psychological stress testing. Regarding hemodynamic measures, significant HR and blood pressure reactivity were induced by psychological stress testing in all five studies. Furthermore, such reactivity was related to disease in two studies (Keys & Taylor, 1971; Schiffer et al., 1976) and suggested in a third (Specchia et al., 1984).

The Buffalo Study

We were fortunate to have access for a time to a suitable patient population and clinical EKG facilities at a large urban hospital to conduct the psychological stress testing research reported in this chapter.[1] A student

---

[1]This study was part of a dissertation (Schiffert, 1985) by a doctoral student in the Department of Health Behavioral Sciences at the State University of New York at Buffalo under our supervision. The data presented in this chapter are based on a reanalysis of the dissertation data reported by Schiffert. A paper based on the reanalyzed data was presented at the annual meeting of the Society for Psychophysiological Research for which an abstract was published (Blascovich, Schiffert, & Katkin, 1989).

of ours had an extensive background in diagnostic exercise stress testing, coronary care nursing, and cardiac rehabilitation. In addition to her graduate studies, she was concurrently employed by the hospital in an administrative role and had access to the necessary resources for psychological stress testing research. Without her, our ideas would have remained hypothetical.

Our purpose was to compare directly the predictive value of traditional diagnostic measures during exercise stress testing and cardiovascular reactivity measures taken during psychological stress testing for coronary artery disease. The traditional exercise stress testing measures were EKG ST-segment depression, presence of premature ventricular contractions, and self-report of pain. The psychological stress testing reactivity measures were HR, DBP, and systolic blood pressure (SBP) changes from rest. Severity of coronary artery disease was measured via cineangiographic techniques in the right (RCA), left anterior descending (LAD), and circumflex (CX) coronary arteries.

Method

Overview

Patients who were referred for coronary angiography underwent both exercise and psychological stress testing in one session in a clinical EKG laboratory at a large university-affiliated hospital. The order of testing was counterbalanced such that half of the patients participated in exercise stress testing first, and the other half participated in psychological stress testing first. Traditional diagnostic and cardiovascular reactivity measures were recorded during each test. Within 3 days, the patients underwent coronary angiography. The traditional diagnostic measures were evaluated by cardiologists who were unaware of the stress condition under which they were recorded, and the angiographic images (films) were evaluated by angiologists who were unaware of the results of the EKG diagnostic evaluations.

Subjects

Thirty male patients who participated in both exercise and psychological stress testing as well as subsequent coronary angiography comprised the sample for this study. Twenty-one other patients who initially were re-cruited for this study were excluded because they were unable to partic-ipate in both stress tests due to physical limitations, safety concerns, or fatigue. Patients were referred by their personal physicians, whose co-operation with the project was solicited by the investigators.

The mean age of the 30-patient sample was 55 years and ranged from 27 to 75 years. A history of MI was reported by 8 patients. Reported risk factors included family history of CHD (14 patients), hypertension (7 patients), smoking within the prior 6 months (6 patients), and diabetes mellitus (4 patients).

Twenty-two of the sample patients reported taking various medi-cations. Two patients reported taking a diuretic only, 4 patients reported taking a beta blocker only, 4 reported taking a calcium channel blocker only, 4 reported taking a beta blocker and a diuretic, 7 reported taking a beta blocker and calcium channel blocker, and 1 reported taking a beta blocker, calcium channel blocker, and a diuretic. Eight of the sample patients reported taking no medications.

Setting

The study was conducted in a well-illuminated, air-conditioned EKG lab-oratory in a large university-affiliated teaching hospital. The laboratory measured approximately $3 \times 4 \times 3$ m. The laboratory contained the exercise stress testing apparatus including a motor-driven, variable ele-vation treadmill surrounded on three sides by balance rails, and the psy-chological stress testing apparatus including a computer, monitor, cush-ioned bench, and response button box. In addition, the laboratory contained an EKG monitoring console and blood pressure measurement equipment.

Stress Testing Measures

Skin preparation for EKG electrode placement consisted of cleansing with Medi-trace abrasive cream. Via-trode disposable EKG electrodes with self-contained electrode gel were attached to the right and left shoulders, right and left iliac crests, and six precordial positions. The EKGs were recorded with an Instrument for Cardiac Research monitoring console. The console displayed three continuous leads at all times as well as a beat-to-beat digital display of HR. HR measurements were made during each baseline, rest, and recovery periods as well as every 2 min during each stress task.

SBP and DBP measurements were obtained peripherally using a Baumann sphygmomanometer with an attached stethoscope. Blood pressure was measured in millimeters of mercury using the same sphygmomanometer and stethoscope on the right arm for all patients during both stress tasks. For SBP measurement, the cuff was inflated until the brachial pulse was not palpable. It was deflated slowly until the first Korotkov sound was audible. The pressure at which this occurred was recorded as SBP. The pressure at which the last Korotkov sound was audible was recorded as DBP. Blood pressure measurements were made during each baseline, rest, and recovery periods as well as every 2 min during each stress task.

Patient pain during the stress tests was ascertained according to a procedure developed by Kattus and MacAlpin (1969). Patients were queried at least every minute throughout the stress tests. Subjects were instructed on how to use the scale, and a chart that depicted the scale levels was available.

Stress Tests

A standardized symptom-limited treadmill exercise test was conducted using the modified Naughton protocol (Naughton, Hellerstein, & Mohler, 1973). Exercise commenced at a workload equivalent of three standard multiples of resting oxygen consumption (METS). The workload was increased every 2 min to a maximum of 12 METS by increases in the angle of elevation of the treadmill bed.

A choice–deadline reaction time task modeled after Goldband (1979) was used in conjunction with mental arithmetic as the psychological stress testing protocol. Repeated choice–deadline trials were presented to each patient via computer monitor in four blocks that lasted from 2 to 4 min depending on speed of patient responses. Each block of trials was followed by a 30-s mental arithmetic task for which the patient was asked to close his eyes, serially subtract the value 7 beginning from a three-digit number, and verbalize each answer.

Each trial of the choice–deadline reaction time task consisted of a foreperiod, a stimulus period, a patient response period with a deadline, a feedback period, and a waiting period. The foreperiod duration varied randomly between 2.5 and 4 s during which the monitor displayed the word *ready* at the top of the screen and a large "plus" sign in the middle of the screen. This was followed by the stimulus period during which only the vertical or horizontal component of the plus sign appeared (i.e., remained) on the screen. The patient's task was to push one of two buttons, which were labeled either *horizontal* or *vertical* according to which component of the plus sign remained on the screen before a deadline occurred, as indicated by a beep generated by the computer. The stimulus period was followed by the feedback period during which the patient was given performance feedback for that trial as well as his overall score (percentage of correct responses) up to that point in the test. The patient was credited with a correct response if he accurately identified the remaining component of the plus sign stimulus before the deadline. There was a waiting period before the subsequent trial that varied randomly between 2 and 4 s.

The reaction time deadline varied within trial blocks as a function of the patient's own reaction time. Specifically, the deadline was the patient's mean reaction time over the three previous trials multiplied by a constant factor for each block of trials. The reaction time deadline varied between trial blocks by the value of the constant multiplier. For the first block, the constant was 1.3; for the second block, 1.15; for the third, 1; and for the fourth, 0.85. Thus, blocks became increasingly difficult.

Procedure

The nature of the study was explained to patients upon their arrival at the EKG department. Patients were informed that they would be participating in both exercise and psychological stress tests and that the latter was an experimental rather than an established procedure. The risks of both tasks were explained. In addition to the standard exercise stress EKG patient consent form, a second form was used to verify informed consent for the psychological stress test. An experimenter then interviewed the patient to ascertain demographic, medication, and risk factor information.

The patient was then escorted to the EKG stress testing laboratory. An EKG technician attached the EKG electrodes and explained their function. The patient was then instructed to sit down and relax for a few minutes (2–6 min) at the end of which a diagnostic baseline EKG was recorded. Next, the technician, per standard clinical procedure, instructed the patient to breathe rapidly for 30 s during which a second diagnostic EKG was recorded to ascertain any changes from baseline likely to have occurred due to respiration. The EKG records were then evaluated by an EKG physician before the patient proceeded any further in the study.

The patient then performed either exercise stress testing or psychological stress testing according to the order condition to which he or she was randomly assigned. The first stress test was followed by a rest period during which recovery HR and blood pressure measurements were recorded until baseline levels were achieved. This was followed by the remaining stress test and a second recovery period.

Instructions for the exercise stress testing were presented by the physician and EKG technician. Instructions for the psychological stress testing were presented by the experimenter and technician. The technician operated the EKG monitoring console and recorded all physiological measurements. The physician remained present in the EKG department during all stress tests.

Angiography

Within 3 days, patients underwent coronary cineangiography, an invasive procedure in which a radio-opaque contrast medium is injected directly into the left ventricle and moving radiographic images of the heart and coronary vasculature are recorded. Estimates of occlusion in three main coronary arteries were subsequently made by trained angiologists who reviewed the angiographic films but were unaware of the results of the stress tests.

Results

Scoring

A score for each of the six predictor variables was determined for both types of stress tests. For the traditional diagnostic measures, ST-segment depressions (STs) were measured by a cardiologist using standard diagnostic algorithms, premature ventricular contractions (PVCs) were scored according to the Lown classification procedure (Lown, Vassaux, & Hood, 1967) on a 7-point scale ranging from 0 (*no PVCs present*) to 6 (*most severe*), and pain (PA) was scored using the patient verbal rating on the 5-point Kattus and MacAlpin (1969) scale. For the cardiovascular reactivity measures, HR delta scores (HRD) were computed as the maximum change from baseline for each test, expressed in beats per minute (bpm), and DPB deltas (DBPD) and SBP deltas (SBPD) were computed as the maximum change from baseline for each test expressed in millimeters of mercury.

Regarding criterion variables, occlusion in the RCA, LAD, and CX arteries were measured by angiologists. The degree of occlusion was scored as the percentage of occlusion in the artery studied. In addition to scores for each artery, three other scores were calculated: the percentage of occlusion in the most occluded artery (MOST), the percentage of occlusion summed across arteries (SUM), and the number of vessels with 50% or greater occlusion (VESSELS). The evaluation of the angiograms revealed that 26 of the sample patients had 50% or greater occlusion of at least one of the three major coronary arteries. Four patients were disease free.

Stress Test Effects on Predictor Variables
To test for effects of stress tests on the traditional and cardiovascular reactivity predictor variables, separate two-way analyses of variance were run on each predictor variable. These analyses included medications as a between-subjects factor with two levels, cardioactive medications (i.e., beta blocker vs. calcium channel blocker) and noncardioactive medications (i.e., no medication vs. diuretic) and type of stress test as the within-subjects factor. Main effects for type of stress test were found for all dependent variables except PA. Relevant means and F values appear in Table 1.

With one exception, no main effects or interactions were found for medication. For HRD, a main effect for medication was found, $F(1, 28) = 8.8$, $p < .01$. Mean HRD was smaller in the cardioactive medication group (24.7 bpm) than in the noncardioactive medication group (41.35 bpm). Pearson product–moment correlations were computed between

TABLE 1
Predictor Variable Means and F Test Values

Predictor	Exercise stress test	Psychological stress test	F[a]
ST	0.92	0.15	20.97***
PVC	0.83	0.37	4.24*
PA	0.23	0.13	0.37
HRD	50.57	9.93	163.64***
DBPD	12.21	4.48	10.03*
SBPD	38.43	22.93	13.37**

Note. ST = ST-segment depression (in millimeters); PVC = premature ventricular contraction (Lown classification 7-point scale); PA = pain (Kattus and MacAlpin 5-point scale); HRD = heart rate delta (in beats per minute); DBPD = diastolic blood pressure delta (in millimeters of mercury); SBPD = systolic blood pressure delta (in millimeters of mercury).
[a]dfs = 1, 28.
*$p < .05$. **$p < .01$. ***$p < .0001$.

predictor values under exercise and psychological stress testing. These values appear in Table 2.

Regression Analyses

Forced regression analyses were used to ascertain the relative predictive value between the traditional diagnostic and cardiovascular measures.

TABLE 2
Pearson Product–Moment Correlations Between Predictor Variables Under Exercise and Psychological Stress Tests

Predictor	r[a]
ST	0.30
PVC	0.54*
PA	−0.01
HRD	0.62**
DBPD	0.09
SBPD	0.47*

Note. ST = ST-segment depression; PVC = premature ventricular contraction; PA = pain; HRD = heart rate delta; DBPD = diastolic blood pressure delta; SBPD = systolic blood pressure delta.
[a]df = 30.
*$p < .01$. **$p < .001$.

Our major point of comparison was between traditional predictors under exercise stress and cardiovascular reactivity predictors under psychological stress. The summary results of the relevant forced multiple regressions for each criterion variable appear in Table 3.

In the regression analyses underlying these summary data, the traditional predictors were entered as a group into the regression model as the first step, followed by the cardiovascular reactivity predictors as the second step. For the MOST, VESSELS, and SUM aggregate measures of occlusion, the cardiovascular reactivity predictors (HRD, DBPD, and SBPD) as a group explained significantly and substantially greater vari-

TABLE 3

Multiple Regression Summary for Traditional (TRAD) Predictors Under Exercise Stress Tests and Reactivity (REACT) Predictors Under Psychological Stress Tests

Criterion variable/ predictor group	R^2	Adjusted R^2	R^2 change	Adjusted R^2 change	F
MOST					
TRAD	0.11	0.00	0.11	0.00	1.73
REACT	0.53	0.41	0.42	0.41	6.65**
VESSELS					
TRAD	0.15	0.04	0.15	0.04	3.00
REACT	0.64	0.55	0.50	0.51	10.23***
SUM					
TRAD	0.18	0.08	0.18	0.08	3.74*
REACT	0.65	0.56	0.48	0.48	10.03***
RCA					
TRAD	0.12	0.02	0.12	0.02	1.39
REACT	0.34	0.17	0.22	0.15	2.46
LAD					
TRAD	0.01	−0.11	0.01	−0.11	0.07
REACT	0.20	−0.01	0.20	0.10	1.81
CX					
TRAD	0.26	0.17	0.26	0.17	5.22**
REACT	0.64	0.54	0.38	0.37	7.73***

Note. Traditional predictors include ST-segment depression, premature ventricular contraction, and pain; reactivity predictors include heart rate deltas, diastolic blood pressure deltas, and systolic blood pressure deltas. MOST = percentage of occlusion in the most occluded coronary artery; VESSELS = the number of coronary vessels with 50% or greater occlusion; SUM = the percentage of occlusion summed across coronary arteries; RCA = right coronary artery; LAD = left anterior descending coronary artery; CX = circumflex coronary artery.
*$p < .05$. **$p < .01$. ***$p < .001$.

ance than did the traditional predictor variables (ST, PVC, and PA) as a group. For the CX occlusion measure, the cardiovascular reactivity predictors explained significantly and substantially greater variance than did the traditional predictors. For the RCA occlusion measure, the cardiovascular reactivity predictors explained marginally significantly greater variance than did the traditional predictors.

Regarding cardiovascular reactivity measures under exercise and psychological stress, the summary results of the relevant forced multiple regressions for each criterion variable appear in Table 4. In the regression analyses underlying these summary data, the cardiovascular reactivity predictors under exercise were entered as a group into the regression

TABLE 4

Multiple Regression Summary for Reactivity Predictors Under Exercise (EXER) and Psychological (PSYCH) Stress Tests

Criterion variable/ predictor group	R^2	Adjusted R^2	R^2 change	Adjusted R^2 change	F
MOST					
EXER	0.34	0.26	0.34	0.26	5.54**
PSYCH	0.55	0.43	0.21	0.17	3.38*
VESSELS					
EXER	0.12	0.02	0.12	0.02	2.45
PSYCH	0.64	0.54	0.51	0.52	10.37***
SUM					
EXER	0.20	0.10	0.20	0.10	3.86*
PSYCH	0.62	0.52	0.42	0.42	8.08***
RCA					
EXER	0.18	0.09	0.18	0.09	2.34
PSYCH	0.42	0.27	0.24	0.18	3.03
LAD					
EXER	0.13	0.03	0.13	0.03	1.25
PSYCH	0.22	0.01	0.09	-0.02	0.81
CX					
EXER	0.11	0.01	0.11	0.01	2.00
PSYCH	0.58	0.47	0.47	0.46	8.33***

Note. Reactivity predictors include heart rate deltas, diastolic blood pressure deltas, and systolic blood pressure deltas. MOST = percentage of occlusion in the most occluded coronary artery; VESSELS = the number of coronary vessels with 50% or greater occlusion; SUM = the percentage of occlusion summed across coronary arteries; RCA = right coronary artery; LAD = left anterior descending coronary artery; CX = circumflex coronary artery.
*$p < .05$. **$p < .01$. ***$p < .001$.

model as the first step, followed by the cardiovascular reactivity predictors under psychological stress as the second step. For the VESSELS and SUM aggregate measures of occlusion, the cardiovascular reactivity predictors under psychological stress explained significantly and substantially greater variance than did the reactivity predictors under exercise. For the MOST measure, the two categories explained significant variance, but the psychological reactivity category of predictors was not substantially greater. For the CX occlusion measure, the cardiovascular reactivity predictors under psychological stress explained significantly and substantially greater variance than did the reactivity predictors under exercise.

Discussion

The results of this study indicate that measures of cardiovascular reactivity to psychological stress are predictive of the severity of coronary artery disease in a patient population referred for coronary angiography. The data indicate that psychological stress testing can present a challenge to the cardiovascular system that is related to the progression of disease even though it does not induce EKG abnormalities to the extent that exercise stress testing does and even though it does not produce hemodynamic changes in the range of those driven by the metabolic demands of exercise stress testing (see Table 1).

The finding that cardiovascular reactivity measures taken during psychological stress testing accounted for significant and substantial variance in coronary occlusion in a regression model over and above that already explained by traditional predictors measured during exercise stress testing (see Table 3) suggests that ischemic changes during exercise challenge can be complemented by cardiovascular reactivity changes during psychological stress to increase the diagnostic sensitivity of clinical stress testing procedures. The finding that reactivity measures during psychological challenge account for significant and substantial variance in occlusion over and above that already explained by cardiovascular reactivity measures during exercise challenge (see Table 4) suggests that exercise-induced changes in hemodynamic reactivity do not subsume the predictive value of psychologically induced changes.

However, there is more to this story. Based on the typical effects of laboratory stressors used in cardiovascular reactivity research, we assumed that the cardiovascular reactivity measures would be positively related to coronary artery occlusion. Our data suggest that the relationship is not so simple. Indeed, HR, DBP, and SBP changes under psychological stress did not individually explain significant variance in coronary occlusion, but they did as a group. However, even here things become more complicated because the pattern of responses across these measures is not unidirectional. Rather, simple correlations indicate a positive relationship between SBP changes and occlusion measures but a negative relationship between HR changes and occlusion and DBP changes and occlusion.

Such a pattern may be consistent with notions of β-adrenergic hyperreactivity to psychological stress based on increased epinephrine production resulting in inotropic effects such as increased contractility and stroke volume, thereby increasing SBP and a vasodilatory effect dropping peripheral resistance and moderating DBP changes. However, this is very speculative, especially without more specific inotropic and vasodilatory measures. What may be a more important explanatory notion regarding this pattern is the presence of coronary artery disease itself. Simply put, the hemodynamic profile of diseased patients may be very different from that of healthy individuals, and it may result in a different pattern of cardiovascular reactivity responses to psychological stress in patients with disease than in healthy young adults.

The question of medications must also be addressed because cardioactive medications tend to obscure cardiosympathetic effects. However, when we examined the data from the 10 patients without cardioactive medications, the pattern of cardiovascular reactivity responses related to disease was even stronger.

General Discussion and Summary

The results of the five prior studies (Deanfield et al., 1984; DeBusk et al., 1979; Keys & Taylor, 1971; Schiffer et al., 1976; Specchia et al., 1984) and the present study taken together raise interesting issues, lead to tentative conclusions, and suggest directions for further research.

One set of issues revolves around the appropriateness of the psychological stress testing/exercise stress testing comparison for which exercise stress testing serves as the comparative standard. The rationale underlying exercise stress testing is that such testing should induce EKG abnormalities such as ST-segment depression and PVCs that are sequelae of the coronary artery disease. The rationale underlying psychological stress testing, on the other hand, is that such testing should induce cardiovascular reactivity responses such as hemodynamic changes that may be antecedents of coronary artery disease.

There are important implications to be derived from the differences in these rationales. Methodologically, using ischemic EKG abnormalities as outcomes is appropriate for exercise stress testing research but not particularly for psychological stress testing research because psychological stress tasks (at least those that are ethical and practical) do not generally induce the metabolic demands that even moderate exercise induces (Rousselle, Blascovich, & Kelsey, 1993) and, hence, are unlikely to induce EKG signs of ischemia. Thus, comparing psychological stress testing to exercise stress testing in terms of outcome data produced simply by the tests themselves is probably inappropriate.

Clinically, exercise stress testing should be equally diagnostic of CHD in all individuals regardless of age or CHD risk factors because it is based on identifying known sequelae of the disease. On the other hand, psychological stress testing should be diagnostic of CHD only for those individuals within whom the disease has had the chance to progress over time because it is based on the antecedents of disease rationale. In the Buffalo study all subjects were at risk for CHD by virtue of age and prior screening, justifying the invasive angiographic procedure. Thus, the utility of psychological stress testing as a diagnostic tool for CHD is probably limited to at least middle-aged and older individuals or individuals who are otherwise at high risk for the disease.

Some tentative conclusions can be drawn from the relatively small psychological stress testing literature. First, psychological stress testing is likely to become useful as a diagnostic test for CHD at least for older patients. Second, exercise stress testing disease predictors do not subsume psychological stress testing predictors when hemodynamic reactivity measures are included in the assessments.

Third, and perhaps most interesting, an individual's pattern of cardiovascular reactivity to psychological stress may change as a function of the progression of disease. Thus, the patterns of hyperreactivity that are demonstrably characteristic of certain individuals who are relatively young and that are implicated in the etiology of cardiovascular disease are not necessarily related to such disease once it develops. This suggests that there may be diagnostic value in repeated psychological stress testing over time such that the change in reactivity patterns to psychological stress may be the most useful diagnostic predictor for the disease.

Future psychological stress testing research should address a number of issues, the most important of which is, of course, establishing beyond doubt the diagnostic sensitivity and specificity of such testing for CHD. Toward this end, the relative effectiveness of various protocols for eliciting patterns of cardiovascular reactivity that are associated with disease needs to be examined. Some are probably less effective than others. For example, DeBusk et al.'s (1979) puzzle task, but neither their emotional visual images nor their interview task, elicited reactivity reliably. Theoretical justification and systematic empirical research are necessary if psychological stress testing is to be standardized for either research or clinical purposes.

The diagnostic value of cardiovascular measures in addition to simple HRD, SBPD, and DBPD should be investigated. Both more sensitive and more revealing measures should be used, including impedance cardiographically derived inotropic and chronotropic indices continuously recorded during psychological stress testing. This is especially important in view of the possible difference in the just-discussed pre- and postdisease cardiovascular reactivity patterns. Finally, larger scale studies should include sufficient numbers of medicated and nonmedicated patients to determine the effects of medications on cardiovascular reactivity to psychological stress.

References

Blascovich, J., Schiffert, J. H., & Katkin, E. S. (1989). A comparison of exercise and psychological stress testing for coronary disease [Abstract]. *Psychophysiology, 26*, 57.

Deanfield, J. E., Kensett, M., Wilson, R., Shea, M., Horlock, P., deLandsheere, C. M., & Selwyn, A. P. (1984). Silent myocardial ischemia due to mental stress. *Lancet, II*, 1001–1004.

DeBusk, R. F., Taylor, C. B., & Agras, W. S. (1979). Comparison of treadmill exercise testing and psychologic stress testing soon after myocardial infarction. *American Journal of Cardiology, 43*, 907–912.

Ernst, A. (1986). Psychophysiological stress to identify cardiovascular risk and for the prediction, differential diagnosis, and treatment of psychosomatic disorders. *Activitas Nervosa Superior, 28*, 61–66.

Goldband, S. (1979). *Environmental specificity of physiological responses to stress in coronary prone subjects.* Unpublished doctoral dissertation, State University of New York at Buffalo.

Janota, M., Lexa, J., Maleckova, M., & Fabian, J. (1987). Mental stress test evaluated by isopotential ST segment mapping. *Activitas Nervosa Superior, 29*, 172–173.

Kattus, A., & MacAlpin, R. (1969). Role of exercise in discovery, evaluation, and management of ischemic heart disease. *Cardiovascular Clinic, 1*, 255.

Keys, A., & Taylor, H. L. (1971). Mortality and coronary heart disease among men studied for 23 years. *Archives of Internal Medicine, 128*, 201–214.

Lown, B., Vassaux, C., & Hood, W. (1967). Unresolved problems in coronary care. *American Journal of Cardiology, 20*, 494–508.

Matthews, K. A., Weiss, S. M., Detre, T., Dembroski, T. M., Faulkner, B., Manuck, S. B., & Williams, R. (Eds.). (1986). *Handbook of stress reactivity and cardiovascular disease.* New York: Wiley.

Naughton, J., Hellerstein, H., & Mohler, I. (1973). *Exercise testing and exercise training in coronary heart disease.* New York: Academic Press.

Rousselle, J. B., Blascovich, J., & Kelsey, R. M. (1993). *Cardiorespiratory reactivity under combined psychological and exercise stress.* Manuscript submitted for publication.

Schiffer, F., Hartley, L. H., Schulman, C. L., & Abelmann, W. H. (1976). The quiz electrocardiogram: A new diagnostic and research technique for evaluating the relation between emotional stress and ischemic heart disease. *American Journal of Cardiology, 37*, 41–47.

Schiffert, J. H. (1985). *Predictive validity of psychological and exercise stress tests for coronary artery disease.* Unpublished doctoral dissertation, State University of New York at Buffalo.

Specchia, G., de Servi, S., Falcone, C., Gavazzi, A., Angoli, L., Bramucci, E., Ardissino, D., & Mussini, A. (1984). Mental arithmetic stress testing in patients with coronary artery disease. *American Heart Journal, 108*, 56–63.

PART TWO

Reactivity and Hypertension

CHAPTER 3

Biobehavioral Stressors, Laboratory Investigation, and the Risk of Hypertension

Patrice G. Saab and Neil Schneiderman

H ypertension is a major risk factor for coronary heart disease and for cerebrovascular disease (Kannel, Gordon, & Schwartz, 1971). High levels of blood pressure maintained over many years are associated with increased risk of target-organ damage and life-threatening disorders of the heart, kidneys, and blood vessels. The risk conveyed by hypertension in these disorders appears to be directly proportional to mean arterial pressure and the length of time that it has been elevated.

Hypertension reflects a disruption of regulatory physiological mechanisms that normally operate to keep blood pressure at healthy levels. Although some cases of hypertension are secondary to known kidney, endocrine, or other specific disorders, approximately 85% of all cases are classified as primary or essential hypertension, in which the exact regulatory disruption leading to the elevated pressure cannot be specified

This research was supported by National Institutes of Health grants HL36588 and HL41335.

(Julius, 1977). Essential hypertension afflicts approximately 20% of the adult American population but has a much greater prevalence among some groups such as African Americans and older individuals (Roberts & Rowland, 1981; U.S. Department of Health and Human Services, 1986).

Although it is conceivable that essential hypertension may be the function of a single regulatory defect, the extensive interrelationships that exist among the multiple dynamic blood pressure regulatory mechanisms in freely breeding populations suggest that the origin and maintenance of hypertension are multifactorily determined (Page, 1949, 1977). Both hereditary and environmental factors have been implicated. Because behavior may be defined in terms of interactions between organisms and their environments, it is appropriate to investigate the role that behavioral factors may play in the pathogenesis of hypertension.

Stress

One behavioral factor that has been shown to be related to blood pressure regulation is stress. Among humans, exposure to stressful living environments (Harburg et al., 1973), life-threatening events (Ruskin, Beard, & Schaffer, 1948), and combat conditions (Ehrstrom, 1945; Graham, 1945) as well as being employed in a high-strain occupation such as air-traffic control (Cobb & Rose, 1973; Rose, Jenkins, & Hurst, 1978) may be associated with persistent elevations in blood pressure. It should be noted, however, that most studies that demonstrated a relationship between stress and elevations in blood pressure have been cross-sectional in nature and that the few longitudinal studies that have been conducted have tended to show that blood pressure typically returns to normotensive levels after termination of the stressor (Graham, 1945; Ruskin et al., 1948).

Perhaps the most compelling evidence of a relationship between stress and hypertension stems from the animal literature. Chronic exposure to stressors (e.g., shock avoidance; auditory, visual, and motion stimuli; and social crowding and disruption) in normotensive animals is accompanied by increased blood pressure (e.g., Henry, Meehan, & Stephens, 1967; Henry, Stephens, & Santisteban, 1975; Herd, Morse, Kelleher, & Jones, 1969; Smookler, Goebel, Siegel, & Clarke, 1973). The research of Henry and colleagues (Henry, Ely, & Stephens, 1972; Henry et al., 1967;

Henry, Stephens, Axelrod, & Mueller, 1971; Henry et al., 1975) has provided the most convincing evidence that exposure to stressors may lead to sustained hypertension. For example, hypertension has been observed after CBA mice that were reared in isolation were placed in a social colony for several months where repeated competitive territorial confrontations resulting in vigorous fighting were likely to occur. On autopsy, evidence of cardiovascular and renal pathology (i.e., increased heart weight, myocardial fibrosis, and arteriosclerosis of the intermural coronary arteries and aorta) was apparent. These data suggest that hypertension can result from exposure to a stressful environment that requires responses that are not in the animal's behavioral repertoire (Henry et al., 1975) or is characterized by threat and uncertainty (Henry & Stephens, 1977). It appears likely that the sustained hypertension and degenerative effects in response to psychosocial stress were a function of sympathetic activation and the release of neurohormones into the circulation (Henry et al., 1971; Vander, Henry, Stephens, Kay, & Mouw, 1978).

Although the animal data relating behavioral stressors to sustained hypertension are provocative, they do leave important questions to be answered before the association of behavioral stress and essential hypertension can be accepted as a generalizable main effect. First, it would be important to determine whether the results obtained by Henry and his collaborators (Henry et al., 1967, 1971, 1972, 1975) could be replicated in mouse strains other than CBA, which appears to be highly emotional. Second, it would be important to ascertain whether blood pressure levels and/or the observed morphological changes tend to regress once the environment is made less stressful.

At present there appears to be insufficient evidence to fully support the view that emotional behavior alone can produce sustained hypertension. A somewhat better case can be made, however, that persistent behavioral conditions that are associated with pronounced increases in sympathetic nervous system activity can interact with genetic predisposition (Dahl, Heine, & Tassinari, 1965; Friedman & Iwai, 1976; Lawler, Barker, Hubbard, & Allen, 1980), dietary factors such as sodium (D. E. Anderson, Kearns, & Better, 1983), or renal infection (Lipman & Shapiro, 1967) to produce sustained hypertension.

Genetic–Behavioral Interactions

Page's (1949, 1977) mosaic theory implies that hereditary factors under-lying hypertension consist of a distribution of variants randomly mixed in the genetic coding of human reproduction. Understanding of ge-netic–behavioral interactions with implications for human hypertension is provided by three lines of research: (a) animal models of hypertension, (b) psychophysiological research examining the influence of family his-tory of hypertension, and (c) psychophysiological research in twin co-horts.

Animal Models

Animal models are frequently used to investigate genetic influences on hypertension. Selectively bred rat strains have provided an important tool for (a) isolating putative genetic variants that might contribute to human hypertension and (b) examining the manner in which these genetic vari-ants are influenced by stress as conveyed by environmental factors. Al-though other models have been developed, the spontaneously hyperten-sive rat (SHR) (Okamato & Aoki, 1963) is the most widely used to study genetic factors in hypertension (see Schneiderman, 1983, for a compre-hensive review of animal models of cardiovascular pathology). The blood pressure of the SHR begins to show marked increases around 5–6 weeks of age and develops established hypertension by 6 months of age. During the early course of hypertension development, young SHRs exhibit a "hyperkinetic" circulation with increased cardiac output related to en-hanced sympathetic discharge that is reminiscent of the defense reaction (Schneiderman & McCabe, 1989; Williams, 1986). In contrast, mature SHRs, like their human counterparts, have normal or subnormal cardiac output with increased total peripheral resistance. Although sympathetic tone appears to be reduced in the older animal, secondary structural changes such as left ventricular hypertrophy and arteriosclerotic changes are apparent (Folkow & Hallbäck, 1977). In response to aversive stimu-lation, the young SHR displays greater sympathetic nervous system ac-tivity and cardiovascular hyperreactivity than do normotensive control rats (e.g., Hallbäck & Folkow, 1974). This stress-induced sympathetically mediated cardiovascular hyperreactivity also characterizes the prehypertensive SHR (Hallbäck, 1975; Hallbäck & Folkow, 1974).

Hallbäck (1975) tested the hypothesis that hypertension is a consequence of the SHR's hyperreactivity to stressful environmental stimulation. The SHRs were socially isolated from weaning until they were 7 months old. Deprived of their usual opportunities for social arousal and confrontation, the blood pressure of these prehypertensive SHRs remained at normotensive levels, whereas the blood pressure of their non-isolated counterparts increased to hypertensive ranges. Cardiovascular responsiveness to acute noisy and vibratory stress, however, was equally exaggerated in both groups in relation to control rats. In a subsequent study, Hallbäck-Norlander and Lundin (1979) found that, although loud noise raised heart rate and cardiac output to a greater extent in SHRs than in control rats, anesthesia lowered heart rate and cardiac output to a larger degree in SHRs than in controls, which suggests that the cardiovascular hyperreactivity may be centrally mediated. Other studies have shown that excessive and prolonged discharge of catecholamines during immobilization (McCarty, Chiveh, Kopin, 1978a, 1978b) or anticipation of footshock (McCarty & Kopin, 1978) are also exhibited by the SHR.

A number of experiments conducted by Cierpial, Konarska, and McCarty (1988) indicate (a) that expression of the hypertensive phenotype in the SHR begins early in life and (b) that this expression is susceptible to perturbation based on experiential factors. These investigators found that cross-fostering SHR pups to Wistar-Kyoto (WKY) normotensive mothers attenuated resting blood pressure levels in the adult SHR.

The borderline hypertensive rat developed by Lawler et al. (1980) is a first-generation cross between the SHR and the WKY rat. This animal model develops frank hypertension when chronically stressed (Lawler et al., 1980) or when fed a high-sodium diet (Lawler, Sanders, Chen, Nagahama, & Oparil, 1987). The stress-induced hypertension can be blocked by exercise (Cox, Hubbard, Lawler, Sanders, & Mitchell, 1985).

Taken together, the experimental findings show that the development of hypertension in the SHR or in the borderline hypertensive rat is facilitated by aversive stimulation, whereas removal of stressful stimulation can impede the development of hypertension. The cardiovascular and catecholamine hyperreactivity characteristics of the SHR also appears to be central in origin, and the hyperreactivity may be involved in the pathogenesis of hypertension.

Family History

In humans, family history of hypertension is recognized as a significant risk factor for hypertension. The young healthy offspring of a hypertensive parent are more likely to become hypertensive than are the offspring of normotensive parents (Feinleib, 1979), and relative risk is greater when both parents are hypertensive (Ayman, 1934). Together with their genetic predisposition for hypertension, individuals with a family history of hypertension are reputed to exhibit exaggerated cardiovascular responsiveness to stressors in relation to individuals with normotensive parents (e.g., Ditto, 1986; Falkner, Onesti, Angelakos, Fernandes, & Langman, 1979; Hastrup, Light, & Obrist, 1982). As such, psychophysiological studies of family history provide an indirect method to evaluate the relationship between stress-induced cardiovascular reactivity and the development of hypertension (Light, 1989).

The psychophysiological literature on family history has received recent attention (see Fredrikson & Matthews, 1990; Matthews & Rakaczky, 1986). For 70% of the 27 studies initially reviewed by Matthews and Rakaczky (1986), groups with a positive history of parental hypertension were characterized by augmented stress-induced blood pressure and/or heart rate responses in relation to those with a negative history of parental hypertension. Results of a recent meta-analytic review show that for 36–43% of the published studies, normotensives with a family history of hypertension exhibited significantly greater blood pressure and heart rate responsivity to stressors than did their counterparts with a negative family history (Fredrikson & Matthews, 1990).

Fredrikson and Matthews (1990) also compared tasks involving active coping and passive coping. Their results demonstrated that active coping tasks elicited more reliable diastolic blood pressure differences between the offspring of hypertensive and normotensive parents. When the cold pressor test was examined separately, the task failed to distinguish reliably the two family history status groups across studies. Variability in significance levels and in effect sizes were also evident as a function of sex and age. More significant diastolic blood pressure effects were obtained for studies that included females and males or females alone than for studies that were restricted to males only. More robust results, especially for heart rate, were also obtained when older (age ≥ 20 years) rather than younger (age < 20 years) individuals were examined.

Fredrikson and Matthews (1990) demonstrated that the genetic–behavioral interaction of family history and cardiovascular responses to laboratory stressors is a robust phenomenon. The importance of the model is underscored by the finding that healthy individuals, with no apparent pathology, who are at risk for hypertension because of their family history, respond to stress in a manner that approximates that of borderline and essential hypertensives (for a review see Fredrikson & Matthews, 1990).

The meta-analytic results also prompt consideration of various factors (e.g., task, age, and sex) when interpreting null effects. First, the failure to find family history differences for the cold pressor test and the pattern of results for the active versus passive coping task comparisons suggest that the nature of the task and its capacity to stimulate myocardial responsivity (Obrist, 1981) may be a critical parameter. Alternatively, it may be that limiting dependent measures to blood pressure and heart rate may not be sufficient to (a) discriminate family history status groups or (b) provide information about underlying cardiovascular differences. Second, the just-mentioned age effects are likely to reflect two sets of difficulties for this type of research: (a) the age-related progression of hypertension and (b) the accurate ascertainment of family history status. More specifically, the family history studies that have examined young individuals (children, adolescents, and young adults) are affected by parents who are relatively young themselves. Although some of the parents may eventually become hypertensive, at the time of study, the disease was not evident (Hastrup, Hotchkiss, & Johnson, 1985; Light, 1989; Obrist, Light, Sherman, & Strogatz, 1987). This situation is further complicated by the relative inaccuracy of knowledge regarding family history of hypertension in younger groups. Hastrup et al. (1985) showed that college students inaccurately report positive as well as negative parental history of hypertension and that accuracy deteriorates further when information on grandparents is requested. This appears to be, in part, related to the subtle nature of the disease. Third, the bias to limit samples to presumably White men only (e.g., Hastrup et al., 1982; Obrist et al., 1987) appears to contribute to less robust family history differences. Given the recent mandate by the National Institutes of Health to include women and minorities in research, the bias in psychophysiological studies examining family history may be resolved.

Although family history of hypertension is viewed as a genetic index, the literature demonstrating family history status differences in cardiovascular responsivity to stressors does not constitute direct support for a heritable component (Smith et al., 1987). Risk for hypertension may also be transmitted by shared environmental factors and learned health behaviors (Durel & Schneiderman, 1991; Light, 1989). The twin cohort literature evaluating cardiovascular responses to stressors addresses this issue and is discussed in the following section.

Twin Studies

Studies comparing monozygotic (MZ) and same-sex dizygotic (DZ) twin pairs have added to current understanding about the relative contributions of familial (genetic and environmental) factors involved in the regulation of cardiovascular responses to stress. A review by Rose (1986) indicates that members of MZ pairs are more likely to show a higher concordance in cardiovascular responding to stressors than are members of DZ pairs. Evidence of heritability has been demonstrated for blood pressure, heart rate, and finger pulse volume responses. However, significant associations vary across cardiovascular parameters and stressors. Carroll and colleagues (Carroll, Hewitt, Last, Turner, & Sims, 1985) demonstrated that heart rate responsivity to a video game challenge in young adult men shows significant heritability (.48) and can best be explained by an additive model of genetic effects plus those effects associated with individual environments rather than the family environment. Other research, including that with older adult men (Carmelli, Chesney, Ward, & Rosenman, 1985; Smith et al., 1987), shows no evidence of genetic effects on heart rate change during serial subtractions or during the hand immersion cold pressor test. Support for the heritability of blood pressure changes from baseline (i.e., delta scores) is also only suggestive in older men and less consistent than that typically observed for task levels (Carmelli et al., 1985; Smith et al., 1987). J. Sims and colleagues (Sims, Hewitt, Kelly, Carroll, & Turner, 1986) proposed that genetic influences on blood pressure change are more robust for younger rather than older adults.

Although the body of research that has compared MZ and DZ twin pairs is rather small in relation to the available data on family history of hypertension, the data support the position that cardiovascular responsivity to stressors is "moderately heritable" (Rose, 1986). Further research in this area, particularly with adequate sample sizes, is warranted. The external validity of these findings to samples that differ on relevant characteristics (e.g., sex and ethnicity) also requires additional examination.

Taken together, the twin, family history, and animal studies suggest that stressors interact with genetic as well as familial factors and influence processes involved in blood pressure regulation. Parallels exist between the stress-induced hyperreactivity of the SHR in relation to normal controls and the individuals with a positive family history in relation to those with a negative family history. What is not explained are the causal processes involved in the association of stress-induced hyperresponsivity and the pathogenesis of hypertension. Several hypotheses have been offered and are presented in the following section.

Hypotheses and Causal Processes

Several plausible theories regarding causal processes have been proposed to address the role of emotional stressors in the development of hypertension. The sympathoadrenomedullary axis figures prominently in most theories. Although the sympathoadrenomedullary axis is not the sole factor, it assumes a critical function in increasing cardiovascular as well as metabolic activity during emotional responding (Schneiderman, 1983). Although sympathetic activation can be adaptive in stressful situations, if the challenge is too severe, prolonged, or frequently repeated, or if the individual has marked organ or tissue pathology, then sympathetic activation could exacerbate existing disorders or initiate new ones.

The precise mechanisms by which sympathetic nervous system activity mediates the relationship between emotional factors and hypertension remains unclear. The relevant working hypotheses include stress-induced cardiovascular reactivity as a marker, arteriolar hypertrophy, autoregulation, and central drive.

Reactivity as a Risk Marker

Sympathetically mediated hyperresponsiveness to stress has been hypothesized to function as a marker for eventual hypertension (Krantz & Manuck, 1984). Support for the association of stress-induced reactivity and hypertension in humans comes from several lines of research including the family history studies and case-control studies referred to earlier (Fredrikson & Matthews, 1990). In addition, prospective studies (concurrent and nonconcurrent) also suggest that hyperresponsiveness to laboratory stressors, such as mental arithmetic or the cold pressor test, may be characteristic of individuals who eventually develop hypertension (Falkner, Kushner, Onesti, & Angelakos, 1981; Menkes et al., 1989; Wood, Sheps, Elveback, & Shirger, 1984).

The postulation that cardiovascular reactivity acts as a marker, however, does not imply a causal role for reactivity (Manuck, Kasprowicz, & Muldoon, 1990). Rather, an additional variable that is associated with both reactivity and hypertension could be implicated. Although this variable remains to be elucidated, Manuck et al. (1990) suggested three possibilities: (a) alteration in autonomic control of the myocardium and vascular system due to a central defect, (b) a higher concentration of intracellular sodium contributing to a decrease in vasodilator capacity, and (c) heightened reactivity of the arteries to vasoconstrictive substances. A discussion of the supportive and refuting arguments for these variables is presented by Manuck et al. (1990).

Arteriolar Structural Changes

Neurogenic factors figure prominently in Folkow's (1978) theory about the development of arteriolar hypertrophy. Folkow and colleagues contend that neurogenic factors contribute to hypertension development by

inducing vessel constriction. The elevated pressure caused by vasoconstriction is thought to produce vascular thickening and mechanically increased resistance that ultimately results in sustained hypertension (Folkow, 1978; Folkow, Grimby, & Thulesius, 1958; Folkow & Neil, 1971).
Folkow's findings suggest that the lumen of maximally dilated vessels is
relatively reduced in hypertensive individuals in relation to normotensive
individuals (Folkow et al., 1958).

Folkow (1978) hypothesized that cardiovascular smooth muscle hypertrophy is due to an adaptive process (over a period of months or years)
that results from exposure to "functional" trigger elements, such as environmental alerting stimuli (i.e., stressors). For example, the central nervous system, by means of stressors, excites the cardiovascular system,
which leads to the defense reaction. Trigger influences, however, are not
necessarily apparent during resting conditions. Furthermore, continuous
exposure to the triggers are not a prerequisite for arteriolar structural
changes. Rather, it is sufficient for exposure to occur repeatedly and
periodically over a fixed interval, as suggested by Manuck and Krantz's
(1986) model of recurrent activation. Thus, repeated excitatory influences
might result in recurrent hyperreactive pressor episodes that ultimately
contribute to adaptations leading to hypertension.

Carruthers (1969) offers another hypothesis by which emotional
stress could lead to hypertension by narrowing the arterial lumina and
increasing vessel wall resistance. Carruthers suggested that emotional
stressors precipitate catecholamine release, which, in turn, mobilizes free
fatty acids in excess of metabolic demands. This results in morphological
changes in the arterial wall in two ways: (a) free fatty acids increase
platelet aggregation, which leads to smooth muscle build-up and vessel
thickening; and (b) free fatty acids are taken up directly by arterial walls
or are converted to triglycerides, which are eventually deposited in the
arterial walls. In this model, blood pressure elevations are a consequence
of changes in vascular resistance.

Autoregulation

Guyton and Coleman (1969) maintain that autoregulatory processes as-
sume a critical function in arterial blood pressure control. Autoregulation

involves the adjustment of the vasculature to regulate blood flow to body tissues in response to alterations in tissue need. Although aspects of the autoregulatory process are rapid, the majority of the adjustments may require days. Renal factors, however, ultimately determine blood pressure level. Guyton (1977) and Guyton and Coleman (1969) contend that sustained hypertension results from the malfunction of renal mechanisms that are involved in fluid volume control. This view is consistent with psychophysiological research that has studied the renal handling of sodium (Light, Koepke, Obrist, & Willis, 1983).

Central Drive

The research of Julius and colleagues (Julius, 1987; Julius & Esler, 1975; Julius, Weder, & Hinderliter, 1986) provides another perspective about the role of autonomic function and behavior in hypertension. Pharmacological blockade studies of hyperkinetic borderline hypertensives, who are characterized by relatively elevated cardiac output, stroke volume, and heart rate, have shown that this condition is due to neurogenic influences (Julius & Esler, 1975). Julius suggests that, for those individuals with neurogenic borderline hypertension, the elevation in blood pressure may be due to behavioral factors. Behavioral factors may in part result in sympathoadrenomedullary activity that contributes to the secretion of renin and increases cardiac output, which lead to myocardial changes (e.g., down-regulation of β-adrenergic receptors) and greater peripheral resistance (Esler et al., 1977). Behavioral factors are presumed to exert their influence via a defect in central nervous system integration of autonomic control of the cardiovascular system (Julius & Esler, 1975) such that greater sympathetic influences cooccur with decreased parasympathetic influences (Julius et al., 1986).

The behavioral factors implicated in Julius's model refer to personality attributes (Julius, 1987). The borderline hypertensive is described by Julius as a submissive, though outward-oriented, individual who suppresses anger. This constellation of personality attributes is hypothesized to manifest in "defense-alerting behaviors." It is the physiological consequences of these behaviors that are purported to contribute to the development of hypertension.

Conclusions

The just-described hypotheses are not necessarily inconsistent with each other. Rather, they underscore different facets of the same issue. This is exemplified by the alternate views regarding the intermediate steps by which neurogenic mechanisms could mediate the relationship between behavioral stress and elevations in blood pressure. The hypotheses of Folkow and Julius offer a rationale for studying this problem in terms of the differential effects proposed for peripheral resistance and cardiac output. Obrist (1981), like Folkow, suggests that recurrent episodes of stress-induced sympathetic activation can contribute to hypertension in vulnerable individuals. However, cardiac output responses in excess of metabolic demands as well as arteriolar hypertrophy are implicated in Obrist's model.

Lund-Johansen (1986), however, maintains that, although young borderline and mild hypertensives are characterized by elevated cardiac output and heart rate with "normal" total peripheral resistance under resting conditions, the cardiac output level is appropriate in relation to oxygen consumption. Lund-Johansen also reports that untreated mild and borderline hypertensives that were followed for 17 years showed a gradual increase in blood pressure over time with a transition to a high total peripheral resistance state and concomitant decreases in cardiac output and stroke volume. Lund-Johansen contends that this transition is more compatible with the Folkow hypothesis than with the autoregulatory hypothesis.

A related issue is the means by which neurogenic events underlying heightened blood pressure responsivity eventually result in sustained hypertension. Sustained hypertension constitutes disrupted control of homeostasis. More specifically, after episodes of elevated responding, baroreceptors should assist in returning blood pressure to normotensive levels. In addition, healthy kidneys would be expected to counteract increased arterial pressure by increasing urinary output, thereby decreasing fluid volume (Shipley & Study, 1951). Folkow's view provides a partial means to understand how neurogenic mechanisms may result in structural changes supporting sustained hypertension; Guyton's hypothesis provides a framework for understanding how the hypertension is maintained.

Although none of the hypotheses unequivocally explain the course of hypertension development, they have had a notable impact on psychophysiological research conducted to clarify factors involved in blood pressure regulation. The strategy that is used in psychophysiological research is discussed in the following section.

Psychophysiological Strategy

Regulatory disorders such as hypertension have traditionally been assessed under basal conditions at either one or a few times. Although assessment under resting conditions provides valuable information, it is limited insofar as it does not address regulatory adjustments that operate in a behaving individual. Psychophysiologists have attempted to address this issue by implementing laboratory and field protocols directed at determining the biobehavioral mechanisms underlying blood pressure in groups at varying risk for hypertension because of factors such as blood pressure status, individual differences, age, ethnicity, sex, and their interaction (N. B. Anderson, 1989; Fredrikson & Matthews, 1990; Light, 1989; Manuck, Kasprowicz, Monroe, Larkin, & Kaplan, 1989; Saab, 1989; Stoney, Davis, & Matthews, 1988).

Just as the exercise stress and glucose tolerance tests have been able to provide important information that cannot be obtained by measurements made under static conditions, likewise, psychophysiological adjustments to challenging laboratory stressors can enhance our understanding of cardiovascular regulatory processes. Data from our laboratory suggest that regulatory mechanisms that are operative under resting conditions become modified as individuals are subjected to stressors. The utility of a psychophysiological strategy is apparent from the just-discussed family history data. For example, the normotensive offspring of hypertensive parents in relation to normotensive parents are indistinguishable on resting cardiovascular measures. It is not until the system is perturbed with a challenge that cardiovascular differences emerge between the family history status groups.

Nonetheless, assessment under resting conditions in the laboratory is critical to psychophysiological strategy because it provides a "control level" by which to compare stress-induced responses. Because resting measures may be affected by such factors as time of day, posture, level of consciousness, experimenter characteristics, prior substance ingestion, aspects of the informed consent, and the like, care and consistency are necessary for the acquisition of resting values. In addition, because habituation to the laboratory and procedures are also likely to influence resting values, attention needs to be paid to the duration of the resting period. The necessity of this is underscored when multiple stressors are presented. In such cases, the length of rest periods between challenges ought to be sufficient to permit recovery of control values. Consideration to the particular response measures also should be given to ensure that the rest-period interval is sufficient to obtain a stable resting level; for example, some neuroendocrine responses such as cortisol take longer to habituate than do measures such as heart rate and blood pressure (Schneiderman & McCabe, 1989). These factors, however, need to be weighed against practical considerations such as subject fatigue when designing and implementing an investigation.

In relation to control levels, stress-induced responses to challenges presented in the laboratory provide a sample of dynamic responses under varying conditions involving precise stimulus control. Although investigators may select stressors for various reasons, the underlying supposition is that responses evoked by the challenges provide useful information about responses to stressors that occur in a freely behaving individual. For example, it has often been assumed that individuals who react with exaggerated responses in the laboratory may react with marked responses to naturally occurring stressors.

Data from an investigation of adolescents conducted by Matthews, Manuck, and Saab (1986) directly bear on this issue. Tenth-grade students completed a standardized laboratory assessment that consisted of three stressors (serial subtraction, mirror tracing, and isometric handgrip). In addition, blood pressure and heart rate measures were obtained before, immediately preceding, and immediately after a required 5-min oral presentation in English class. For comparison purposes, assessments were also made during the student's subsequent English class. Reactor status (high vs. low reactor) to the laboratory stressors was related to cardiovascular responses during the evaluative speaking stressor. Those who displayed hyperreactivity to the laboratory tasks showed greater blood pressure and/or heart rate levels over the course of the presentation period (though this was not entirely consistent across laboratory stressors) but were not distinguished from low reactors during the next day English class period. These findings suggest that psychophysiological assessment in the laboratory can index responsivity in the field to naturally occurring stressors.

Several studies have also examined the relationship between responses to laboratory stressors and blood pressure measurements made during usual activities in naturalistic settings. Taken together, the data are mixed with respect to the association between the ambulatory blood pressure variability and laboratory task responses (for a review see Pickering & Gerrin, 1990). Although some investigators have reported significant associations between absolute task levels and ambulatory blood pressure levels (e.g., Harshfield et al., 1988; McKinney et al., 1985), Harshfield and colleagues (Harshfield et al., 1988) report that the correlations do not exceed those obtained between baseline and ambulatory blood pressure levels.

Research from our laboratory (Ironson et al., 1989) was undertaken to determine whether responses to laboratory challenges can improve prediction of ambulatory blood pressure responses beyond that obtained by initial blood pressure measurements. Although the correlations for ambulatory blood pressure levels and stressor-evoked blood pressure levels were in the moderate range, they did not exceed the obtained association for baseline and ambulatory levels. Regression analyses showed that baseline systolic blood pressure predicted 41% of the variance in systolic blood pressure at work for the total sample. Of the four tasks that were presented (structured interview, foot immersion cold pressor test, video game, and bicycle ergometry), only the change in systolic blood pressure during the structured interview added significantly, but it predicted only an additional 3% of the variance. When analyses were repeated separately for Whites, African Americans, men, and women, the structured interview continued to predict work systolic blood pressure for Whites and men (accounting for an additional 6% and 7% of the variance, respectively) beyond that predicted by baseline. For diastolic blood pressure at work, responses to the cold pressor test predicted an additional 5% of the variance above baseline for the African Americans, whereas responses to the structured interview predicted an additional 4% of the variance above baseline for the women. Only video game responses added to the prediction of systolic blood pressure at home, accounting for an additional 7% of the variance in women.

It is clear from these data that a carefully defined baseline is a powerful predictor of ambulatory blood pressure (Ironson et al., 1989). Although the amount of the variance accounted for by the laboratory stressors above and beyond the baseline levels was relatively low, the findings underscore the importance of evaluating factors such as subject ethnicity and sex. The finding that the cold pressor test, a stressor known to elicit vasoconstrictor activity (e.g., Allen & Crowell, 1989), differentially predicted diastolic blood pressure significantly better for African Americans than for Whites is perhaps more important than finding that the task can predict a small increase above ambulatory levels. The African American–White differences detected by the cold pressor test suggest that continued exploration into the mechanisms involved in differential blood pressure regulation in African Americans and Whites can be productive. Findings that blood pressure responses to laboratory tasks can be related to ambulatory blood pressure measures are likely to be important because several studies have reported relationships between field measurements of blood pressure, subsequent hypertension (Rose et al., 1978), and the complications of hypertension (Devereux et al., 1982; Perloff, Sokolow, & Cowan, 1983; Pickering, Harshfield, Devereux, & Laragh, 1985; Sokolow, Werdegar, Kain, & Hinman, 1966). Moreover, these studies have pointed out that ambulatory measurements add important information beyond that obtained by casual blood pressure readings in the clinic.

The rationale for using the psychophysiological strategy was outlined earlier. To the extent that it involves concomitant analyses of resting control levels, responses to a variety of laboratory tasks, and adjustments made under field conditions, it permits one to gain a comprehensive view of the relationships that exist among stressors, behavior, and cardiovascular regulation. The strategy does pose some risk, however, because erroneous inferences can be made, generalizations can be drawn too broadly, and superficial similarities or differences can be easily misinterpreted. To minimize such risks, it is necessary to specify stimulus–response relationships as precisely as possible and to use comprehensive measurement strategies that can allow the adequate identification of response patterns and their variations. In the subsequent section, we address the selection of laboratory stressors and the use of appropriate response measures to assess differential patterns of response.

Situational Stereotypy and Differential Patterns of Response

A wide variety of stressors have been used by researchers to elicit cardiovascular reactivity in the laboratory. Conceptual schemes that are used to categorize tasks include, but are not limited to, comparisons of sensory rejection versus sensory intake (Lacey, 1967), active coping versus passive coping (Obrist, 1981), defense reaction or striving versus aversive vigilance (e.g., Schneiderman, 1978, 1983; Schneiderman & McCabe, 1989), and Pattern 1 versus Pattern 2 (Williams, 1986). Schemes are imposed because it is implicitly assumed that certain physiological response patterns can be reliably elicited by specific tasks, that is, situational stereotypy (Lacey, 1967).

Williams (1986) and Schneiderman (1978, 1983) offered a theoretical model that encompasses Hilton's (1975) view that the organization of the central nervous system acts in concert in response to stimulation such that "integrated response patterns" rather than isolated responses occur. Response patterns, by definition, would be expected to be few in number. Therefore, a large body of stimuli would be expected to elicit similar responses patterns. Based on animal and human research, defensive reactions, striving, or Pattern 1–type reactions are associated with skeletal muscle vasodilation, blood pressure increases primarily due to elevations in cardiac output, tachycardia, increased β1-adrenergic activity, and decreased vagal tone. In contrast, vigilance or Pattern 2–type reactions are characterized by muscle vasoconstriction, blood pressure increases primarily due to elevations in total peripheral resistance, bradycardia, increased α-adrenergic activity, and increased vagal tone (Schneiderman & McCabe, 1989; Williams, 1986). Laboratory stressors thought to evoke the first patterns of responses are those that involve active coping, mental work, or defense behavior, whereas those associated with the second pattern of responses are characterized by aversive vigilance, inhibitory coping, or passive avoidance.

Although situational stereotypy is acknowledged, the similarities and differences evoked by laboratory stressors are not completely understood. For example, there are a number of factors that appear to moderate the Pattern 1 response pattern (e.g., instructions, incentives, harassment, controllability, predictability, and individual differences) and mixed patterns of response are often apparent (Schneiderman & McCabe, 1989). In part, the lack of clarity in understanding the stressor attributes and various other factors that influence response patterns is largely attributable to the manner in which cardiovascular reactivity is typically evaluated, that is, by assessments limited to blood pressure and heart rate. Inferences about response patterns have often been based on only two or three parameters. This has historically been a shortcoming of most of the psychophysiological literature on response patterns.

Instead of limiting the assessment to convenient measures, it is important to evaluate judiciously an adequate number of relevant measures to allow for the response pattern and its variations to be sufficiently identified. Impedance cardiography can be of considerable value in this regard because it provides a noninvasive means to calculate cardiac output and total peripheral resistance in addition to estimates of contractility. As such, impedance cardiography provides a methodology to identify the factor(s) underlying the blood pressure and heart rate responses to laboratory stressors and the response pattern emitted by the cardiovascular system. The recent research of Allen and colleagues (Allen & Crowell, 1989; Allen, Obrist, Sherwood, & Crowell, 1987; Allen, Sherwood, & Obrist, 1986) is illustrative in this regard. Allen has studied responses evoked by foot, as well as hand, immersion cold pressor tests, reaction time with and without threat of shock, and mental arithmetic requiring verbal responses (i.e., serial subtraction) as well as nonverbal responses (i.e., computer-delivered stimuli). Allen and Crowell (1989) demonstrated that the use of systolic and diastolic blood pressure and heart rate alone are insufficient to distinguish among cold pressor, mental arithmetic, and reaction time stressors because all tasks evoke increases above resting levels. However, total peripheral resistance evoked by the cold pressor test exceeds levels evoked by the reaction time and mental arithmetic tasks, whereas the opposite was true for cardiac output. The cardiac output results were a function of augmented stroke volume and heart rate for reaction time, no change in stroke volume with increased heart rate for mental arithmetic, and a large decrease in stroke volume with increased heart rate for the cold pressor test. Mental arithmetic and reaction time were also characterized by a faster preinjection period than was the cold pressor test. Together with respiratory variables, these data were interpreted as being consistent with a β-adrenergic or Pattern 1 response pattern for reaction time, an α-adrenergic or Pattern 2 response pattern for the cold pressor test, and a mixed response pattern for mental arithmetic.

Recent research in our laboratory examined the response patterns evoked by three additional tasks that we routinely use in our cardiovascular psychophysiology investigations, that is, the evaluated speaking task, mirror tracing task, and the forehead stimulation cold pressor test (Saab et al., 1992). The evaluative speaking task involves preparing and presenting a story about a given situation. The task has a salient social–evaluative component. Instructions specify that the presention will be videotaped and later rated on the basis of poise, articulation, and appearance of the subject. The mirror tracing task requires tracing the outline of a star while looking at its mirror image, which inverts the star. As such, the task requires inhibiting certain motor responses in relation to visual feedback. For the forehead stimulation cold pressor test, an ice pack is situated over the subject's forehead and temple region. This version of the cold pressor test involves stimulation of the opthalmic–trigeminal dermatome.

Our interest, like that of Allen's (e.g., Allen & Crowell, 1989), was to identify the response patterns that characterize the three tasks. In addition, given our longstanding interest in ethnic differences, we were concerned as to whether response patterns differ as a function of ethnicity. To this end, we studied White and African American men who were 25–44 years old. All three tasks significantly raised systolic and diastolic blood pressure above resting levels in the White and African American men. The heart rate acceleration during the preparation and presentation phases of the evaluated speaking task, and to a smaller extent during the mirror tracing task, contrasted with the deceleration during forehead stimulation that was observed for both ethnic groups. The African American and White men were essentially indistinguishable on the basis of the blood pressure and heart rate parameters alone. In contrast, the impedance cardiography–derived measures, including cardiac output, stroke volume, total peripheral resistance, and the Heather index, assisted in understanding the processes supporting the task blood pressure and heart rate responses (see Figure 1). White men increased cardiac output during speech preparation and maintained the response during the presentation phase. The cardiac output response occurred with no alteration in total peripheral resistance for the preparation phase but coincided with an increase in total peripheral resistance during the presentation period. In contrast, the mirror tracing task and cold pressor test were associated with a slight elevation in total peripheral resistance with no change in cardiac output. The Heather index data showed evidence of increased cardiac contractility during periods of greater cardiac output. Thus, for the White men, the response pattern that was evoked during the speech preparation period suggests a myocardial response pattern, whereas the response pattern during the presentation phase seems to represent a mixed challenge that appears to have both myocardial and vascular components. The mirror tracing task and cold pressor test evoked a vascular response pattern.

For the African American men, cardiac output decreased during all task periods. The decreased cardiac output was largely a function of decreased stroke volume. Sympathetic drive on the myocardium, as reflected by the Heather index, was also attenuated across all tasks in the African Americans. Total peripheral resistance, however, was consistently elevated across task periods in the African Americans, which suggests

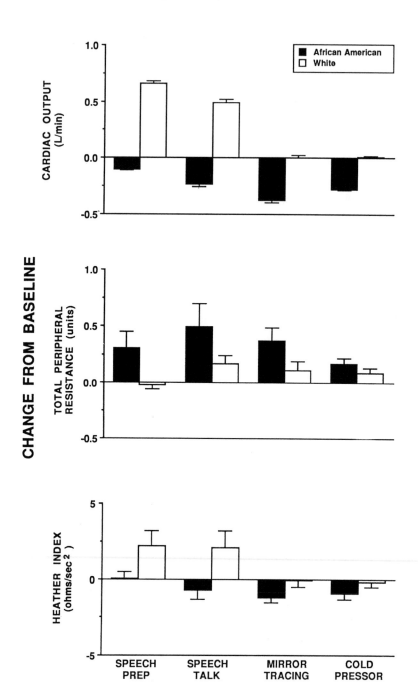

FIGURE 1. Mean change from baseline (±*SE*) of cardiac output, total peripheral resistance, and the Heather index for African American and White men. From "Myocardial and Peripheral Vascular Responses to Behavioral Challenges and Their Stability in Black and White Americans" by P. G. Saab, M. M. Llabre, B. E. Hurwitz, C. A. Frame, L. J. Reineke, A. I. Fins, J. McCalla, L. K. Cieply, and N. Schneiderman, 1992, *Psychophysiology, 29,* 384–397; copyright 1992 by the Society for Psychophysiological Research; reprinted by permission.

that the overall blood pressure responsivity of the African American men was due to arteriolar vasoconstriction.

Both the mirror tracing task, which is a psychological challenge, and forehead cold stimulation, which is a physical challenge with a measurable psychological component (Peckerman et al., 1991), appeared to evoke a vascularly mediated response pattern in the African American and White men. It is also noteworthy that the preparation period of the speech, which elicited a myocardial response pattern in the White men, evoked a vasoconstrictive response pattern in the African American men. Thus, the preparation period results demonstrate that ethnicity moderates response patterns for some tasks. It is necessary to recognize that we would have been unable to identify these relationships had we limited our measurements to blood pressure and heart rate. Although these relationships are intriguing, we recognize the necessity of replicating these relationships in larger samples that include older individuals and women. This research is currently under way in our laboratory.

The value of implementing the psychophysiological strategy as a potential means for understanding these group differences and their utility as a marker for hypertensive risk in part depends on a demonstration of temporal stability (Pickering & Gerrin, 1990). Therefore, we retested the participants in the Saab et al. (1992) study 2 weeks later under identical circumstances. The results indicated that cardiac output, stroke volume, total peripheral resistance, and the Heather index could be reliably assessed over this interval. The reliabilities of the baseline and task levels of the impedance-derived parameters were comparable to or greater (0.72–0.92) than the values typically associated with blood pressure and heart rate in the literature (for a review of the blood pressure and heart rate stability literature see Manuck et al., 1989). Although the reliabilities of the delta scores for impedance-derived parameters tended to be greater than those for blood pressure, as expected, the reliabilities for the delta scores were somewhat attenuated in relation to task levels for all parameters. Nonetheless, they compare quite favorably with other research that has used impedance cardiography (Fahrenberg, Schneider, & Safian, 1987; Kasprowicz, Manuck, Malkoff, & Krantz, 1990; McKinney et al., 1985; Myrtek, 1985). A recently completed 1-year retest of a subsample of these men also showed that the physiological responses remain stable over the longer follow-up interval (Llabre et al., 1992). Taken together, these findings demonstrate that impedance cardiography is a reliable and powerful tool for characterizing the response patterns of laboratory tasks that are used in cardiovascular reactivity research.

Total Peripheral Resistance and Hypertensive Risk

To the extent that hypertension appears to be in large measure a disorder of peripheral resistance, our finding (Saab et al., 1992) that African Americans, who in relation to Whites are at greater risk for hypertension, primarily respond to a variety of stressors with an increase in peripheral resistance, even while normotensive, is of considerable interest. These data are consistent with the findings of Light and Sherwood (1989), who showed that in relation to White college men, African American college men responded to a competitive reaction time task (a purported β-adrenergic challenge for Whites) with greater total peripheral resistance responses both before and after beta blockade. Trieber and colleagues (Trieber et al., 1990) also reported that African American men (medical students) exhibit greater total peripheral resistance responses than do their White counterparts to the forehead stimulation cold pressor test.

Recent research by Girdler, Turner, Sherwood, and Light (1990) agrees with the view that increased total peripheral resistance responding characterizes groups at high risk for hypertension. In response to two speech tasks (evaluated speaking and reading text aloud) and two math tasks (serial subtraction and nonverbal computerized math), total peripheral resistance increased for the normotensive men and decreased for the normotensive women in a predominantly White sample. In contrast, the cardiac output responses of women surpassed those of men. Designation of myocardial and vascular hyperreactors (based on cardiac output and total peripheral resistance changes) for the serial subtraction and reading-aloud stressors demonstrated that a higher percentage of women were represented among the myocardial reactors, whereas more men were represented among the vascular reactors.

Although we are unaware of any published study that has directly examined vascular resistance responding as a function of age, blood pressure (especially for systolic blood pressure) responsivity to stressors is typically greater in older groups in relation to younger groups (Garwood, Engel, & Capriotti, 1982; Johansson & Hjalmarson, 1988; Matthews & Stoney, 1988; Palmer, Ziegler, & Lake, 1978; Steptoe, Moses, & Edwards, 1990). Arterial stiffening is reputed to play a primary role in the age-related increase in resting systolic blood pressure. In fact, Lakatta (1987) suggested that "vascular aging" represents a "muted hypertension."

When considered together, the data from studies that examined cardiovascular responsiveness as a function of ethnicity, gender, and age suggest that hypertensive risk may be related to the tendency of elevating blood pressure in challenging situations by increasing peripheral resistance. This suggests that earlier descriptions of hypertensive development that were based primarily on examination of White men (e.g., Esler et al., 1977; Lund-Johansen, 1986) may be incomplete. Along these lines, it is interesting to note that Julius's group (Julius, Pascual, Sannerstedt, & Mitchell, 1971) has pointed out that even when blood pressure elevations appear to be driven by an increase in cardiac output in borderline hypertensive patients, the failure to reflexively decrease blood pressure levels reflects a dysregulation of peripheral resistance.

Research Agenda

The data available on the pathogenesis of hypertension suggest that it is multifactorily determined (Page, 1977). For this reason it is difficult to assess the contribution made by individual variables or their specific interactions with other variables. Animal models such as the Dahl sodium-sensitive rat, the SHR, and the borderline hypertensive rat appear to be good candidates for future studies examining genetic–behavioral interactions. Social interaction studies such as those carried out by Henry and colleagues (e.g., Henry et al., 1975) need to be conducted on rats and mice with strain as a variable.

Several studies that examined the contributions made by psychosocial factors to the development of hypertension have identified socioecologic stress, low socioeconomic status, and being African American as major variables (e.g., Harburg et al., 1973). The precise biobehavioral factors driving these variables have not been adequately identified. Thus, the exact manner in which an unhealthy life-style, poor nutrition, and inadequate health care interact with the harsh environmental conditions experienced by many African Americans is yet to be determined. Particular attention needs to be paid to adiposity because obese adults are almost twice as likely to be hypertensive as age-matched nonobese subjects (E. A. H. Sims, 1982), and adult African American women have been found to weigh significantly more than their White counterparts at every age (Gartside, Khoury, & Glueck, 1984). The relationship between excessive alcohol use and stress in the development of hypertension also deserves attention.

A body of evidence has recently begun to emerge relating obesity and blood pressure elevations to insulin resistance and hyperinsulinemia (e.g., Reaven, 1988). Behaviorally related research needs to focus on the metabolic interrelationships that are involved because it appears likely that hyperinsulinemia affects sympathetic nervous system activity and the renal handling of sodium. It would be particularly interesting, for example, to determine whether hyperinsulinemia is related to (a) the increased α-adrenergic responsivity to norepinephrine infusion seen in hypertensive African Americans (Dimsdale, Graham, Ziegler, Zusman, & Berry, 1987) and/or (b) the increased peripheral resistance and α-adrenergic reactivity in response to the cold pressor test (N. B. Anderson, Lane, Muranaka, Williams, & Houseworth, 1988) and other behavioral stressors in African Americans (Alpert, Dover, Booker, Martin, & Strong, 1981; Light & Sherwood, 1989).

Laboratory research into the study of blood pressure regulation in humans has now reached a point at which (a) technology exists for noninvasively evaluating hemodynamic response patterns to behavioral stressors and (b) well-characterized stressors have been identified that are capable of differentially eliciting various response patterns. Although the resting blood pressure baseline may well be the best predictor of blood pressure in nonlaboratory situations, it appears likely that a study of hemodynamic factors in the laboratory may facilitate an understanding of how blood pressure is differentially regulated under conditions of relaxation, sleep, and job strain under field conditions. Such studies may prove to be particularly useful in the future prediction of hypertensive risk.

References

Allen, M. T., & Crowell, M. D. (1989). Patterns of autonomic response during laboratory stressors. *Psychophysiology, 26,* 603–614.

Allen, M. T., Obrist, P. A., Sherwood, A., & Crowell, M. D. (1987). Evaluation of myocardial and peripheral vascular responses during reaction time, mental arithmetic, and cold pressor tasks. *Psychophysiology, 24,* 648–656.

Allen, M. T., Sherwood, A., & Obrist, P. A. (1986). Interactions of respiratory and cardiovascular adjustments to behavioral stressors. *Psychophysiology, 23,* 532–541.

Alpert, B. S., Dover, E. V., Booker, D. L., Martin, A. M., & Strong, W. B. (1981). Blood pressure response to dynamic exercise in healthy children: Black versus White. *Journal of Pediatrics, 99,* 556–560.

Anderson, D. E., Kearns, W. D., & Better, W. E. (1983). Progressive hypertension in dogs by avoidance conditioning and saline infusion. *Hypertension, 5,* 286–291.

Anderson, N. B. (1989). Ethnic differences in resting and stress-induced cardiovascular and humoral activity: An overview. In N. Schneiderman, S. M. Weiss, & P. Kaufmann (Eds.), *Handbook of research methods in cardiovascular behavioral medicine* (pp. 433–451). New York: Plenum.

Anderson, N. B., Lane, J. D., Muranaka, M., Williams, R. B., Jr., & Houseworth, S. J. (1988). Racial differences in blood pressure and forearm vascular responses to the cold face stimulus. *Psychosomatic Medicine, 50,* 57–63.

Ayman, D. (1934). Heredity in arteriolar (essential) hypertension: A clinical study of blood pressure of 1,524 members of 277 families. *Archives of Internal Medicine, 53,* 792–798.

Carmelli, D., Chesney, M. A., Ward, M. M., & Rosenman, R. H. (1985). Twin similarity in cardiovascular stress response. *Health Psychology, 4,* 413–423.

Carroll, D., Hewitt, J. K., Last, K. R., Turner, J. R., & Sims, J. (1985). A twin study of cardiac reactivity and its relationship to parental blood pressure. *Physiology and Behavior, 34,* 103–106.

Carruthers, M. E. (1969). Aggression and atheroma. *Lancet, 2,* 1170–1171.

Cierpial, M. A., Konarska, M., & McCarty, R. (1988). Maternal effects on the development of spontaneous hypertension. *Health Psychology, 7,* 125–135.

Cobb, S., & Rose, R. M. (1973). Hypertension, peptic ulcer, and diabetes in air traffic controllers. *Journal of the American Medical Association, 224,* 489–492.

Cox, R. H., Hubbard, J. W., Lawler, J. E., Sanders, B. J., & Mitchell, V. P. (1985). Exercise training attenuates stress-induced hypertension in the rat. *Hypertension, 7,* 747–751.

Dahl, L. K., Heine, M., & Tassinari, L. J. (1965). Effects of chronic salt ingestion: Further demonstration that genetic factors influence the development of hypertension. Evidence from experimental hypertension due to cortisone and to adrenal regeneration. *Journal of Experimental Medicine, 122,* 533–545.

Devereux, R., Pickering, T., Harshfield, G., Denby, L., Clark, L., Kleinert, H., Pregibon, D.,

Borer, J., & Laragh, J. (1982). Does home blood pressure improve prediction of change in patients with hypertension? *Circulation, 66*(Suppl. II), II-63.

Dimsdale, J. E., Graham, R. M., Ziegler, M. G., Zusman, R. M., & Berry, C. C. (1987). Age, race, diagnosis, and sodium effects on the pressor response to infused norepinephrine. *Hypertension, 10,* 564–569.

Ditto, B. (1986). Parental history of essential hypertension, active coping, and cardiovascular reactivity. *Psychophysiology, 23,* 62–70.

Durel, L., & Schneiderman, N. (1991). Biobehavioral bases of hypertension in Blacks. In P. M. McCabe, T. Field, & N. Schneiderman (Eds.), *Stress, coping and disease* (pp. 3–34). Hillsdale, NJ: Erlbaum.

Ehrstrom, M. D. (1945). Psychogene kriegshypertonien [Psychogenic hypertension]. *Acta Medica Scandinavica, 122,* 546–570.

Esler, M., Julius, S., Zweifler, A., Randall, O., Harburg, E., Gardiner, H., & De Quattro, V. (1977). Mild high-renin essential hypertension: Neurogenic hypertension? *New England Journal of Medicine, 296,* 405–411.

Falkner, B., Kushner, H., Onesti, G., & Angelakos, E. (1981). Cardiovascular characteristics in adolescents who develop essential hypertension. *Hypertension, 3,* 521–527.

Falkner, B., Onesti, G., Angelakos, E. T., Fernandes, M., & Langman, C. (1979). Cardiovascular response to mental stress in normal adolescents with hypertensive parents. *Hypertension, 1,* 23.

Fahrenberg, J., Schneider, H. J., & Safian, P. (1987). Psychophysiological assessments in a repeated-measurement design extending over a one-year interval: Trends and stability. *Biological Psychology, 24,* 49–66.

Feinleib, M. (1979). Genetics and familial aggregation of blood pressure. In G. Onesti & C. R. Klimt (Eds.), *Hypertension: Determinants, complications and intervention* (pp. 35–48). New York: Grune & Stratton.

Folkow, B. (1978). Cardiovascular structural adaptation: Its role in the initiation and maintenance of primary hypertension. *Clinical Science and Molecular Medicine, 55,* 3s–22s.

Folkow, B., Grimby, G., & Thulesius, O. (1958). Adaptive structural changes of the vascular walls in hypertension and their relation to the control of the peripheral resistance. *Acta Physiologica Scandinavica, 44,* 255–272.

Folkow, B., & Hallbäck, M. (1977). Physiopathology of spontaneous hypertension in rats. In J. Genest, E. Koiw, & O. Kuchel (Eds.), *Hypertension: Physiopathology and treatment* (pp. 507–529). New York: McGraw-Hill.

Folkow, B., & Neil, E. (1971). *Circulation.* London: Oxford University Press.

Fredrikson, M., & Matthews, K. A. (1990). Cardiovascular responses to behavioral stress and hypertension: A meta-analytic review. *Annals of Behavioral Medicine, 12,* 30–39.

Friedman, R., & Iwai, J. (1976). Genetic predisposition and stress-induced hypertension. *Science, 193,* 161–172.

Gartside, P. S., Khoury, P., & Glueck, C. J. (1984). Determinants of high density lipoprotein cholesterol in Blacks and Whites: The Second National Health and Nutrition Examination Survey. *American Heart Journal, 108*, 641–653.

Garwood, M., Engel, B. T., & Capriotti, R. (1982). Autonomic nervous system function and aging: Response specificity. *Psychophysiology, 19*, 378–385.

Girdler, S. S., Turner, J. R., Sherwood, A., & Light, K. C. (1990). Gender differences in blood pressure control during a variety of behavioral stressors. *Psychosomatic Medicine, 52*, 571–591.

Graham, J. D. P. (1945). High blood pressure after battle. *Lancet, 248*, 239–240.

Guyton, A. C. (1977). Personal views on mechanisms of hypertension. In J. Genest, E. Koiw, & O. Kuchel (Eds.), *Hypertension: Physiopathology and treatment.* New York: McGraw-Hill.

Guyton, A. C., & Coleman, T. G. (1969). Quantitative analysis of the pathophysiology of hypertension. *Circulation Research, 24*(Suppl. I), I-1–I-19.

Hallbäck, M. (1975). Consequence of social isolation on blood pressure, cardiovascular reactivity and design in spontaneously hypertensive rats. *Acta Physiologica Scandinavica, 93*, 455–465.

Hallbäck, M., & Folkow, B. (1974). Cardiovascular responses to acute mental "stress" in spontaneously hypertensive rats. *Acta Physiological Scandinavica, 90*, 684–698.

Hallbäck-Norlander, M., & Lundin, S. (1979). Background of hyperkinetic circulatory state in young spontaneously hypertensive rats. In P. Meyer & H. Schmitt (Eds.), *Nervous system and hypertension.* New York: Wiley.

Harburg, E., Erfurt, J. C., Hauenstein, L. S., Chape, C., Schull, W. J., & Schork, M. A. (1973). Socioecological stress, suppressed hostility, skin color, and black–white male blood pressure: Detroit. *Psychosomatic Medicine, 35*, 276–296.

Harshfield, G. A., James, G. D., Schlussel, Y., Yee, L. S., Blank, S. G., & Pickering, T. G. (1988). Do laboratory tests of blood pressure reactivity predict blood pressure variability in real life? *American Journal of Hypertension, 1*, 168–174.

Hastrup, J. L., Hotchkiss, A. P., & Johnson, C. A. (1985). Accuracy of knowledge of family history of cardiovascular disorders. *Health Psychology, 4*, 291–306.

Hastrup, J. L., Light, K. C., & Obrist, P. A. (1982). Parental hypertension and cardiovascular response to stress in healthy young adults. *Psychophysiology, 19*, 615–622.

Henry, J. P., Ely, D. L., & Stephens, P. M. (1972). Changes in catecholamine-controlling enzymes in response to psychosocial activation of the defence and alarm reactions: Physiology, emotion and psychosomatic illness. *Ciba Foundation Symposium, 8*, 225–251.

Henry, J. P., Meehan, J. P., & Stephens, P. M. (1967). The use of psychosocial stimuli to induce prolonged systolic hypertension in mice. *Psychosomatic Medicine, 29*, 408–432.

Henry, J. P., & Stephens, P. M. (1977). *Stress, health and the social environment: A sociobiologic approach to medicine.* New York: Springer.

Henry, J. P., Stephens, P. M., Axelrod, J., & Mueller, R. A. (1971). Effect of psychosocial stimulation on the enzymes involved in the biosynthesis and metabolism of noradrenaline and adrenaline. *Psychosomatic Medicine, 33,* 227–237.

Henry, J. P., Stephens, P. M., & Santisteban, G. A. (1975). A model of psychosocial hypertension showing reversibility and progression of cardiovascular complications. *Circulation Research, 36,* 156–164.

Herd, J. A., Morse, W. H., Kelleher, R. T., & Jones, L. G. (1969). Arterial hypertension in the squirrel monkey during behavioral experiments. *American Journal of Physiology, 217,* 24–29.

Hilton, S. M. (1975). Ways of viewing the central nervous control of the circulation: Old and new. *Brain Research, 87,* 213–219.

Ironson, G. H., Gellman, M. D., Spitzer, S. B., Llabre, M. M., Pasin, R. D., Weidler, D. J., & Schneiderman, N. (1989). Predicting home and work blood pressure measurements from resting baselines and laboratory reactivity in Black and White Americans. *Psychophysiology, 26,* 174–184.

Johansson, S. R., & Hjalmarson, A. (1988). Age and sex differences in cardiovascular reactivity to adrenergic agonists, mental stress and isometric exercise in normal subjects. *Scandinavian Journal of Clinical Laboratory Investigation, 48,* 183–191.

Julius, S. (1977). Classification of hypertension. In J. Genest, E. Koiw, & O. Kuchel (Eds.), *Hypertension: Physiopathology and treatment* (pp. 9–14). New York: McGraw-Hill.

Julius, S. (1987). Hemodynamic, pharmacologic and epidemiologic evidence for behavioral factors in human hypertension. In S. Julius & D. R. Bassett (Eds.), *Handbook of hypertension: Vol. 9. Behavioral factors in hypertension* (pp. 59–74). Amsterdam: Elsevier Science.

Julius, S., & Esler, M. (1975). Autonomic nervous cardiovascular regulation in borderline hypertension. *American Journal of Cardiology, 36,* 685–695.

Julius, S., Pascual, A. V., Sannerstedt, R., & Mitchell, C. (1971). Relationship between cardiac output and peripheral resistance in borderline hypertension. *Circulation, 43,* 382–390.

Julius, S., Weder, A. B., & Hinderliter, A. L. (1986). Does behaviorally induced blood pressure variability lead to hypertension? In K. A. Matthews, S. M. Weiss, T. Detre, T. M. Dembroski, B. Falkner, S. B. Manuck, & R. B. Williams, Jr. (Eds.), *Handbook of stress, reactivity, and cardiovascular disease* (pp. 71–82). New York: Wiley.

Kannel, W. B., Gordon, T., & Schwartz, M. J. (1971). Systolic versus diastolic blood pressure and risk of coronary heart disease. *American Journal of Cardiology, 27,* 335–343.

Kasprowicz, A. L., Manuck, S. B., Malkoff, S. B., & Krantz, D. S. (1990). Individual differences in behaviorally evoked cardiovascular response: Temporal stability and hemodynamic patterning. *Psychophysiology, 27,* 605–619.

Krantz, D. S., & Manuck, S. B. (1984). Acute psychophysiologic reactivity and risk of cardiovascular disease: A review and methodologic critique. *Psychological Bulletin, 96,* 435–464.

Lacey, J. I. (1967). Somatic response patterning and stress: Some revisions of activation theory. In M. H. Appley & R. Trumbull (Eds.), *Issues in research* (pp. 14–44). New York: Appleton-Century-Crofts.

Lakatta, E. G. (1987). Do hypertension and aging have a similar effect on the myocardium? *Circulation, 75*(Suppl. I), I-69.

Lawler, J. E., Barker, G. F., Hubbard, J. W., & Allen, M. T. (1980). The effects of conflict on tonic levels of blood pressure in the genetically borderline hypertensive rat. *Psychophysiology, 17*, 363–370.

Lawler, J. E., Sanders, B. J., Chen, Y. F., Nagahama, S., & Oparil, S. (1987). Hypertension produced by a high sodium diet in the borderline hypertensive rat. *Clinical and Experimental Hypertension, A9*, 1713–1731.

Light, K. C. (1989). Constitutional factors relating to differences in cardiovascular response. In N. Schneiderman, S. M. Weiss, & P. Kaufmann (Eds.), *Handbook of research methods in cardiovascular behavioral medicine* (pp. 417–431). New York: Plenum.

Light, K. C., Koepke, J. P., Obrist, P. A., & Willis, P. W. (1983). Psychological stress induces sodium and fluid retention in men at high risk for hypertension. *Science, 220*, 429–431.

Light, K. C., & Sherwood, A. (1989). Race, borderline hypertension, and hemodynamic responses to behavioral stress before and after beta-adrenergic blockade. *Health Psychology, 8*, 577–595.

Lipman, R. L., & Shapiro, A. (1967). Effects of a behavioral stimulus on the blood pressure of rats with experimental pyelonephritis. *Psychosomatic Medicine, 29*, 612–618.

Llabre, M. M., Saab, P. G., Hurwitz, B., Frame, C., Spitzer, S., Phillips, D., & Schneiderman, N. (1992, March). *Stability of stroke volume, cardiac output, total periperhal resistance and Heather index under different laboratory challenges: One year follow-up*. Paper presented at the annual meeting of the Society of Behavioral Medicine, New York.

Lund-Johansen, P. (1986). Hemodynamic patterns in the natural history of borderline hypertension. *Journal of Cardiovascular Pharmacology, 8*(Suppl. 5), S8–S14.

Manuck, S. B., Kasprowicz, A. L., Monroe, S. M., Larkin, K. T., & Kaplan, J. R. (1989). Psychophysiologic reactivity as a dimension of individual differences. In N. Schneiderman, S. M. Weiss, & P. Kaufmann (Eds.), *Handbook of research methods in cardiovascular behavioral medicine* (pp. 365–382). New York: Plenum.

Manuck, S. B., Kasprowicz, A. L., & Muldoon, M. F. (1990). Behaviorally-evoked cardiovascular reactivity and hypertension: Conceptual issues and potential associations. *Annals of Behavioral Medicine, 12*, 17–29.

Manuck, S. B., & Krantz, D. S. (1986). Psychophysiologic reactivity in coronary heart disease and essential hypertension. In K. A. Matthews, S. M. Weiss, T. Detre, T. M. Dembroski, B. Falkner, S. B. Manuck, & R. B. Williams, Jr. (Eds.), *Handbook of stress, reactivity, and cardiovascular disease* (pp. 11–34). New York: Wiley.

Matthews, K. A., Manuck, S. B., & Saab, P. G. (1986). Predictors of cardiovascular responses to a naturally occurring stressor: Characteristics of the reactive adolescent during public speaking. *Psychophysiology, 23,* 198–209.

Matthews, K. A., & Rakaczky, C. J. (1986). Familial aspects of the Type A behavior pattern and physiologic reactivity to stress. In T. H. Schmidt, T. M. Dembroski, & G. Blumchen (Eds.), *Biological and psychological factors in cardiovascular disease* (pp. 228–245). Berlin: Springer-Verlag.

Matthews, K. A., & Stoney, C. M. (1988). Influences of sex and age on cardiovascular responses during stress. *Psychosomatic Medicine, 50,* 46–56.

McCarty, R., Chiveh, C. C., & Kopin, I. J. (1978a). Behavioral and cardiovascular responses of spontaneously hypertensive and normotensive rats to inescapable footshock. *Behavioral Biology, 22,* 405.

McCarty, R., Chiveh, C. C., & Kopin, I. J. (1978b). Spontaneously hypertensive rats: Adrenergic hyper-reactivity to anticipation of electric shock. *Behavioral Biology, 23,* 180.

McCarty, R., & Kopin, I. J. (1978). Alterations in plasma catecholamines and behavior during acute stress in spontaneously hypertensive and Wistar-Kyoto normotensive rats. *Life Science, 22,* 997.

McKinney, M. E., Milner, M. H., Rüddel, H., McIlvain, H. E., Witte, H., Buell, J. C., & Eliot, R. S. (1985). The standardized mental stress test protocol: Test–retest reliability and comparison with ambulatory blood pressure monitoring. *Psychophysiology, 22,* 453–463.

Menkes, M. S., Matthews, K. A., Krantz, D. S., Lundberg, U., Mead, L. A., Qaqish, B., Liang, K.-Y., Thomas, C. B., & Pearson, T. A. (1989). Cardiovascular reactivity to the cold pressor test as a predictor of hypertension. *Hypertension, 14,* 524–530.

Myrtek, M. (1985). Adaptation effects and the stability of physiological responses to repeated testing. In A. Steptoe, H. Rüddel, & H. Neus (Eds.), *Clinical and methodological issues in cardiovascular psychophysiology* (pp. 93–106). Berlin: Springer-Verlag.

Obrist, P. A. (1981). *Cardiovascular psychophysiology: A perspective.* New York: Plenum.

Obrist, P. A., Light, K. C., Sherman, A. J., & Strogatz, D. S. (1987). Cardiovascular responses to stress: I. Measures of myocardial response and relationship to high resting systolic pressure and parental hypertension. *Psychophysiology, 24,* 65–78.

Okamoto, K., & Aoki, K. (1963). Development of a strain of spontaneously hypertensive rat. *Japanese Circulation Journal, 27,* 282–293.

Page, I. H. (1949). Pathogenesis of arterial hypertension. *Journal of the American Medical Association, 140,* 451–458.

Page, I. H. (1977). Some regulatory mechanisms of renovascular and essential hypertension. In J. Genest, E. Koiw, & O. Kuchel (Eds.), *Hypertension: Physiopathology and treatment* (pp. 576–597). New York: McGraw-Hill.

Palmer, G. J., Ziegler, M. G., & Lake, C. R. (1978). Response of norepinephrine and blood pressure to stress increases with age. *Journal of Gerontology, 33,* 482–487.

Peckerman, A., Saab, P. G., McCabe, P. M., Skyler, J. S., Winters, R. W., Llabre, M. M., & Schneiderman, N. (1991). Blood pressure reactivity and perception of pain during the forehead cold pressor test. *Psychophysiology, 28,* 485–495.

Perloff, D., Sokolow, M., & Cowan, R. (1983). The prognostic value of ambulatory blood pressures. *Journal of the American Medical Association, 249,* 2792–2798.

Pickering, T. G., & Gerrin, W. (1990). Cardiovascular reactivity in the laboratory and the role of behavioral factors in hypertension: A critical review. *Annals of Behavioral Medicine, 12,* 3–16.

Pickering, T. G., Harshfield, G. A., Devereux, R. B., & Laragh, J. H. (1985). What is the role of ambulatory blood pressure monitoring in the management of hypertensive patients? *Hypertension, 7,* 171.

Reaven, G. M. (1988). Role of insulin resistance in human disease. *Diabetes, 37,* 1595–1607.

Roberts, J., & Rowland, M. (1981). *Hypertension in adults 25–74 years of age. United States: 1971–1975* (Series 11, No. 221). Washington, DC: U.S. Department of Health, Education, and Welfare, National Center for Health Statistics.

Rose, R. J. (1986). Familial influences on cardiovascular reactivity to stress. In K. A. Matthews, S. M. Weiss, T. Detre, T. M. Dembroski, B. Falkner, S. B. Manuck, & R. B. Williams, Jr. (Eds.), *Handbook of stress, reactivity, and cardiovascular disease* (pp. 259–272). New York: Wiley.

Rose, R., Jenkins, C., & Hurst, M. (1978). *Air traffic controller health change study.* Boston: Boston University School of Medicine.

Ruskin, A., Beard, O. W., & Schaffer, R. L. (1948). Blast hypertension: Elevated arterial pressure in victims of the Texas City disaster. *American Journal of Medicine, 4,* 228–236.

Saab, P. G. (1989). Cardiovascular and neuroendocrine responses to challenge in males and females. In N. Schneiderman, S. M. Weiss, & P. Kaufmann (Eds.), *Handbook of research methods in cardiovascular behavioral medicine* (pp. 453–481). New York: Plenum.

Saab, P. G., Llabre, M. M., Hurwitz, B. E., Frame, C. A., Reineke, L. J., Fins, A. I., McCalla, J., Cieply, L. K., & Schneiderman, N. (1992). Myocardial and peripheral vascular responses to behavioral challenges and their stability in Black and White Americans. *Psychophysiology, 29,* 384–397.

Schneiderman, N. (1978). Animal models relating behavioral stress and cardiovascular pathology. In T. M. Dembroski, S. M. Weiss, J. L. Shields, S. G. Haynes, & M. Feinleib (Eds.), *Coronary-prone behavior* (pp. 155–182). New York: Springer-Verlag.

Schneiderman, N. (1983). Behavior, autonomic function and animal models of cardiovascular pathology. In T. M. Dembroski & T. H. Schmidt (Eds.), *Biobehavioral bases of coronary heart disease* (pp. 304–364). New York: Karger.

Schneiderman, N., & McCabe, P. M. (1989). Psychophysiologic strategies in laboratory research. In N. Schneiderman, S. M. Weiss, & P. G. Kaufmann (Eds.), *Handbook of research methods in cardiovascular behavioral medicine* (pp. 349–364). New York: Plenum.

Shipley, R. E., & Study, R. S. (1951). Changes in renal blood flow, extraction of insulin, glomerular filtration rate, tissue pressure, and urine flow with acute alterations of renal artery blood pressure. *American Journal of Physiology, 167,* 676–682.

Sims, E. A. H. (1982). Mechanisms of hypertension in the overweight. *Hypertension, 4*(Suppl. III), III-43–III-49.

Sims, J., Hewitt, J. K., Kelly, K. A., Carroll, D., & Turner, J. R. (1986). Familial and individual influences on blood pressure. *Acta Geneticae Medicae et Gemellologiae, 35,* 7–21.

Smith, T. W., Turner, C. W., Ford, M. H., Hunt, S. C., Barlow, G. K., Stults, B. M., & Williams, R. R. (1987). Blood pressure reactivity in adult male twins. *Health Psychology, 6,* 209–220.

Smookler, H. H., Goebel, K. H., Siegel, M. I., & Clarke, D. E. (1973). Hypertensive effects of prolonged auditory, visual, and motion stimulation. *Federation Proceedings, 32,* 2105–2110.

Sokolow, M., Werdegar, D., Kain, H., & Hinman, A. (1966). Relationships between level of blood pressure measured casually and by portable recorder and severity of complications in essential hypertension. *Circulation, 34,* 279.

Steptoe, A., Moses, J., & Edwards, S. (1990). Age-related differences in cardiovascular reactions to mental tests in women. *Health Psychology, 9,* 18–34.

Stoney, C. M., Davis, M. C., & Matthews, K. A. (1988). Sex differences in physiological responses to stress and in coronary heart disease: A causal link? *Psychophysiology, 24,* 127–131.

Treiber, F. A., Musante, L., Branden, D., Arensman, F., Strong, W. B., Levy, M., & Leverett, S. (1990). Racial differences in hemodynamic responses to the cold face stimulus in children and adults. *Psychosomatic Medicine, 52,* 286–296.

U.S. Department of Health and Human Services. (1986). *Report of the Secretary's Task Force on Black and Minority Health: Cardiovascular and cerebrovascular disease.* Washington, DC: U.S. Government Printing Office.

Vander, A. J., Henry, J. P., Stephens, P. M., Kay, L. L., & Mouw, D. R. (1978). Plasma renin activity in psychosocial hypertension of CBA mice. *Circulation Research, 42,* 496–502.

Williams, R. B., Jr. (1986). Patterns of reactivity and stress. In K. A. Matthews, S. M. Weiss, T. Detre, T. M. Dembroski, B. Falkner, S. B. Manuck, & R. B. Williams, Jr. (Eds.), *Handbook of stress, reactivity, and cardiovascular disease* (pp. 109–125). New York: Wiley.

Wood, D. L., Sheps, S. G., Elveback, L. R., & Schirger, A. (1984). Cold-pressor test as a predictor of hypertension. *Hypertension, 6,* 301.

CHAPTER 4

A Biopsychosocial Model of Race Differences in Vascular Reactivity

Norman B. Anderson, Maya McNeilly, and Hector Myers

O ne of the most consistent findings in the cardiovascular epidemiological literature is the higher resting blood pressure and greater
prevalence of essential hypertension among Black adults compared with
White adults (Folkow, 1982, 1987). The higher rates of hypertension among
Blacks has been documented for men between the ages of 25 and 64
years and for women between the ages of 25 and 74 years (Obrist, 1981).
Not surprisingly, given the extraordinarily high rate of hypertension morbidity among Blacks, this group also suffers disproportionately higher
rates of hypertension-related mortality from heart disease, cerebral vascular disease, and renal disease (Obrist, 1981; Matthews et al., 1986).

Given the higher rates of hypertension in Blacks than in Whites,
researchers in the past decade began to examine racial differences in
stress reactivity as one potential contributor to excessive hypertension
morbidity in Blacks. In this chapter, we review studies of racial differences
in stress-induced reactivity. This review is based in part on studies of
racial differences in autonomic reactivity by Anderson (1989) and An-

derson, McNeilly, and Myers (1991). After this review, we present a model describing a contextual perspective for understanding the possible biopsychosocial interactions that might underlie the racial differences in reactivity and hypertension prevalence. We hope that this model might serve as a guide for future research.

Black–White Differences in Reactivity

Cardiovascular Responses

Numerous investigations have been conducted on Black–White differences in autonomic reactivity. These investigations, which have included both children and adults, have used a wide variety of laboratory stressors, experimental designs, physiological measures, and population subgroups. Despite the diversity of approaches, most of these studies demonstrated that Black children show higher levels or greater increases in cardiovascular activity in response to laboratory stressors compared with White children (Alpert, Dover, Booker, Martin, & Strong, 1981; Arensman, Trieber, Gruber, & Strong, 1989; Berenson, Voors, Webber, Dalferes, & Harsha, 1979; Hohn et al., 1983; Murphy, Alpert, Moses, & Somes, 1986; Murphy, Alpert, Walker, & Willey, 1988; Murphy, Alpert, Willey, & Somes, 1988; Trieber et al., 1990; Trieber, Musante, Strong, & Levy, 1989; Voors, Webber, & Berenson, 1980) and compared with Black and White adults (Anderson, Lane, Monou, Williams, & Houseworth, 1988; Anderson, Lane, Muranaka, Williams, & Houseworth, 1988; Anderson, Lane, Taguchi, & Williams, 1989; Anderson, Lane, Taguchi, Williams, & Houseworth, 1989; Dimsdale, Graham, Ziegler, Zusman, & Berry, 1987; Durel et al., 1989; Light, Obrist, Sherwood, James, & Strogatz, 1987; Light & Sherwood, 1989; McAdoo, Weinberger, Miller, Fineberg, & Grim, 1990; McNeilly & Zeichner, 1989; Morrell, Myers, Shapiro, Goldstein, & Armstrong, 1989; Myers, Shapiro, McClure, & Daims, 1989; Tischenkel et al., 1989; Trieber et al., 1990).

Perhaps more important, however, are the findings that the hemodynamic mechanisms producing the stress-induced blood pressure responses may be different in Blacks and Whites. For example, two patterns of cardiovascular adjustment to stress have been reported: the myocardial and the vascular. The myocardial reactivity pattern is characterized by an increase in blood pressure associated with increases in cardiac output, stroke volume, heart rate, epinephrine, and norepinephrine and a decrease in total peripheral resistance. In contrast, the vascular pattern produces an increase in blood pressure via the release of norepinephrine and an increase in total peripheral resistance—the hallmark of the α-adrenergic pattern.

Research suggests that blood pressure reactivity in Blacks is mediated substantially more by vascular peripheral vasoconstriction compared with that in Whites. This heightened vasoconstrictive response in Blacks has been observed among children (Arensman et al., 1989; Trieber et al., 1989) and among normotensive and hypertensive adults (Anderson, Lane, Taguchi, Williams, & Houseworth, 1989; Light et al., 1987; McAdoo et al., 1990; Tischenkel et al., 1989; Trieber et al., 1990) and has been most clearly seen in studies that used the forehead cold pressor task—a stimulus that produces a profound vascular vasoconstrictive pattern of reactivity (Anderson, Lane, Muranaka, Williams, & Houseworth, 1988; Anderson, Lane, Taguchi, & Williams, 1989; Anderson, Lane, Taguchi, Williams, & Houseworth, 1989; Trieber et al., 1990).

In contrast to the augmented vascular reactivity in Blacks, most studies have shown that young Black adults show either similar or diminished heart rate reactivity in relation to their White counterparts (Anderson, Lane, Monou, Williams, & Houseworth, 1988; Anderson, Lane, Taguchi, & Williams, 1989; Anderson, Lane, Taguchi, Williams, & Houseworth, 1989; Durel et al., 1989; Falkner & Kushner, 1989; Fredrikson, 1986; Light et al., 1987; Light & Sherwood, 1989; McAdoo et al., 1990; Morrell et al., 1989; Myers et al., 1989; Strickland, Myers, & Lahey, 1989; Tischenkel et al., 1989). The data on cardiac reactivity among children, however, are less consistent. Some studies have indicated higher levels of exercise-induced heart rate responses among White children in relation to Black children (Arensman et al., 1989; Berenson et al., 1979; Hohn et al., 1983; Trieber et al., 1989), whereas others have yielded nonsignificant race differences in cardiac responses to exercise, postural tilt, and the forehead cold pressor task (Alpert et al., 1981; Tell, Prineas, & Gomez-Marin, 1988; Trieber et al., 1990).

On the other hand, studies that used psychological challenges such as video games have consistently elicited greater heart rate reactivity among Black children compared with White children (Murphy et al., 1986; Murphy, Alpert, Walker, & Willey, 1988; Murphy, Alpert, Willey, & Somes, 1988). Two of these studies, in which the effects of experimenter's race on heart rate responses were observed in children, particularly Blacks, showed greater heart rate reactivity when the children were paired with a same-race experimenter (Murphy et al., 1986; Murphy, Alpert, Walker, & Willey, 1988). There was also a tendency for White children to have higher resting heart rates than Black children when paired with a Black experimenter. These investigators speculated that same-race pairings possibly elicit an increased effort to perform well on the tasks, whereas the mixed-race pairings result in decreased challenge and involvement.

Predictors of Reactivity Among Blacks

To identify predictors of reactivity within the Black population, researchers have begun to investigate the effects of factors such as blood pressure status, family history of hypertension, and personality.

With few exceptions, most of the studies that compared Blacks at different levels of blood pressure have shown that children and adults with higher blood pressure show greater reactivity to a variety of stressors compared with individuals with lower blood pressure (Berenson et al., 1979; Light et al., 1987; Light & Sherwood, 1989; McAdoo et al., 1990; McNeilly & Zeichner, 1989; Voors et al., 1980). The one study that did not observe blood pressure status effects on reactivity (Falkner, Kushner, Khalsa, Canessa, & Katz, 1986) observed numerous interactive effects of race, gender, and task on reactivity, which may have overshadowed any blood pressure status effects. Conversely, although a number of studies have shown that family history of hypertension predicts cardiovascular reactivity among Whites (Matthews & Rakacksky, 1986), this effect has been less consistent among Blacks. In fact, most studies with Black men and women have shown no significant effects of family history on reactivity (Anderson, Lane, Monou, Williams, & Houseworth, 1988; Anderson, Lane, Taguchi, Williams, & Houseworth, 1989; Anderson et al., 1986; Falkner et al., 1986; Morrell et al., 1989). Most studies that have shown effects of history on reactivity have examined group differences in absolute levels of blood pressure responses during stress (Falkner et al., 1986; Hohn et al., 1983; Johnson, 1989) or recovery (Myers et al., 1989) rather than changes in measures from baseline to stress. Only two studies obtained significant effects of family history on blood pressure as measured by delta scores. In one of these, Black women with a positive family history showed smaller systolic blood pressure (SBP) and forearm blood flow responses to mental arithmetic compared with White women—a finding that was interpreted to suggest that Blacks may show diminished cardiac responsivity and increased vascular responsivity (Anderson, Lane, Muranaka, Williams, & Houseworth, 1988) to stressors. In another study, positive correlations were seen between type A behavior in Black women with a positive family history and SBP responses to the structured interview (Durel et al., 1989).

Studies of personality characteristics and cardiovascular activity have shown that among Blacks elevated resting blood pressure and hypertension have been associated with suppressed anger and hostility (Gentry, Chesney, Gary, Hall, & Harburg, 1982; Harburg, Blakelock, & Roper, 1979; Harburg et al., 1973a, 1973b; Johnson, Schork, & Spielberger, 1978; Johnson, Spielberger, Worden, & Jacobs, 1987). Similarly, investigations of cardiovascular reactivity and personality among Blacks suggest that anger, hostility, and type A behavior are associated with greater reactivity (Anderson et al., 1986; Armstead, Lawler, Gorden, Cross, & Gibbons, 1989; Clark & Harrell, 1982; Durel et al., 1989; Johnson, 1989). These relationships, however, may depend on gender, family history of hypertension, the personality constructs measured, and the experimental tasks used. For example, Durel et al. (1989) found that among Black women, trait anger was associated with greater SBP and greater diastolic blood pressure (DBP) at rest in the laboratory and at work and with greater DBP during the cold pressor task. Among Black men, however, positive correlations were observed only between cognitive anger and DBP at rest.

Johnson (1989) observed interactive effects of personality and family history of hypertension on blood pressure for which Black men with a positive family history showed higher levels of trait anger, anger-out, and submissiveness compared with those with a negative family history. Importantly, these men also showed the highest blood pressure levels at rest and during stress. Finally, Armstead et al. (1989) tested the effects of exposure to racist stimuli on anger and cardiovascular reactivity among

Blacks. They observed that blood pressure increases were significantly greater to video clips depicting anger-provoking racist scenes than those showing nonracist anger-provoking and neutral scenes. In addition, blood pressure responses were positively correlated with trait anger.

Summary of Research Findings

As demonstrated by the previous review, there have been a substantial number of studies on Black–White differences in autonomic reactivity. Yet, despite the diversity of approaches used, most studies have demonstrated that Blacks show greater blood pressure reactivity to laboratory stressors compared with their White counterparts. Perhaps more important, though, is that the mechanisms responsible for producing the stress-induced blood pressure response may be different in Blacks than in Whites. Blacks have been found to exhibit greater blood pressure reactivity mediated by peripheral vasoconstriction (characteristic of the α-adrenergic pattern), whereas the blood pressure response of Whites has shown greater cardiac involvement (characteristic of the β-adrenergic pattern). These results, particularly the heightened peripheral vasoconstrictive responses in the Blacks, have been observed among children, adults, normotensives, and borderline hypertensives. It has been most clearly seen in studies that used stressors, such as the forehead cold pressor test, that are specifically designed to produce a predominantly α-adrenergic pattern of reactivity. Fewer studies have been conducted on the variability of responses to laboratory stressors among Blacks. The exception is the research on family history of hypertension and reactivity among Blacks for which the studies have not consistently uncovered greater reactivity in Black adults with a positive family history. The possible reasons for the lack of findings for family history are discussed in a later section.

Augmented Reactivity in Blacks: A Contextual Model

Context of Autonomic Reactivity

Thus far, research using the reactivity paradigm has been largely concerned with describing racial differences in reactivity. It is now apparent that the next logical scientific imperative is to ascertain the factors responsible for the greater vascular reactivity among Blacks in relation to Whites and, perhaps more importantly, to identify what variables are predictive of heightened vascular reactivity within the Black population. It is these issues that the proposed contextual model is designed to address. Anderson and McNeilly (1991), in their discussion of a contextual perspective of psychophysiological research, note that physiological and psychophysiological responses obtained in an experimental laboratory are partly a function of the socioecological niche that the individual occupies at that time. With regard to racial differences in reactivity, it is our contention that the degree to which there are Black–White differences in vascular reactivity and essential hypertension is due in large part to racial differences in the socioecological niches that the two groups occupy in the United States.

Figure 1 illustrates a proposed working contextual model for investigations of stress-induced vascular reactivity in Blacks. The principal tenet of the proposed contextual model is that the exaggerated peripheral vascular reactivity observed in many Blacks in relation to Whites is a function of a number of biological, psychological, behavioral, environmental, and sociocultural factors. The model begins with the premise that in reactivity research race should be viewed as a proxy for the effects of differential exposure to chronic social and environmental stressors rather than as a proxy for the effects of genetic differences. Black Americans, on average, are exposed to a wider array of chronic stressors than are their White counterparts. These chronic stressors interact with biological, behavioral, and psychological risk factors to increase sympathetic nervous system activity, which in turn leads to the release of neuroendocrine substances including norepinephrine and adrenocorticotropin hormone (ACTH), augmented sodium retention, and enhanced vasoconstriction. The resultant higher levels of endogenous sodium and ACTH not only increase blood volume but act to potentiate the vasoconstrictive effects of norepinephrine on the peripheral vasculature. Over time, the repeated stressor-induced episodes of vascular reactivity may lead to structural changes in the vascular wall (e.g., increased wall-to-lumen ratio), which further augments reactivity. If repeated frequently over a number of years, this process has the potential to lead to the development of sustained

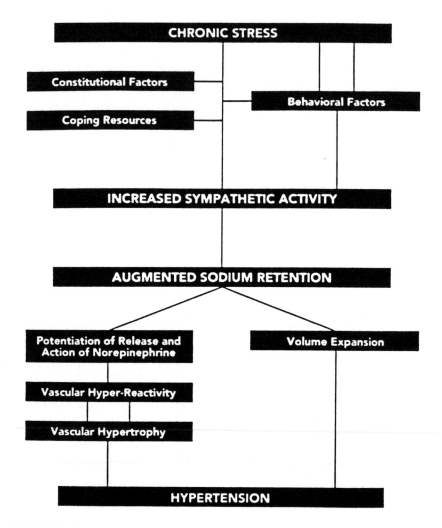

FIGURE 1.   Contextual model of reactivity and hypertension in Blacks. From "Autonomic Reactivity and Hypertension in Blacks: A Review and Proposed Model" by N. B. Anderson, M. McNeilly, and H. Myers, 1991, *Ethnicity and Disease, 1,* p. 159; copyright 1991 by the International Society on Hypertension in Blacks; reprinted by permission.

hypertension. The remainder of this chapter is devoted to explicating each component of this model and delineating its relevance to research on reactivity in Blacks.

Chronic Stressors

Many researchers have voiced the view of race as a sociological designation that indicates exposure to common life experiences. According to the current model, one distinguishing feature of the life experiences between Black and White Americans is the greater exposure to chronic life stressors. As Cooper and David (1986) noted, "Blacks in the United States have a historically determined structural relationship to the social system" (p. 113). This structural relationship has involved several hundred years of institutional discrimination and government-sanctioned racism (Katz & Taylor, 1988; Wilson, 1973), which has only recently been remediated through the civil rights legislation of the 1960s. As a consequence of this history and the continued race consciousness of our society, Blacks currently experience a greater array of chronic stressors in relation to Whites. These chronic stressors include, among others, higher unemployment, higher poverty rates, higher low-income levels, lower status occupations, lower social status, residential crowding, and substandard housing (Blackwell, 1975; Farley, 1984; Farley & Allen, 1989; Harris, 1982; Jaynes & Williams, 1989; Lawrence, 1981; Wilson, 1989).

Many of these chronic social and environmental stressors have been associated with hypertension among Blacks. For example, socioeconomic status (SES) shows a strong inverse relationship with hypertension among Blacks (Hypertension Detection and Follow-up Program Cooperative Group, 1977). In addition, Harburg et al. (1973a, 1973b) found that Blacks residing in neighborhoods high in socioecologic stress, characterized by low SES and high social instability (SIS; defined as high crime and divorce rates), exhibit significantly higher blood pressures than Blacks living in low SES but more stable neighborhoods. Among Whites, socioecological stress did not influence blood pressure. Similarly, James and Kleinbaum (1976) found that, for Black men 45–54 years old, high-stress counties (low SES, high SIS) of North Carolina were associated with significantly higher hypertension-related mortality (e.g., hypertensive heart disease and stroke) than were low-stress counties. As in Harburg's (1973a, 1973b, 1979) Detroit studies, no stress–mortality relationship was found for White males. Thus, not only are Blacks exposed more frequently to chronic stressors, but these social and environmental factors may have greater health consequences for Blacks.

Chronic Stress and Vascular Reactivity: Physiological Mediators

If the differential exposure to chronic stressors is related to acute cardiovascular reactivity as we have proposed, then it should be possible to identify specific physiological mechanisms linking these phenomena in Blacks. It is proposed that exposure to chronic stressors enhances sympathetic nervous system activity, which results in augmented sodium retention and neuroendocrine release. Augmented sodium retention and neuroendocrine release may, in addition to increasing blood volume, contribute to the greater vascular responses in Blacks.

Sympathetic Nervous System Effects
Of critical importance is whether exposure to chronic stress is associated with this hypothesized physiological scenario. In support of this, research from animal and human studies has demonstrated that exposure to acute and chronic uncontrollable stress may augment resting sympathetic tone; enhance sympathetic reactivity to acute, novel stressors; elevate plasma levels of catecholamines, ACTH, and opioid peptides; and augment sodium retention (Baum, Gatchel, & Schaeffer, 1983; Davidson, Fleming, & Baum, 1987; Fleming, Baum, Davidson, Rectanus, & McArdle, 1987; Fleming, Baum, & Wess, 1987; Guillemin et al., 1977; Koepke & DiBona, 1985; Koepke, Light, & Obrist, 1983; Light, Koepke, Obrist, & Willis, 1983; McCarthy, Horwatt, & Konarska, 1988; Rossier et al., 1977). For example, in a study of residential crowding, Fleming, Baum, and Wess (1987) found that individuals who lived in more crowded neighborhoods had greater blood pressure and heart rate reactivity during a challenging behavioral task than those who lived in less crowded neighborhoods. Studies of the biochemical mechanisms underlying blood pressure reactivity indicate that norepinephrine elicits elevations in blood pressure through vasoconstrictive effects on the peripheral vasculature (Goldstein & Shapiro,

1990). ACTH has been shown to potentiate norepinephrine's vasocon-strictive effects, particularly in humans and animals with reduced renal excretory capacity (Bassett, Strand, & Cairncross, 1978; Kurland & Free-berg, 1951; Schomig, Luth, Dietz, & Gross, 1976; Strand & Smith, 1980; Whitworth, Coghlan, Denton, Hardy, & Scoggins, 1979), and to augment norepinephrine-induced contractions of atrial muscle (Bassett et al., 1978; Strand & Smith, 1980). Importantly, ACTH also induces sodium and water retention (Lohmeier & Carroll, 1985).

In a series of studies at the University of North Carolina at Chapel Hill, investigators examined the role of stress and sodium retention in dogs and spontaneously hypertensive rats (Gringnolo, Koepke, & Obrist, 1982; Koepke & DiBona, 1985; Koepke et al., 1983; Light, 1987). In these studies, animals that were exposed to chronic stress showed significant reductions in sodium and fluid excretion and an associated rise in blood pressure, which was mediated by renal sympathetic nerves. In perhaps the first study of stress and sodium retention in humans, Light et al. (1983) discovered that a stressful laboratory task (competitive reaction time) decreased urinary sodium excretion in both borderline hypertensives and individuals with a parental history of hypertension.

Sodium Effects

There are at least four lines of research that implicate sodium as a prin-cipal physiological mediator of heightened vascular reactivity in Blacks. First, there is now considerable evidence that heightened sympathetic activity may induce sodium retention (Weinberger, Luft, & Henry, 1982). Second, although the dietary sodium intake of Blacks may not be signif-icantly higher than that of Whites (Grim et al., 1980), Blacks excrete less sodium in urine and exhibit greater pressor responses to sodium loading (Luft, Grim, Fineberg, & Weinberger, 1979; Luft, Grim, & Weinberger, 1985). Thus, Blacks may be more susceptible to the blood pressure effects of sodium, despite a similar dietary intake in relation to Whites. Third, research suggests that sodium may augment cardiovascular reactivity in subjects at risk for hypertension (Ambrosioni, Costa, Montebugnoli, Borghi, & Margnani, 1981; Ambrosioni et al., 1982; Falkner, Onesti, &

Angelakos, 1981). Finally, studies in both humans and spontaneously hypertensive rats indicate that sodium may exert its effects on blood pressure via heightened vasoconstriction rather than by increasing cardiac output (Mark et al., 1975; Nilsson, Fly, Friberg, Kalstrom, & Folkow, 1985). Thus, given the influence of the sympathetic nervous system on sodium retention, the greater sodium sensitivity among Blacks, and the effects of sodium on both reactivity and vascular resistance, sodium may be the pivotal physiological mechanism responsible for the observed race differences in vascular reactivity.

How might sodium contribute to increased vascular resistance? As shown in Figure 1, sodium may lead to heightened vascular resistance through its effects on plasma norepinephrine release and action. Although in normotensive individuals sodium loading has been shown to decrease plasma and urinary norepinephrine levels, the opposite effect has been observed for salt-sensitive and hypertensive individuals. In these individuals, sodium loading increases plasma and urinary norepinephrine levels, whereas sodium deprivation has the inverse effect (Koolen & Van Brummelen, 1984; Luft, Rankin et al., 1979; Takeshita, Imaizumi, Ashirara, & Nakamura, 1982). Furthermore, high sodium intake has been shown to potentiate the effects of norepinephrine on the vasculature (Rankin, Luft, Henry, Gibbs, & Weinberger, 1981). High dietary sodium intake has also been associated with increased pressor responses to infused norepinephrine in Black hypertensives in relation to White hypertensives (Dimsdale et al., 1987). Thus, if Blacks exhibit an exaggerated antinatriuresis, then this may lead to an increased release or vasoconstrictive action of plasma norepinephrine. This chain of events would increase peripheral vascular resistance in Blacks. Moreover, chronic stressors, that in themselves stimulate the release of plasma norepinephrine, would interact with higher prevailing sodium levels to further stimulate vascular reactivity. It is hypothesized that the heightened vascular reactivity observed in Blacks may ultimately result in structural changes (i.e., hypertrophy) in the peripheral vasculature, which in turn may further augment vascular hyperreactivity (Folkow, 1982, 1987). A long-term consequence of this process could be sustained hypertension (Folkow, 1982, 1987).

In summary, there is compelling evidence that Blacks in American society are systematically exposed to a wider array of chronic social stressors compared with their White counterparts. These stressors involve lower SES, higher rates of poverty, higher unemployment, lower status occupations, exposure to racism, and more crowded and ecologically stressful residential environments. Many of these stressors have been related to elevated blood pressure and increased hypertension prevalence. Research with humans and animals suggests that exposure to chronic stress may increase tonic sympathetic nervous system activity, acute autonomic reactivity, and urinary sodium retention. Future studies may determine whether the types of stressors to which many Blacks are confronted on a daily basis are related to these potentially pathological sequelae.

Behavioral and Psychological Factors

It is conceivable that chronic social stressors may increase neuroendocrine release and sodium retention through specific behavioral or psychological factors. Early research demonstrated an association between anger, type A behavior, and higher levels of plasma norepinephrine and blood pressure among Whites (Friedman, Byers, Diamant, & Rosenman, 1975). To date, only one study has examined these relationships in Blacks (Durel et al., 1989). Although this recent study yielded nonsignificant relationships between norepinephrine and anger for both Blacks and Whites, it did demonstrate positive correlations between anger and cardiovascular reactivity in these individuals.

A number of studies have shown that behavioral and psychological factors are linked to elevated blood pressure and hypertension among Blacks (Anderson, Myers, Pickering, & Jackson, 1989; James, 1985). For example, suppressed anger and hostility have been associated with elevated blood pressure and hypertension in both adolescents and adults (Harburg et al., 1979; Johnson et al., 1978, 1987). In general, this literature has indicated that Blacks who frequently suppress their anger when provoked or who express their anger without reflection have higher resting blood pressure levels than those who routinely express their anger or those who express it only after some reflection (Gentry et al., 1982; Johnson et al., 1978). Durel et al. (1989) recently found that the experience of frequent anger is related to higher ambulatory blood pressures among Black women while at work. At this time, research has not examined whether inhibited anger expression is related to sodium excretion or neuroendocrine release among Blacks. It is clear, however, that the social milieu in which many Blacks exist not only contributes to the experience of angry feelings but simultaneously punishes their expression.

Another behavioral factor that is associated with high blood pressure among Blacks is the "John Henryism" behavioral pattern of hard work and determination against overwhelming odds. James and colleagues speculated that Blacks who exhibit this type of determination, but who also have few resources to help them achieve their goals, may be at greatest risk for developing hypertension (James, Hartnett, & Kalsbeek, 1983; James, LaCroix, Kleinbaum, & Strogatz, 1984). Furthermore, it has been found that Blacks who are high in John Henryism and low in SES have a higher percentage of hypertension than persons who are low in John Henryism or higher in SES (James, Strogatz, Wing, & Ramsey, 1987). Interestingly, no interaction of John Henryism with education or blood pressure has been found for Whites, which suggests, as James (1985) noted, that this coping style may be particularly relevant to Black populations.

As depicted in Figure 1, the behavior of individuals who are high in John Henryism may actually increase their exposure to stressful social and environmental circumstances. That is, these individuals may continually strive to gain control over their environment in spite of numerous barriers, thereby potentially exposing themselves more frequently to frustrating and stressful situations. Whether this exposure to behaviorally mediated chronic stress results in enhanced sympathetic nervous system activity and altered sodium regulation remains to be empirically determined. It has been reported, however, that active behavioral coping with acute laboratory stressors enhances sodium retention (Light et al., 1983). It is this active coping with real-life stressors that is the sine qua non of the John Henryism pattern.

Chronic social stressors may also have other psychological and emotional effects that could potentially influence sodium retention and neuroendocrine release. For example, low-income Blacks have been found to report more psychological distress than lower and higher income Whites and higher income Blacks, perhaps because of the combined burden of poverty and racism (Kessler & Neighbors, 1986). In addition, the stressful residential environments to which many Blacks are exposed, (e.g., crowding, crime) are related to stress symptoms such as anxiety, depression, somatic complaints, lower levels of perceived control, and enhanced sympathetic nervous system activity (Baum et al., 1983; Davidson et al., 1987; Fleming, Baum, Davidson, Rectanus, & McArdle, 1987; Fleming, Baum, & Wess, 1987; Schaeffer & Baum, 1984).

Biological/Genetic Factors

Although genetic variables have been identified as important in determining sodium excretion in both Blacks and Whites (Grim et al., 1984), epidemiological evidence suggests that the association of parental history and risk for hypertension may not be as strong among Blacks in relation to Whites (Luft, Rankin et al., 1979). In fact, no published studies have demonstrated the expected relationship between parental history of hypertension and cardiovascular reactivity among Black adults (Anderson, Lane, Taguchi, & Williams, 1989; Anderson, Lane, Taguchi, Williams, & Houseworth, 1989; Anderson et al., 1986; Rowlands et al., 1982), although this relationship has been found fairly consistently among Whites (Fredrickson & Matthews, 1990). A possible explanation for these somewhat puzzling findings may be the substantial influence of psychosocial factors in the development of hypertension among Blacks (Anderson, Myers, Pickering, & Jackson, 1989). That is, psychosocial factors, such as chronic stress, may overshadow the influence of parental history such that risk for hypertension and hyperreactivity are augmented even in persons with a negative parental history. This would result in a diminished ability to detect differences between parental history groups among Blacks (Anderson & McNeilly, 1991).

Second, as we have discussed, although sodium retention has a clear genetic component (Grim et al., 1984), it may also be stimulated by psychosocial stress. To the degree that Blacks, particularly low-income Blacks, experience more psychological stress than do Whites or upper income Blacks (Kessler & Neighbors, 1986), they may consequently be more susceptible to inhibited sodium excretion.

Finally, the genetic distinction between Black and White Americans is, at best, ambiguous. It has been noted that the gene pool of American Blacks is composed of a heterogeneous mixture from genetically diverse populations of Africans (Hiernaux, 1975; Mourant, 1983) and American Whites (Glass & Li, 1953; Pollitzer, 1958). In fact, Reed (1969) estimates that up to 50% of the genes of Black Americans are derived from White ancestors, whereas Lewontin and colleagues (Lewontin, 1973; Lewontin, Rose, & Kamin, 1984) reported that genetic differences between individuals within a race have a substantially greater impact on the total species genetic variation than genetic differences between races. Therefore, although genetic factors no doubt play a role in reactivity among Blacks, their influence on between-race differences is likely to be considerably less.

Coping Resources

Thus far, we have been discussing the various physiological, social, and behavioral factors that may contribute to the augmented sodium retention, greater vascular reactivity, and higher hypertension prevalence among Blacks compared with Whites. It is important to note, however, that there may be factors inherent in the culture and traditions of Black Americans that may counteract the sympathetic and hypertensinogenic effects of chronic stress. A number of researchers have advocated the view that Black Americans share many characteristics, both social and behavioral, that have their origin in African traditions (Jones, 1980; King, Dixon, & Nobles, 1976; Nobles, 1974). As summarized by Anderson (1989), these African traditions include, among other things, a strong spiritual orientation; a deep sense of kinship and identification with the "tribe" and larger group, rather than a strictly individualistic orientation; a reverence toward the oral tradition and the spoken word; a flexible concept of time, which is marked by events rather than the clock or calendar; an emphasis on the past and present rather than the future; and an unashamed use of emotional expressiveness.

The presence of these African traditions in the Black culture are apparent, for example, in the expression of both verbal and nonverbal behaviors (Kochman, 1981; Smith, 1981); the importance of the extended family, which may include in addition to blood relatives, individuals who are given the same status and responsibilities as blood relatives (Nobles, 1974); the central role of religion and spirituality; the unique style and emotional expressiveness of the Black church service, even though the content of the hymns and readings may be European American (Jones, 1980); and the strong sense of group solidarity, racial identity, or "we-ness" in the Black community (Jones, 1980).

According to our contextual model, certain of these cultural traditions could well decrease the effects of stress and, consequently, the effects of stress on sympathetic nervous system activity, sodium retention, and blood pressure level. It has been found, for example, that among Whites, regular church attendance is associated with lower resting blood pressure levels than is less frequent attendance (Graham et al., 1978). It would be of interest to determine whether Blacks who are exposed to chronic life stressors (e.g., low-income Blacks), but who also have a high cultural "buffer" (e.g., strong religious orientation, social support, or extended family network), exhibit lower tonic sympathetic nervous system activity, lower sodium retention, and lower cardiovascular reactivity than do those individuals who are less connected to cultural resources.

Testing the Contextual Model: Directions for Research

The contextual model presented herein was designed to provide a stimulus for examining both the basis for racial differences in vascular reactivity as well as for exploring within-race variability in vascular responses among Blacks. Toward these ends, the model suggests a number of testable hypotheses and research questions. Various components of the model could be tested using either field or laboratory methodologies. For example, the model would predict that Blacks who are exposed to higher levels of chronic stress should have higher resting stress hormone levels (e.g., catecholamines, ACTH) and exaggerated responses to novel stimuli, which suggests increased sympathetic nervous system activity compared with Blacks who experience lower levels of chronic stress. Second, chronic stress should also be positively associated with increased sodium retention (i.e., slower sodium excretion rates) and greater vascular reactivity in Blacks. Third, the combination of chronic stress exposure and behavioral and psychological factors such as anger suppression and John Henryism should be positively associated with both increased sympathetic nervous system activity and greater sodium retention. Furthermore, dietary sodium loading (or saline infusions) should potentiate vascular reactivity in Blacks who experience chronic stress. Finally, the contextual model would predict that Blacks with more coping resources (e.g., high social support, strong religious orientation, and strong racial identity) will show lower sympathetic nervous system activity and decreased sodium retention in relation to those with fewer coping resources.

Summary and Conclusions

In summary, according to the proposed model, race is viewed as a sociocultural designation that denotes differential exposure to chronic social stressors. It is proposed that Blacks are exposed to significantly more chronic social stressors than are White Americans. Many of these chronic social stressors have been associated with hypertension prevalence in epidemiological studies. Furthermore, chronic stress has been shown to augment cardiovascular reactivity to acute stress in both animals and humans and to increase sodium retention in spontaneously hypertensive rats. Acute stress has also been demonstrated to increase sodium retention in humans. The essential element of our model is that chronic social stressors that are more represented within the Black American population due to historical factors are related to an increase in sodium sensitivity and retention. This altered sodium metabolism may be further augmented by biological, behavioral, and psychological risk factors for hypertension and modulated by stress coping resources. It is hoped that this model will serve as a stimulus for further research on the biopsychosocial aspects of autonomic reactivity and hypertension in Blacks.

References

Alpert, B. S., Dover, E. V., Booker, D. L., Martin, A. M., & Strong, W. B. (1981). Blood pressure response to dynamic exercise in healthy children—Black versus White. *Journal of Pediatrics, 99,* 556–560.

Ambrosioni, E., Costa, F. V., Borghi, C., Montebugnoli, L., Giordani, M. F., & Magnani, B. (1982). Effects of moderate salt restriction on intralymphocytic sodium and pressor response to stress in borderline hypertension. *Hypertension, 4,* 789–794.

Ambrosioni, E., Costa, F. V., Montebugnoli, L., Borghi, C., & Margnani, B. (1981). Intralymphocytic sodium concentration as an index of response to stress an exercise in young subjects with borderline hypertension. *Clinical Science, 61*(Suppl. 7), 25.

Anderson, N. B. (1989). Racial differences in stress-induced cardiovascular reactivity and hypertension: Current status and substantive issues. *Psychological Bulletin, 105,* 89–105.

Anderson, N. B., Lane, J. D., Monou, H., Williams, R. B., Jr., & Houseworth, S. J. (1988). Racial differences in cardiovascular reactivity to mental arithmetic. *International Journal of Psychophysiology, 6,* 161–164.

Anderson, N. B., Lane, J. D., Muranaka, M., Williams, R. B., Jr., & Houseworth, S. J. (1988). Racial differences in blood pressure and forearm vascular responses to the cold face stimulus. *Psychosomatic Medicine, 50,* 57–63.

Anderson, N. B., Lane, J. D., Taguchi, F., & Williams, R. B., Jr. (1989). Patterns of cardiovascular responses to stress as a function of race and parental hypertension in men. *Health Psychology, 8,* 525–540.

Anderson, N. B., Lane, J. D., Taguchi, F., Williams, R. B., Jr., & Houseworth, S. J. (1989). Race, parental history of hypertension, and patterns of cardiovascular reactivity in women. *Psychophysiology, 26,* 39–47.

Anderson, N. B., & McNeilly, M. (1991). Age, gender, and race variables in psychophysiological assessment: Sociodemographics in context. *Psychological Assessment: A Journal of Clinical and Consulting Psychology, 3,* 376–384.

Anderson, N. B., McNeilly, M., & Myers, H. (1991). Autonomic reactivity and hypertension in Blacks: A review and proposed model. *Ethnicity and Disease, 1,* 154–170.

Anderson, N. B., Myers, H., Pickering T., & Jackson, J. (1989). Hypertension in Blacks: Psychosocial and biological perspectives. *Journal of Hypertension, 7,* 161–172.

Anderson, N. B., Williams, R. B., Jr., Lane, J. D., Haney, T., Simpson, S., & Houseworth, S. J. (1986). Type A behavior, family history of hypertension, and cardiovascular responses among Black women. *Health Psychology, 5,* 393–406.

Arensman, F. W., Trieber, F. A., Gruber, M. P., & Strong, W. B. (1989). Exercise induced differences in cardiac output, blood pressure and systemic vascular resistance in a healthy biracial population of ten year old boys. *American Journal of Disorders of Children, 143,* 212–216.

Armstead, C. A., Lawler, K. A., Gorden, G., Cross, J., & Gibbons, J. (1989). Relationship of racial stressors to blood pressure responses and anger expression in Black college students. *Health Psychology, 8,* 541–556.

Bassett, J. R., Strand, F. L., & Cairncross, K. D. (1978). Glucocorticoids, adrenocorticotropic hormone and related polypeptides on myocardial sensitivity to noradrenaline. *European Journal of Pharmacology, 49,* 243–249.

Baum, A., Gatchel, R. J., & Schaeffer, M. A. (1983). Emotional, behavioral, and physiological effects of chronic stress at Three Mile Island. *Journal of Consulting and Clinical Psychology, 51,* 565–572.

Berenson, G. S., Voors, A. W., Webber, L. S., Dalferes, E. R., Jr., & Harsha, D. W. (1979). Racial differences of parameters associated with blood pressure levels in children—The Bogalusa Heart Study. *Metabolism, 28,* 1218–1228.

Blackwell, J. E. (1975). *The Black community, diversity and unity.* New York: Harper & Row.

Clark, V., & Harrell, J. (1982). The relationship among type A behavior, styles used in coping with racism, and blood pressure. *Journal of Black Psychology, 8,* 89–99.

Cooper, R., & David, R. (1986). The biological concept of race and its application to public health and epidemiology. *Journal of Health Politics, Policy and Law, 11,* 97–116.

Davidson, L. M., Fleming, R., & Baum, A. (1987). Chronic stress, catecholamines, and sleep disturbance at Three Mile Island. *Journal of Human Stress, 13,* 75–83.

Dimsdale, J. E., Graham, R., Ziegler, M. G., Zusman, R., & Berry, C. C. (1987). Age, race, diagnosis and sodium effects on the pressor response to infused norepinephrine. *Hypertension, 10,* 564–569.

Durel, L. A., Carver, C. S., Spitzer, S. B., Llabre, M. M., Weintraub, J. K., Saab, P. G., & Schneiderman, N. (1989). Associations of blood pressure with self-report measures of anger and hostility among Black and White men and women. *Health Psychology, 8,* 557–575.

Falkner, B., & Kushner, H. (1989). Race differences in stress-induced reactivity in young adults. *Health Psychology, 8,* 613–627.

Falkner, B., Kushner, H., Khalsa, D. K., Canessa, M., & Katz, S. (1986). Sodium sensitivity, growth and family history of hypertension in young Blacks. *Journal of Hypertension, 4,* S381–S383.

Falkner, B., Onesti, G., & Angelakos, E. T. (1981). Effect of salt loading on the cardiovascular response to stress in adolescents. *Hypertension, 3*(Suppl. II), 195–199.

Farley, R. (1984). *Blacks and Whites: Narrowing the gap?* Cambridge, MA: Harvard University Press.

Farley, R., & Allen, W. R. (1989). *The color line and the quality of life in America.* New York: Oxford University Press.

Fleming, I., Baum, A., Davidson, L. M., Rectanus, E., & McArdle, S. (1987). Chronic stress as a factor in psychologic reactivity to challenge. *Health Psychology, 6,* 221–238.

Fleming, I., Baum, A., & Wess, L. (1987). Social density and perceived control as mediators of crowding stress in high-density residential neighborhoods. *Journal of Personality and Social Psychology, 52,* 899–906.

Folkow, B. (1982). Physiological aspects of primary hypertension. *Psychological Review, 62,* 347.

Folkow, B. (1987). Psychosocial and central nervous influences in primary hypertension. *Circulation, 76*(Suppl. I), I-10–I-19.

Fredrikson, M. (1986). Racial differences in reactivity to behavioral challenge in essential hypertension. *Journal of Hypertension, 4,* 325–331.

Fredrickson, M., & Matthews, K. A. (1990). Cardiovascular responses to behavioral stress and hypertension: A meta-analytic review. *Annals of the Society of Behavioral Medicine, 12*, 30–39.

Friedman, M., Byers, S. O., Diamant, J., & Rosenmann, R. H. (1975). Plasma catecholamine response of coronary prone subjects (type A) to a specific challenge. *Metabolism, 24*, 205–210.

Gentry, W. D., Chesney, A. P., Gary, H. E., Hall, P. P., & Harburg, E. (1982). Habitual anger-coping styles: Effects on mean blood pressure and risk for essential hypertension. *Psychosomatic Medicine, 44*, 195–202.

Glass, B., & Li, C. C. (1953). The dynamics of racial intermixture: An analysis based on the American Negro. *American Journal of Human Genetics, 5*, 1–20.

Goldstein, I. B., & Shapiro, D. (1990). Cardiovascular response during postural change in the elderly. *Journal of Gerontology: Medical Sciences, 45*, M20–M25.

Graham, T. W., Kaplan, B. H., Cornoni-Huntley, J. C., James, S. A., Becker, C., Hames, C. G., & Heyden, S. (1978). Frequency of church attendance and blood pressure elevation. *Journal of Behavioral Medicine, 1*, 37–43.

Grim, C., Luft, F., Miller, J., Meneely, G., Batarbee, H., Hames, C., & Dahl, K. (1980). Racial differences in blood pressure in Evans County, Georgia: Relationship to sodium and potassium intake and plasma renin activity. *Journal of Chronic Diseases, 33*, 87–94.

Grim, C., Luft, F., Weinberger, M., Miller, J., Rose, R., & Christia, J. (1984). Genetic, familial, and racial influences on blood pressure control systems in man. *Australian and New Zealand Journal of Medicine, 14*, 453–457.

Gringnolo, A., Koepke, J. P., & Obrist, P. A. (1982). Renal function, heart rate and blood pressure during exercise and shock avoidance in dogs. *American Journal of Physiology, 242*, R482.

Guillemin, R., Vargo, T., Rossier, J., Minick, S., Ling, N., Rivier, C., Vale, W., & Bloom, F. (1977). Beta-endorphin and adrenocorticotropin are secreted concomitantly by the pituitary gland. *Science, 197*, 1367–1369.

Harburg, E., Blakelock, E. H., & Roper, P. J. (1979). Resentful and reflective coping with arbitrary authority and blood pressure: Detroit. *Psychosomatic Medicine, 41*, 189–202.

Harburg, E., Erfurt, J. C., Hauenstein, L. S., Chape, C., Schull, W. J., & Schork, M. A. (1973a). Socioecological stress, suppressed hostility, skin color and Black–White male blood pressure: Detroit. *Psychosomatic Medicine, 35*, 276–296.

Harburg, E., Erfurt, J., Hauenstein, L., Chape, C., Schull, W., & Schork, M. (1973b). Socioecological stressor areas and Black–White blood pressure: Detroit. *Journal of Chronic Diseases, 26*, 595–611.

Harris, W. H. (1982). *The harder we run: Black workers since the Civil War.* New York: Oxford University Press.

Hiernaux, J. (1975). *The people of Africa.* New York: Scribner.

Hohn, A. R., Riopel, D. A., Keol, J. E., Loadholt, C. B., Margolius, H. S., Halushka, P. V., Privitera, P. J., Webb, J. G., Medley, E. S., Schuman, S. H., Rubin, M. I., Pantell, R. H., & Braustein, M. L. (1983). Childhood familial and racial differences in physiologic and biochemical factors related to hypertension. *Hypertension, 5,* 56–70.

Hypertension Detection and Follow-up Program Cooperative Group. (1977). Race, education and prevalence of hypertension. *American Journal of Epidemiology, 106,* 351–361.

James, S. A. (1985). Psychosocial and environmental factors in Black hypertension, In W. Hall, E. Saunders, & N. Schulman (Eds.), *Hypertension in Blacks: Epidemiology, pathophysiology and treatment* (pp. 132–143). Chicago: Yearbook Publishers.

James, S. A., Hartnett, S. A., & Kalsbeek, W. D. (1983). John Henryism and blood pressure differences among Black men. *Journal of Behavioral Medicine, 6,* 259–278.

James, S. A., & Kleinbaum, D. G. (1976). Socioecologic stress and hypertension-related mortality rates in North Carolina. *Journal of Public Health, 66,* 354–358.

James, S. A., LaCroix, A. Z., Kleinbaum, D. G., & Strogatz, D. S. (1984). John Henryism and blood pressure differences among Black men: II. The role of occupational stressors. *Journal of Behavioral Medicine, 7,* 259–275.

James, S. A., Strogatz, D. S., Wing, S. B., & Ramsey, D. L. (1987). Socioeconomic status, John Henryism, and hypertension in Blacks and Whites. *American Journal of Epidemiology, 126,* 664–673.

Jaynes, G. D., & Williams, R. M., Jr. (1989). *A common destiny: Blacks and American society.* Washington, DC: National Academy Press.

Johnson, E. H. (1989). Cardiovascular reactivity, emotional factors, and home blood pressures in Black males with and without a parental history of hypertension. *Psychosomatic Medicine, 51,* 390–403.

Johnson, E. H., Schork, N. J., & Spielberger, C. D. (1978). Emotion and familial determinants of elevated blood pressure in Black and White adolescent females. *Journal of Psychosomatic Research, 31,* 731–741.

Johnson, E. H., Spielberger, C. D., Worden, T. J., & Jacobs, G. A. (1987). Emotional and familial determinants of elevated blood pressure in Black and White adolescent males. *Journal of Psychosomatic Research, 31,* 287–300.

Jones, R. L. (Ed.). (1980). *Black psychology* (2nd ed.). New York: Harper & Row.

Katz, P., & Taylor, D. (Eds.). (1988). *Eliminating racism.* New York: Plenum.

Kessler, R. C., & Neighbors, H. W. (1986). A new perspective on the relationships among race, social class, and psychological distress. *Journal of Health and Social Behavior, 27,* 107–115.

King, L., Dixon, F. J., & Nobles, W. (Eds.). (1976). *African philosophy: Assumptions and paradigms for research on Black persons.* Los Angeles, CA: Fanon Center.

Kochman, T. (1981). *Black and White styles in conflict.* Chicago: University of Chicago Press.

Koepke, J. P., & DiBona, G. F. (1985). High sodium intake enhances renal nerve and antinatriuretic responses to stress in SHR. *Hypertension, 7,* 357.

Koepke, J. P., Light, K. C., & Obrist, P. A. (1983). Neural control of renal excretory function during behavioral stress in conscious dogs. *American Journal of Physiology, 245,* R251.

Koolen, M. I., & Van Brummelen, P. (1984). Adrenergic activity and peripheral hemodynamics in relation to sodium sensitivity in patients with essential hypertension. *Hypertension, 6,* 820–825.

Kurland, G. S., & Freeberg, A. S. (1951). The potentiating effect of ACTH and of cortisone on pressor response to intravenous infusion of L-nor-epinephrine. *Proceedings of the Society of Experimental Biology and Medicine, 78,* 28.

Lawrence, G. (Ed.). (1981). *The Black male.* Beverly Hills, CA: Sage.

Lewontin, R. C. (1973). The appointment of human diversity. *Evolutionary Biology, 6,* 381–398.

Lewontin, R. C., Rose, S., & Kamin, L. J. (1984). *Not in our genes: Biology, ideology, and human nature.* New York: Pantheon Books.

Light, K. C. (1987). Psychosocial precursors of hypertension: Experimental evidence. *Circulation, 76*(Suppl. I), I-67–I-76.

Light, K. C., Koepke, J. P., Obrist, P. A., & Willis, P. W. (1983). Psychological stress induces sodium and fluid retention in men at high risk for hypertension. *Science, 220,* 429.

Light, K. C., Obrist, P. A., Sherwood, A., James, S., & Strogatz, D. (1987). Effects of race and marginally elevated blood pressure on cardiovascular responses to stress in young men. *Hypertension, 10,* 555–563.

Light, K. C., & Sherwood, A. (1989). Race, borderline hypertension, and hemodynamic responses to behavioral stress before and after beta-adrenergic blockade. *Health Psychology, 8,* 577–596.

Lohmeier, T. E., & Carroll, R. G. (1985). Adrenocortical hormones and their interaction with angiotensin II and catecholamines in the production of hypertension. In F. Mantero, E. G. Biglieri, J. W. Funder, & B. A. Scoggins (Eds.), *The adrenal gland and hypertension* (Vol. 27, pp. 159–176). New York: Raven Press.

Luft, F., Grim, C., Fineberg, N., & Weinberger, M. (1979). Effects of volume expansion and contraction in normotensive Whites, Blacks, and subjects of different ages. *Circulation, 59,* 643–650.

Luft, F., Grim, C., & Weinberger, M. (1985). Electrolyte and volume homeostasis in Blacks. In W. Hall, E. Saunders, & N. Shulman (Eds.), *Hypertension in Blacks: Epidemiology, pathophysiology, and treatment* (pp. 115–131). Chicago: Yearbook Medical.

Luft, F. C., Rankin, L. I., Henry, D. P., Bloch, R., Grim, C. E., Weyman, A. E., Murry, R. H., & Weinberger, M. H. (1979). Plasma and urinary norepinephrine values at extremes of sodium intake in normal man. *Hypertension, 1,* 261.

Mark, A. L., Lawton, W. J., Abboud, F. M., Fitz, A. E., Cannor, W. E., & Heistad, D. D. (1975).

Effects of high and low sodium intake on arterial pressure and forearm vascular resistance in borderline hypertension. *Circulation Research, 36*(Suppl. I), I-194–I-198.

Matthews, K., Weiss, S., Detre, T., Dembroski, T., Falkner, B., Manuck, S., & Williams, R. (Eds.). (1986). *Handbook of stress reactivity and cardiovascular disease.* New York: Wiley.

Matthews, K. A., & Rakacksky, C. J. (1986). Familial aspects of the type A behavioral pattern and physiologic reactivity to stress. In T. H. Schmidt, T. M. Dembroski, & G. Blumchen (Eds.), *Biological and psychological factors in cardiovascular disease* (pp. 228–245). Berlin: Springer-Verlag.

McAdoo, W. G., Weinberger, M. H., Miller, J. Z., Fineberg, N. S., & Grim, C. E. (1990). Race and gender influence hemodynamic responses to psychological and physical stimuli. *Journal of Hypertension, 8,* 961–967.

McCarthy, R., Horwatt, K., & Konarska, M. (1988). Chronic stress and sympathetic–adrenal medullary responsiveness. *Social Science in Medicine, 26,* 333–341.

McNeilly, M., & Zeichner, A. (1989). Neuropeptide and cardiovascular responses to intravenous catheterization in normotensive and hypertensive Blacks and Whites. *Health Psychology, 8,* 487–501.

Morrell, M. A., Myers, H., Shapiro, D., Goldstein, I., & Armstrong, M. (1989). Cardiovascular reactivity to psychological stressors in Black and White normotensive males. *Health Psychology, 7,* 479–496.

Mourant, A. E. (1983). *Blood relations: Blood groups and anthropology.* New York: Oxford University Press.

Murphy, J., Alpert, B., Moses, D., & Somes, G. (1986). Race and cardiovascular reactivity: A neglected relationship. *Hypertension, 8,* 1075–1083.

Murphy, J. K., Alpert, B. S., Walker, S. S., & Willey, E. S. (1988). Race and cardiovascular reactivity: A replication. *Hypertension, 11,* 308–311.

Murphy, J. K., Alpert, B. S., Willey, E. S., & Somes, G. W. (1988). Cardiovascular reactivity to psychological stress in healthy children. *Psychophysiology, 25,* 144–152.

Myers, H. F., Shapiro, D., McClure, F., & Daims, R. (1989). Impact of caffeine and psychological stress on blood pressure in Black and White men. *Health Psychology, 8,* 597–612.

Nilsson, H., Fly, D., Friberg, P., Kalstrom, G. E., & Folkow, B. (1985). Effects of high and low sodium diets on the resistance of vessels and their adrenergic vasoconstrictor fibre control in normotensive (WKY) and hypertensive (SHR) rats. *Acta Physiologica Scandinavica, 125,* 323–334.

Nobles, W. (1974, June). Africanity: Its role in Black families. *Black Scholar,* pp. 10–16.

Obrist, P. A. (1981). *Cardiovascular psychophysiology: A perspective.* New York: Plenum.

Pollitzer, W. S. (1958). The Negroes of Charleston, SC: A study of hemoglobin types, serology, and morphology. *American Journal of Physical Anthropology, 16,* 241–263.

Rankin, L. I., Luft, F. C., Henry, D. P., Gibbs, P. S., & Weinberger, M. H. (1981). Sodium intake alters the effects of norepinephrine on blood pressure. *Hypertension, 3,* 650–656.

Reed, T. (1969). Caucasian genes in American Negroes. *Science, 165,* 762–768.

Rossier, J., French, E. D., Rivier, C., Ling, N., Guillemin, R., & Bloom, R. E. (1977). Foot-shock induced stress increases β-endorphin levels in blood but not brain. *Nature, 270,* 618–620.

Rowlands, D., De Givanni, J., McLeay, R., Watson, R., Stallard, T., & Littler, W. (1982). Cardiovascular response in Black and White hypertensives. *Hypertension, 4,* 817–820.

Schaeffer, M. A., & Baum, A. (1984). Adrenal cortical response to stress at Three Mile Island. *Psychosomatic Medicine, 46,* 227–237.

Schomig, A., Luth, B., Dietz, R., & Gross, F. (1976). Changes in vascular smooth muscle sensitivity to vasoconstrictor agents induced by corticosteroids, adrenalectomy and differing salt intake in rats. *Clinical Science and Molecular Medicine, 51*(Suppl. 3), 61.

Smith, E. J. (1981). Cultural and historical perspectives in counseling Blacks. In D. W. Sue (Ed.), *Counseling the culturally different: Theory and practice* (pp. 141–185). New York: Wiley.

Strand, F. L., & Smith, C. M. (1980). LPH, ACTH, MSH and motor system. *Pharmacology and Therapeutics, 11,* 509–533.

Strickland, T. L., Myers, H. F., & Lahey, B. B. (1989). Cardiovascular reactivity with caffeine and stress in Black and White normotensive females. *Psychosomatic Medicine, 51,* 381–389.

Takeshita, A., Imaizumi, T., Ashihara, T., & Nakamura, M. (1982). Characteristics of responses to salt loading and deprivation in hypertensive subjects. *Circulation Research, 51,* 457–464.

Tell, G. S., Prineas, R. J., & Gomez-Marin, D. (1988). Postural changes in blood pressure and pulse rate among Black adolescents and White adolescents: The Minneapolis children's blood pressure study. *American Journal of Epidemiology, 128,* 360–369.

Tischenkel, N. J., Saab, P. G., Schneiderman, N., Nelsen, R. A., Pasin, R. D., Goldstein, D. A., Spitzer, S. B., Woo-Ming, R., & Weidler, D. J. (1989). Cardiovascular and neuro-humoral responses to behavioral challenge as a function of race and sex. *Health Psychology, 8,* 503–524.

Trieber, F. A., Musante, L., Braden, D., Arensman, F., Strong, W. B., Levy, M., & Leverett, S. (1990). Racial differences in hemodynamic responses to the cold face stimulus in children and adults. *Psychosomatic Medicine, 52,* 286–296.

Trieber, F. A., Musante, L., Strong, W. B., & Levy, M. (1989). Racial differences in young children's blood pressure. *American Journal of Diseases of Children, 143,* 720–723.

Voors, A., Webber, L., & Berenson, G. (1980). Racial contrasts in cardiovascular response tests for children from a total community. *Hypertension, 2,* 686–694.

Weinberger, M., Luft, F., & Henry, D. (1982). The role of the SNS in the modulation of sodium excretion. *Clinical Experimental Hypertension, A4,* 719–735.

Whitworth, J. A., Coghlan, J. P., Denton, D. A., Hardy, K. J., & Scoggins, B. A. (1979). Effect of sodium loading and ACTH on blood pressure of sheep with reduced renal mass. *Cardiovascular Research, 13,* 9.

Wilson, W. (1973). *Power, racism, and privilege.* New York: Free Press.

Wilson, W. J. (Ed.). (1989). The ghetto underclass: Social science perspectives. *Annals of the American Academy of Political and Social Science, 501.*

PART THREE

Patterns of Cardiovascular Reactivity

CHAPTER 5

Stability and Patterning of Behaviorally Evoked Cardiovascular Reactivity

Stephen B. Manuck, Thomas W. Kamarck, Alfred S. Kasprowicz, and Shari R. Waldstein

People vary greatly in the magnitude of their heart rate and blood pressure reactions to behavioral stimuli. This observation has prompted speculation that the exaggerated cardiovascular responses to stress seen in certain "hyperreactive" individuals promote development of coronary heart disease or essential hypertension (Krantz & Manuck, 1984; Manuck, Kaplan, & Matthews, 1986; Manuck, Kasprowicz, & Muldoon, 1990). Most such hypotheses presume that this interindividual variability of cardiovascular reactions can be evaluated using standard laboratory protocols and that response differences among individuals are reproducible, both over time and under different stimulus conditions (Manuck, Kasprowicz, Monroe, Larkin, & Kaplan, 1989). Yet, as a construct, cardiovascular reactivity is frequently criticized on just these grounds—namely, for lack of temporal and cross-stimulus consistency

The preparation of this chapter was supported, in part, by National Institutes of Health grant HL40962.

(e.g., Parati et al., 1991; Pickering & Gerin, 1990). It has also been suggested that the primary focus on blood pressure reactions to stress seen in much of the reactivity literature obscures an underlying heterogeneity of hemodynamic patterns that may give rise to the pressor response and that such variability, in turn, may be differentially related to parameters of disease risk (Manuck et al., 1990). Accordingly, in this chapter, we address several issues that are pertinent to cardiovascular reactivity as a dimension of individual differences but pay particular attention to questions of response consistency and hemodynamic patterning. The principal conclusions of this discussion are threefold: (a) A sufficient assessment of cardiovascular reactivity may require aggregation of responses over multiple test stimuli and possibly over multiple testing sessions, (b) individuals do differ reliably in the pattern of hemodynamic adjustments supporting their pressor responses to behavioral challenge, and (c) individual differences in blood pressure response to a given task or stimulus reflects an interaction between the hemodynamic response propensities of the individual and certain response-eliciting attributes of the stimulus itself.

Reactivity as a Trait

We have previously proposed that *psychophysiological reactivity* be defined as a portion of the variability among individuals that is seen on measurement of a physiological parameter during subjects' exposure to behavioral stimuli (e.g., psychomotor, cognitive, or interpersonal challenges), which cannot be predicted from a knowledge of the variability that exists in the same parameter and among the same individuals in the absence of notable behavioral stimulation (as at rest) (Manuck et al., 1989). One quantitative expression of such reactivity may be found in the residual derived from regression of stimulus-related physiological measurements onto corresponding baseline values. In this context, the "residualized" change score reflects the extent to which an individual's task value (e.g., heart rate during performance of a difficult cognitive test) is either greater or less than that predicted on the basis of the same subject's baseline measurement and of the overall association between baseline and task values for the group as a whole. A more commonly reported index of psychophysiological reactivity is the simple change score, which is typically calculated as the arithmetic difference between measurements obtained during subjects' exposure to the eliciting stimulus and a (usually) preceding baseline recording. Of course, the arithmetic difference score will be "contaminated" by baseline influences whenever these two parameters are correlated, although this seems to occur infrequently among studies involving healthy (normotensive) individuals and for which adequate conditions of baseline measurement have been achieved.

However quantified, psychophysiological reactivity conveys unique information about the physiological functioning of individuals, information that cannot be obtained when measuring the same variables among quiescent and resting subjects. Because of the absence of standardized protocols for psychophysiological assessment, statements regarding the relative reactivity of individuals can at present be made only in relation to the responsivity of other persons who are subjected to identical conditions of measurement. As a result, there is currently no criterion response—such as a specific magnitude of blood pressure rise on subjects' exposure to a particular stimulus—that may be taken as indicative of the hyperreactive individual. Measurements of reactivity are therefore still largely sample dependent.

In a manner reminiscent of the state–trait distinction in personality psychology, either of two meanings may be used when referring to reactivity. As a state variable, reactivity reflects the variability of responses that is seen on subjects' exposure to a particular stimulus on a particular occasion. The (more common) trait use of this term denotes a response characteristic of individuals, namely a propensity to respond to behavioral stimuli with cardiovascular reactions of greater or lesser magnitude. In this sense, reactivity is a dispositional attribute, a characteristic of an individual that can be presumed to exert pervasive influence on cardiovascular responses seen under various conditions of behavioral stimulation.

Interestingly, most of the reactivity literature purports to deal with this construct in its trait aspect but in doing so infers the reactivity of individuals from their responses to a single stimulus, such as mental arithmetic or the cold pressor test, or to a few different stimuli that, on analysis, are treated independently. An obvious difficulty when inferring dispositional reactivity from single observations is that subjects' cardio-vascular responses to any specific task are likely to be determined, in part, by factors other than the reactivity trait. Such determinants will variably influence different subjects and may be largely random (e.g., presence of distractions, fatigue) or peculiar to the test stimulus; examples of the latter would include familiarity with the stimulus or level of skill (e.g., psychomotor and cognitive challenges) or pain sensitivity (e.g., the cold pressor test). Furthermore, the relative influences of these extra-neous factors cannot be separated from the reactivity "trait" of the in-dividual (as just defined) when only a single observation is available.

To state the problem another way, when reactivity is construed as an enduring, or stable, characteristic, reactivity is understood to be a phenomenon having consistency—consistency under different eliciting conditions and consistency over time (Manuck et al., 1989). When reac-tivity is defined operationally by reference to responses to a single stim-ulus, it is done so without evidence of consistency, and therefore, it must be assumed that the cardiovascular reactions that were observed on this one occasion were not influenced significantly by any factor other than the reactive "characteristic" of the individual. Whether this is a fair as-sumption can be known only if, at some point, the consistency of re-sponses (or of response distributions among individuals) is actually eval-uated, as seen over time and across different eliciting stimuli.

Table 1 enumerates the reasonable bases for inferring dispositional reactivity. It is similar to Fishbein and Ajzen's (1975; Ajzen, 1988) aggre-gation model of behavioral disposition. The columns refer to occasions

TABLE 1

Aggregation Model of Dispositional Cardiovascular Reactivity

Task	Occasion			Response tendency
	1	2	n	
1	T_{11}	$T_{12} \dots T_{1n}$		R_1
2	T_{21}	$T_{22} \dots T_{2n}$		R_2
3	T_{31}	$T_{32} \dots T_{3n}$		R_3
$\downarrow$	$\downarrow$	$\downarrow \dots \downarrow$		$\downarrow$
m	T_{m1}	$T_{m2} \dots T_{mn}$		R_m
Multiple-task criteria	M_1	$M_2 \dots M_n$		Dispositional reactivity

of measurement (1–n). For convenience, we define *dispositional cardiovascular reactivity* as the propensity to experience cardiovascular reactions of greater or lesser magnitude, in relation to other individuals, when exposed to behavioral stimuli—stimuli that may be aversive, challenging, or simply engaging (i.e., across the array of behavioral tasks that have been administered in studies purporting to evaluate such reactivity). In Table 1, each cell reflects responsivity to a single task on a single occasion; when defining reactivity, the cell can be referred to as a single-act criterion for reactivity assessment.

If the single-act criterion is adequate to evaluate cardiovascular reactivity, then subjects' responses to the criterion task should correlate highly with response distributions representing any other entry in the table (e.g., the same stimulus administered at a different time or a different stimulus presented on either the same or another occasion). Regarding consistency of response distributions across stimuli, pertinent literature is relatively sparse. This is due again to a preponderance of studies that used only one eliciting stimulus, as well as absence of reported intertask correlations when more than one task was administered. The evidence that exists, though, suggests only mild-to-moderate consistency over tasks. As reviewed previously, intertask correlations for heart rate and blood pressure tend to range from about 0.20 to about 0.60 and average in the 0.40–0.50 range across common laboratory stressors such as mental arithmetic, reaction time tasks, and the cold pressor test (Manuck et al., 1989). Intertask correlations of this magnitude are not inconsistent with a dispositional model of reactivity; indeed, in psychometric assessment, interitem correlations may range from 0.10 to 0.40 and still constitute a reliable unifactorial scale (Nunnally, 1967). Given this magnitude of association, however, it is unlikely that the use of any single experimental challenge will be sufficient to evaluate the response characteristics of individuals, just as a single item is rarely a sufficient index of a personality trait.

To the extent that low intertask correlations are due to influences of random or stimulus-specific factors such as those cited earlier, the reliability of reactivity assessments might be enhanced by aggregating individuals' responses over several different tasks. In computing average behavioral tendencies derived from subjects' exposure to multiple stimuli, the extraneous influences of factors that may differ from task to task should tend to cancel each other out (Ajzen, 1988; Epstein, 1979, 1980), thereby yielding a less "contaminated" index of reactivity. Returning to Table 1, a multiple-act (or multiple-task) evaluation of cardiovascular reactivity can be achieved by aggregating responses over rows (tasks) within a column (occasion of testing) (e.g., T_{11}, T_{12}, T_{13}, etc.).

One caution regarding response aggregation, however, is that averaging can also potentially obscure, rather than reveal, individual differences if various eliciting stimuli (or classes of stimuli) evoke largely uncorrelated cardiovascular reactions. For example, two laboratory stressors might both raise blood pressure but because of different hemodynamic mechanisms: Blood pressure may rise in one instance because the stimulus evokes an increase in cardiac output, and in the other, it may rise because it raises the peripheral resistance. If interindividual variability within the two tasks reflects differences in subjects' myocardial (cardiac output) and resistance responses, respectively, then these two eliciting stimuli may well tap into different dimensions of reactivity. If such dimensions are sufficiently correlated, then the presence of reactivity "subtypes" (e.g., cardiac vs. vascular reactors) should not preclude the detection of a single underlying response propensity (overall magnitude of response), in the same manner that a measure of various intellectual abilities may still be meaningfully summarized by a single-factor score (O'Grady, 1983). If different dimensions of reactivity are largely uncorrelated, however, then aggregation across tasks that evoke different patterns of response may not yield a single factor. Whether individual differences in cardiovascular reactivity do exhibit such multidimensionality is currently unknown, although later we return briefly to this issue. At this time, we conclude only that reactions to typical laboratory stressors share sufficient variance to postulate a single continuum of cardiovascular reactivity for which reliability of measurement may be improved by aggregating responses across multiple stimuli.

When responses to the same stimulus are assessed on two or more occasions, the temporal stability of response distributions is evaluated, which is another indicator of consistency. In contrast to the paucity of

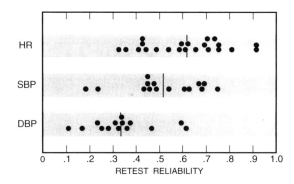

FIGURE 1. Retest reliability of heart rate (HR), systolic blood pressure (SBP), and diastolic blood pressure (DBP) in studies that used adult subject samples. Each filled circle corresponds to the retest reliability observed in a single sample. Vertical lines depict the average of all retest correlations.

published evidence addressing intertask relationships, there is now considerable literature on the retest reliability of cardiovascular reactivity. These studies typically report correlations between measurements obtained on two occasions (generally separated by 2 days to a few months) and are based on subjects' reactions to a single stimulus or to several tasks analyzed individually. Figure 1 summarizes the results of available studies of retest reliability in adult samples[1]; most of these investigations involved young adult subjects (generally college students), although a few of the studies included hypertensive patients. The continuum of test–retest correlations is indicated at the bottom of the figure. For each study, the observed test–retest correlation (or the average of such correlations, if more that one task was administered) is plotted for measures of heart rate and systolic and diastolic blood pressure. The correlations are based on some index of response to the eliciting stimulus, usually a

[1]Arena, Blanchard, Andrasik, Cotch, & Myers, 1983; Carroll, Turner, Lee, & Stephenson, 1984; Fahrenberg, Schneider, Foerester, Myrtek, & Muller, 1985; Faulstich et al., 1986; Giaconi et al., 1987; Glass, Lake, Contrada, Kehoe, & Erlanger, 1983; Kamarck et al., 1992; Kamarck, Jennings, Stewart, & Eddy, 1991; Kasprowicz, Manuck, Malkoff, & Krantz, 1990; Langewitz, Ruddel, Noack, & Wachtarz, 1989; Lovallo, Pincomb, & Wilson, 1986; Manuck & Garland, 1980; Manuck & Schaefer, 1978; McKinney et al., 1985; Myrtek, 1985; Rombouts, 1982; Seraganian et al., 1985; Sharpley, Scuderi, & Heffernan, 1989; Sherwood, Turner, Light, & Blumenthal, 1990; Turner, Carroll, Sims, Hewitt, & Kelly, 1986; van Egeren & Sparrow, 1989.

simple change score that reflects the difference in heart rate or blood pressure between periods of task presentation and an appropriate baseline measurement. Also, for each of the three response variables, the mean retest correlation across all studies is indicated by placement of a vertical line through the axis of plotted coefficients.

There is clearly great variability among studies: Correlations range from 0.32 to 0.91 for heart rate, with a mean test–retest correlation of 0.61. The situation with respect to systolic blood pressure is similar, if somewhat weaker, with an average correlation of 0.51. Diastolic blood pressure is the weakest of the three response variables, with an average coefficient of 0.34; in many individual studies, the test–retest correlation for diastolic reactivity does not reach significance. Overall, the evidence that individual differences in behaviorally evoked cardiovascular reactions are reproducible over time is mixed and, at best, moderate (for heart rate); in the case of diastolic blood pressure, retest reliability is frankly equivocal. The wide differences in outcome between ostensibly similar studies suggest that methodological features of these investigations might account, in part, for the difficulty of demonstrating reproducible response distributions in some laboratories. Such factors may include use of extremely small samples, inadequate pretest adaptation and baseline measurements, or substantial between-sessions habituation to particular test stimuli (Manuck et al., 1989). Nonetheless, when taken as a whole, it must be concluded that this literature provides rather less support for retest reliability than would ordinarily be expected of a robust dispositional construct.

It is possible, of course, that aggregating measurements over repeated observations will yield a more stable index of reactivity. Averaging responses recorded on multiple occasions will diminish the effects of nonsystematic, session-to-session influences on cardiovascular responses, such as fluctuations of mood, fatigue, or other distractions. Even when obtaining measurements on repeated occasions, though, if a researcher has used a single eliciting stimulus, then he or she can aspire only to demonstrate consistent individual differences in reactivity to that particular task. Recall that by our definition dispositional reactivity presumes cross-situational, or cross-stimulus, consistency, as well as retest

stability. Following Ajzen (1988), temporally stable distributions of responses to single tasks might then be referred to as "response tendencies,"
as shown in the row margins of Table 1.

There is some evidence that estimates of retest reliability are improved when subjects' responses to several tasks are averaged to yield
an aggregated index of reactivity. Kamarck and colleagues administered
a battery of three computerized cognitive and psychomotor tasks to three
different subject samples (Kamarck et al., 1991, 1992). One study used
college-age men, one used a community sample of men of widely different ages (24–76 years old) and education, and the third used another
community sample of Black and White women (25–44 years old). Because
the aim of this research was to develop a test protocol of adequate reliability for use in a population-based epidemiological investigation, ef-
forts were made to standardize all features of the component tasks. This
included standard delivery of instructions and practice trials, exclusion
of verbalized responses, minimization of the motor elements of response
execution (e.g., use of low-pressure microswitches), and computerized
titration of task difficulty in accordance with subjects' skill levels (both
within and across sessions). Test–retest intervals varied from 1 week to
1 month.

Figure 2 presents the main findings of these studies with respect to
retest reliability. Note that in the panels for heart rate and systolic and
diastolic blood pressure there are four sets of data points; these correspond to the three just-mentioned samples, with data for the study of
Black and White women presented separately by race. The filled circles
indicate the mean test–retest correlation for a particular sample, as calculated over the test battery's three component tasks. The vertical line
in each panel is the same as that shown in Figure 1 and again depicts the
mean test–retest correlation reported in prior literature. It is apparent
that the retest reliability of the current tasks exceeds the mean for the
literature in nearly all instances. It should be noted, too, that three of the
four samples were composed of relatively homogeneous groups, so that
enhanced reliability cannot be attributed simply to the diversity of the
samples. Extending from each filled circle (i.e., mean correlation) is a
line that terminates with the point of an arrow. This latter point corre-

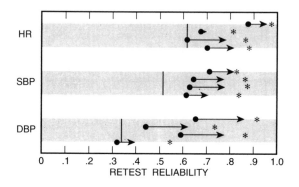

FIGURE 2. Retest reliability of heart rate (HR), systolic blood pressure (SBP), and diastolic blood pressure (DBP) in four adult samples that were administered a standardized multitask protocol. Filled circles depict retest reliability averaged over all tasks. Arrows depict retest reliability of reactivity indices aggregated over all tasks. Asterisks denote generalizability coefficients for reactivity indices aggregated over two occasions of testing. Vertical lines depict the average of all retest correlations.

sponds to the test–retest correlation achieved when using an index of reactivity aggregated over the three stimulus tasks. Note that in every case there is some improvement in retest reliability, which is sometimes rather appreciable; indeed, all but two correlations based on the aggregated tasks exceed 0.70.

Generalizability coefficients may be calculated to assess the effect on reliability of aggregating across sessions as well as tasks. A generalizability coefficient is an intraclass coefficient that indicates how well a sample of measures with specified characteristics (items, raters, occasions of testing, etc.) generalizes to a hypothetical population of measures from which the sample is assumed to be drawn (see Crocker & Algina, 1986; Cronbach, Gleser, Nanda, & Rajaratnaw, 1972; Llabre et al., 1988). In Figure 2, the star depicted on each line denotes the generalizability coefficient associated with measures of cardiovascular reactivity aggregated across two sessions (equivalent to a hypothetical test–retest correlation in which each test score is derived from two testing sessions). With two exceptions, these coefficients surpass 0.80 for all measures and on all samples.

The foregoing data persuade us that there may truly exist a reliable dimension of individual differences in cardiovascular reactivity, although prior literature and the predominant methodologies it reflects may have only imperfectly captured this phenomenon. The single-task protocol, administered on a single occasion (which, incidentally, characterizes the entire prospective literature bearing on the reactivity–hypertension association) (Manuck et al., 1990), may simply be inadequate to reliably characterize the dispositional reactivity of individuals. If this is so, then the ability of response distributions based on single-task protocols to correlate with or to predict other variables of interest (like hypertension or coronary ischemic events) will be constrained correspondingly. As implied in Table 1, cardiovascular reactivity may be assessed best by administering multiple eliciting stimuli on multiple occasions. Although application of test batteries as extensive as this may not be practicable in many instances, we nonetheless conclude that, as in other areas of psychology dealing with behavioral dispositions, much may be gained by the use of aggregated measurements. Just as reliability is a precondition for validity, so too the value of aggregation lies not only in the assessment of cardiovascular reactivity itself but in an improved ability to evaluate the relationship of such reactivity to aspects of cardiovascular disease.

Patterning of Hemodynamic Response

Generally, only a few physiological variables are recorded in studies of individual differences, and these are often treated as equivalent, or effectively interchangeable, indices of cardiovascular function (Manuck et al., 1989). Among the typically recorded measurements, blood pressure is perhaps of greatest interest because of its role as the pathognomonic indicator of hypertension. It should be recalled, however, that blood pressure actually expresses a relationship between varying hemodynamic processes—namely, the pumping actions of the heart and forces that impede, or resist, the flow of blood out of the arterial circulation. Hence, blood pressure is a parameter of a somewhat different quality than cardiovascular measurements that may be expressed as discrete events, intervals, rates, or quantities (e.g., heart rate, systolic time intervals, stroke volume).

The derivative nature of blood pressure is illustrated in Figure 3, which depicts the hemodynamic reactions of 2 individuals to a 3-min mental arithmetic task (serial subtraction) (Manuck et al., 1990). The values are change scores (task minus baseline) and reflect the magnitude of subjects' responses, as averaged over the 3-min task period. The cardiovascular measurements that were recorded are systolic, diastolic, and mean blood pressure, heart rate, the cardiac preejection period, stroke volume (evaluated noninvasively by impedance cardiography and expressed as an index [divided by body surface area]), and calculated values of cardiac output (index) and total peripheral resistance. Note that, al-

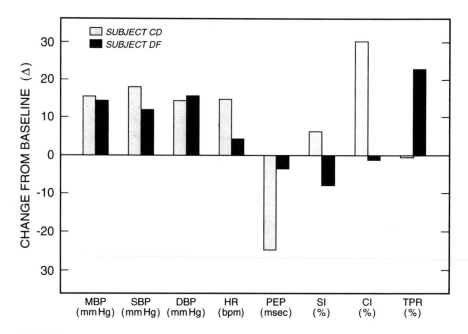

FIGURE 3. Cardiovascular responses to mental arithmetic in two individuals, subjects CD and DF. Values are expressed as change from baseline measurements. MBP = mean blood pressure; SBP = systolic blood pressure; DBP = diastolic blood pressure; HR = heart rate; PEP = cardiac preejection period; SI = stroke index; CI = cardiac index; TPR = total peripheral resistance. From "Behaviorally-Evoked Cardiovascular Reactivity and Hypertension: Conceptual Issues and Potential Associations" by S. B. Manuck, A. L. Kasprowicz, and M. F. Muldoon, 1990, *Annals of Behavioral Medicine, 12,* 17–29; copyright 1990 by the Society of Behavioral Medicine; reprinted by permission.

though these 2 individuals exhibited nearly identical elevations in mean blood pressure, their cardiovascular responses differed dramatically in almost every other respect. Subject CD alone, for example, showed a marked heart rate acceleration, an attenuation of the preejection period, and a substantial rise in the cardiac index, whereas only subject DF reacted to mental arithmetic with an appreciable increase in peripheral resistance.

The comparable blood pressure elevations observed in subjects CD and DF therefore appear to be achieved by entirely different mechanisms. The pressor response of subject CD is sustained by concomitant cardiac reactions to mental arithmetic, whereas vascular influences predominate in subject DF. This hemodynamic differentiation is also reflected to a small degree in the pattern of subjects' systolic and diastolic responses, which reveal a slight widening of the pulse pressure in subject CD and a narrowing of the same index in subject DF. The data data depicted in Figure 3 thus demonstrate the variability of hemodynamic responses that may give rise to behaviorally evoked pressor reactions.

Of course, if these 2 individuals reflect only isolated instances of relatively "pure" cardiac-dependent (output) and vascular-dependent (resistance) blood pressure responses, then these observations are of less interest than was such variability to describe an important dimension of individual differences in cardiovascular reactivity. Addressing this issue, Figure 4 summarizes the hemodynamic responses to mental arithmetic seen in groups of clearly differentiated cardiac and vascular reactors, as well as in persons whose cardiovascular responsivity reflects a combination (mixture) of cardiac and vascular influences. Together, these three subject groups comprise about 60% of an unselected sample of 39 young adult men who participated in a recent study of psychophysiological reactivity (Kasprowicz et al., 1990).

For purposes of classification, the subject groupings depicted in Figure 4 were identified solely on the basis of impedance-derived measurements of cardiac output (index) and peripheral resistance. From the change score distributions for these two parameters, we identified as cardiac output (CI) reactors all individuals who had shown (a) a rise in the cardiac index during mental arithmetic that exceeded the mean re-

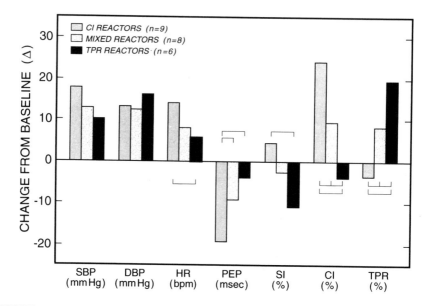

FIGURE 4. Cardiovascular reactions to mental arithmetic during Session 1 for cardiac index (CI) reactors, mixed reactors, and total peripheral resistance (TPR) reactors. Brackets indicate significant pairwise contrasts ($p <$ .05). SBP = systolic blood pressure; DBP = diastolic blood pressure; HR = heart rate; PEP = cardiac preejection period; SI = stroke index. From "Individual Differences in Behaviorally Evoked Cardiovascular Response: Temporal Stability and Hemodynamic Patterning" by A. L. Kasprowicz, S. B. Manuck, S. B. Maldoff, and D. S. Krantz, 1990, *Psychophysiology, 27,* 605–619; copyright 1990 by the Society for Psychophysiological Research; reprinted by permission.

sponse of all subjects by at least one standard deviation and (b) a change in peripheral resistance that was less than the sample mean. Conversely, resistance (TPR) reactors were identified as subjects who had shown (a) a change in the cardiac index that was less than the sample mean and (b) an increase in the total peripheral resistance that exceeded the mean the mean response of all subjects by at least a standard deviation.

Defining mixed cardiac and vascular reactors was less straightforward because we wanted to identify individuals who had exhibited concomitant, and roughly comparable, increases in both the cardiac index and total peripheral resistance. First, we standardized the change scores for each of the two index variables, which generated distributions having a mean of 0.0 and standard deviation of 1.0. We then subtracted the standardized score reflecting each subject's change in peripheral resistance from that denoting his change in cardiac index. The smaller this difference, the more comparable should be a subject's responses on the two variables; of course, a small difference between the cardiac index and resistance "scores" would also characterize nonreactive individuals who simply failed to respond in any way to the eliciting stimulus. Therefore, we identified as *mixed reactors* all subjects in whom (a) the foregoing difference was less than ±1.0 and (b) both the cardiac index and total peripheral resistance increased (i.e., showed a positive change) over baseline measurements during subject's performance of the task. In all, 23 subjects were classified by these various criteria, which yielded 9 CI reactors, 6 TPR reactors, and 8 mixed reactors.

As shown in Figure 4, the changes in cardiac index and total peripheral resistance evoked by mental arithmetic differed as expected between our three subject groups. TPR reactors showed no mean change in the cardiac index, nor did CI reactors exhibit any elevation in peripheral resistance; at the same time, CI reactors showed appreciable elevations in the cardiac index, as did TPR reactors in their total peripheral resistance. Also, mixed reactors exhibited intermediate responses on both variables and differed significantly from CI and TPR reactors on each. Mean changes in the preejection period, heart rate, and stroke index paralleled those for cardiac index and peripheral resistance, but only the CI and TPR reactive groups differed significantly with respect to the latter two variables. Although neither systolic nor diastolic blood pressure reactions differentiated the three groups, it is apparent that the pulse pressure rose during mental arithmetic among CI reactors and fell in TPR reactors; when calculated separately, this group difference in pulse pressure response is also significant. Thus, impedance-derived assessments of the cardiac index and total peripheral resistance reveal a heterogeneity of underlying hemodynamic responsivity, at least among healthy young men. This heterogeneity of response is also paralleled by changes in heart rate and stroke index and corroborated by two measurements that do not directly contribute to impedance evaluations: pulse pressure and the cardiac preejection period.

As with individual response measures such as heart rate or blood pressure, we wanted to determine whether such differences in the patterning of individuals' hemodynamic reactions are stable over time. For this purpose, we also compared the cardiovascular responses to mental arithmetic recorded 1 month later among the same three groups (i.e., among the subjects identified as CI, mixed, and TPR reactors based on their first-session reactions to the same task). As shown in Figure 5, group means at follow-up were all in the same direction as those seen on subjects' initial exposure to the eliciting stimulus, despite an overall habituation of responses between the two sessions. Statistically, the CI and TPR reactors differed significantly with respect to changes in the cardiac index, peripheral resistance, stroke volume, and preejection period but not in heart rate. The responses of mixed reactors again fell between

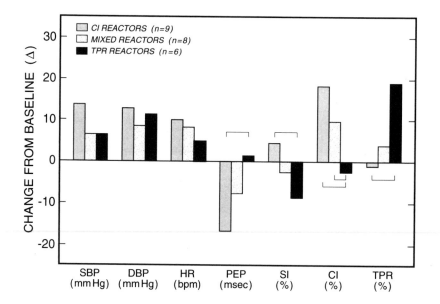

FIGURE 5. Cardiovascular reactions to mental arithmetic during Session 2 for cardiac index (CI) reactors, mixed reactors, and total peripheral resistance (TPR) reactors. Brackets indicate significant pairwise contrasts ($p < .05$). SBP = systolic blood pressure; DBP = diastolic blood pressure; HR = heart rate; PEP = cardiac preejection period; SI = stroke index. From "Individual Differences in Behaviorally Evoked Cardiovascular Response: Temporal Stability and Hemodynamic Patterning" by A. L. Kasprowicz, S. B. Manuck, S. B. Maldoff, and D. S. Krantz, 1990, *Psychophysiology, 27,* 605–619; copyright 1990 by the Society for Psychophysiological Research; reprinted by permission.

those of CI and TPR reactors but differed reliably only from TPR reactors and on only one measure of change—the cardiac index. Thus, differences in subjects' behaviorally evoked hemodynamic reactions show some degree of reproducibility, at least on retesting at 1 month and among individuals who exhibited the most divergent patterns of response (i.e., CI and TPR reactors). It may be noted, too, that these observations are based on use of a single eliciting stimulus (mental arithmetic). Our prior discussion of psychometric considerations that constrain the assessment of reactivity suggests, of course, that aggregating subjects' reactions over multiple stimuli would yield a more reliable evaluation of this typology.

Actually, we did expose subjects to a second laboratory task in this experiment but one that differed in an important respect from mental arithmetic. In this regard, an interesting feature of mental arithmetic (as operationalized in this study) was its failure to evoke a uniform pattern of cardiovascular response across all subjects. We might consider this stimulus to be a weak "cardiac" task, insofar as it elicited a significant, but small, overall increase in cardiac output and was associated with substantial variability among individuals. Our second task, mirror tracing, required subjects to trace with a stylus the outline of a geometric figure (star), guided only by the mirror image of the target design. This perceptual reversal makes the task distinctly frustrating, and subjects' pressor reactions during task performance are generally of the same magnitude as those seen under mental arithmetic. However, virtually all subjects showed a marked rise in the total peripheral resistance, accompanied by a net drop in cardiac index. It was therefore of interest to determine whether our typology of cardiovascular reactivity, which was defined by individuals' reactions to mental arithmetic, would predict any aspect of subjects' responses to mirror tracing—again, a predominantly vascular stimulus.

Illustrated in Figure 6 are mean responses recorded during mirror tracing among the CI, TPR, and mixed reactors. Because subjects' reactions did not vary between the two data collections conducted 1 month apart, the mean changes were collapsed across the two experimental sessions. It is apparent that the three groups showed similar increases in total peripheral resistance but differed in their cardiac output responses.

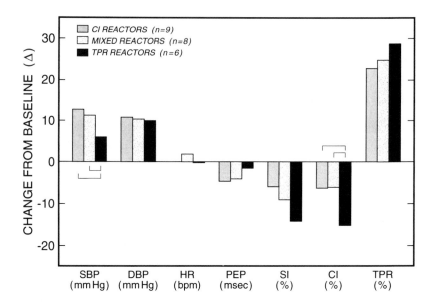

FIGURE 6.   Cardiovascular reactions to the mirror tracing task, collapsed across Sessions 1 and 2, for cardiac index (CI) reactors, mixed reactors, and total peripheral resistance (TPR) reactors. Brackets indicate significant pairwise contrasts ($p < .05$). SBP = systolic blood pressure; DBP = diastolic blood pressure; HR = heart rate; PEP = cardiac preejection period; SI = stroke index. From "Individual Differences in Behaviorally Evoked Cardiovascular Response: Temporal Stability and Hemodynamic Patterning" by A. L. Kasprowicz, S. B. Manuck, S. B. Maldoff, and D. S. Krantz, 1990, *Psychophysiology, 27,* 605–619; copyright 1990 by the Society for Psychophysiological Research; reprinted by permission.

In particular, the cardiac index decreased in TPR reactors to a greater extent that among either the CI or mixed reactors. We speculate that this more modest fall in the cardiac index in CI and mixed reactors reflects an "attempt" by these subjects to mount a cadiac response, in accord with their response propensities (as demonstrated under mental arithmetic). However, such a response failed to achieve an actual rise in the cardiac output during mirror tracing (in relation to baseline) because of an increased cardiac afterload associated with the markedly elevated peripheral resistance that was seen in all three groups. Interestingly, the net effect of these influences may be a more pronounced pressor response among subjects whose hemodynamic reactions subsume both a vascular and a cardiac component. Indeed, as shown in Figure 6, the CI and mixed reactors did exhibit significantly greater systolic blood pressure elevations during mirror tracing than did their resistance-reactive counterparts.

From the latter observations, we conclude that both stimulus attributes and individual response propensities determine cardiovascular reactions to a given stimulus. A tentative model describing such associations is illustrated in Figure 7, which attempts to account for behaviorally evoked blood pressure responses (the ordinate) in terms of individual and stimulus-specific attributes. On the stimulus side, behavioral challenges differ in the extent to which they elicit a primarily cardiac or vascular response, as well as in the strength of these response-eliciting tendencies: This dimension is labeled *stimulus type* in the figure. As described previously, in our own data, mental arithmetic might be considered a weak cardiac task, and mirror tracing might be considered a strong vascular stimulus.

In addition to variations in cardiovascular response due to stimulus type, the reactions of individuals also vary greatly. Moreover, we propose that this interindividual variability reflects the influence of various trait-

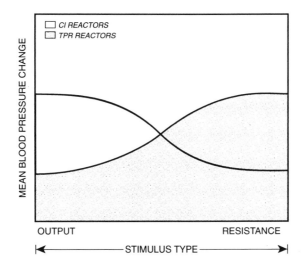

FIGURE 7. A model of stimulus influences on the behaviorally evoked blood pressure responses of cardiac index (CI) and total peripheral resistance (TPR) reactors.

like response propensities. These propensities, in turn, will be most readily observed as discriminable patterns of hemodynamic adjustment when
subjects are exposed to stimuli (like mental arithmetic) that do not tend
to evoke cardiovascular reactions that are either strongly cardiac or
strongly vascular in nature. Under such conditions, CI reactors will respond primarily with increases in cardiac output, and TPR reactors will
respond primarily with elevations in peripheral resistance.

Our data also suggest, however, that the individual response propensity will affect cardiovascular reactions even to stimuli that do tend
to elicit predominantly cardiac or vascular adjustments. Thus, on performance of mirror tracing, subjects whose response propensities were
incongruent with the strong vascular nature of the stimulus (e.g., CI reactors) showed a partial cardiac response, in addition to the increased
peripheral resistance "pulled for" by this task. Again, the net outcome
was a greater systolic blood pressure reaction among the CI and mixed
reactors than among TPR reactors. The response propensity of the TPR
reactors (resistance) was congruent with, and hence possibly preempted
by, resistance-eliciting aspects of mirror tracing itself. These relationships
are shown on the right side of the model in Figure 7, which depicts output
reactors as experiencing the more pronounced blood pressure response
to a "resistance-type" task.

Conversely, it is conceivable that the responses of TPR reactors to
a strong cardiac task would entail both a stimulus-evoked cardiac response and (unlike CI reactors) some residual vascular involvement,
which may possibly appear as a failure to show compensatory decreases
in peripheral resistance. In this instance, it might be expected that the
largest pressor responses would be found among TPR reactors because
of the additive influences of these particular stimulus and subject attributes (Figure 7, left side). Thus, one nonintuitive implication of our model
is that differences in the magnitude of blood pressure responses seen
among cardiac- and resistance-reactive individuals may change, even reverse, under highly different stimulus conditions.

Summarizing the preceding observations, our data persuade us that
mean cardiovascular reactions to behavioral stimuli, as seen among
groups of individuals, obscure an underlying heterogeneity of hemody-

namic responses. In addition, under some stimulus conditions, such as mental arithmetic in this experiment, subsets of individuals may be identified whose pressor responses are supported by changes in either the cardiac output or total peripheral resistance or by a combination of cardiac and vascular influences. When derived from impedance measurements of output and resistance, these differentiated patterns of response are also corroborated by corresponding group differences on other cardiovascular parameters (e.g., the cardiac preejection period and pulse pressure). Preliminary evidence suggests, too, that this typology of hemodynamic response reflects a stable, or reproducible, dimension of individual differences. Moreover, these differences generalize, in this experiment, to a different stimulus, mirror tracing, which (unlike mental arithmetic) tends to induce a uniformly elevated peripheral resistance. Cardiac-reactive individuals show both the vascular response that may be "dictated" by attributes of the task and an attenuated fall in the cardiac output (at least in relation to resistance-reactive subjects). This finding is consistent with the notion that cardiac-reactive subjects try to mount a cardiac response, even when this attempt may not find expression as a true increase in the cardiac output due to resistance-dependent afterload. The net effect, however, is an enhanced pressor response among cardiac-reactive individuals. Finally, these results suggest to us a more general model by which both individual response propensities and stimulus attributes interact to determine cardiovascular adjustments seen under various behavioral challenges.

References

Ajzen, I. (1988). *Attitudes, personality and behavior*. Chicago: Dorsey.

Arena, J. G., Blanchard, E. B., Andrasik, R., Cotch, P., & Myers, P. (1983). Reliability of psychophysiological assessment. *Behaviour Research and Therapy, 21*, 447–460.

Carroll, D., Turner, J. R., Lee, H. J., & Stephenson, J. (1984). Temporal consistency of individual differences in cardiac response to a video game. *Biological Psychology, 19*, 81–93.

Crocker, L., & Algina, J. (1986). *Introduction to classical and modern test theory*. New York: Holt, Rinehart & Winston.

Cronbach, L. J., Gleser, G. C., Nanda, H., & Rajaratnaw, N. (1972). *The dependability of behavioral measurements: Theory of generalizability for scores and profiles*. New York: Wiley.

Epstein, S. (1979). The stability of behavior: I. On predicting most of the people much of the time. *Journal of Personality and Social Psychology, 37,* 1097–1126.

Epstein, S. (1980). The stability of behavior: II. Implications for psychological research. *American Psychologist, 35,* 790–807.

Fahrenberg, J., Schneider, H., Foerester, F., Myrtek, M., & Muller, W. (1985). The quantification of cardiovascular reactivity in longitudinal studies. In A. Steptoe, H. Ruddel, & H. Neus (Eds.), *Clinical and methodological issues in cardiovascular psychophysiology* (pp. 107–120). Berlin: Springer-Verlag.

Faulstich, M. E., Williamson, D. A., McKenzie, S J., Duchmann, E. G., Hutchinson, K. M., & Blouin, D. C. (1986). Temporal stability of psychophysiological responding: A comparative analysis of mental and physical stressors. *International Journal of Neuroscience, 30,* 65–72.

Fishbein, M., & Ajzen, I. (1975). *Belief, attitude, intention, and behavior: An introduction to theory and research.* Reading, MA: Addison-Wesley.

Giaconi, S., Palombo, C., Genovesi-Ebert, A., Marabotti, C., Mezzasalma, L., & Ghione, S. (1987). Medium-term reproducibility of stress tests in borderline arterial hypertension. *Journal of Clinical Hypertension, 3,* 654–660.

Glass, D. C., Lake, C. R., Contrada, R. J., Kehoe, K., & Erlanger, L. R. (1983). Stability of individual differences in physiologic response to stress. *Health Psychology, 4,* 317–342.

Kamarck, T. W., Jennings, J. R., Debski, T. T., Glickman-Weiss, E., Johnson, P. S., Eddy, M. J., & Manuck, S. B. (1992). Reliable measures of behaviorally-evoked cardiovascular reactivity from a PC-based test battery: Results from student and community samples. *Psychophysiology, 29,* 17–28.

Kamarck, T. W., Jennings, J. R., Stewart, C. J., & Eddy, M. J. (1991). Reliable responses to a PC-based reactivity protocol: The effects of gender, race, and obesity [Abstract]. *Psychophysiology, 28*(Suppl. 33), 33.

Kasprowicz, A. L., Manuck, S. B., Malkoff, S. B., & Krantz, D. S. (1990). Individual differences in behaviorally evoked cardiovascular response: Temporal stability and hemodynamic patterning. *Psychophysiology, 27,* 605–619.

Krantz, D. S., & Manuck, S. B. (1984). Acute psychophysiological reactivity and risk of cardiovascular disease: A review and methodologic critique. *Psychological Bulletin, 96,* 435–464.

Langewitz, W., Ruddel, H., Noack, H., & Wachtarz, K. (1989). The reliability of psychophysiological examinations under field conditions: Results of repetitive mental stress testing in middle-aged men. *European Heart Journal, 10,* 657–665.

Llabre, M. M., Ironson, G. H., Spitzer, S. B., Gellman, M. D., Weidler, D. J., & Schneiderman, N. (1988). How many blood pressure measurements are enough?: An application of generalizability theory to the study of blood pressure reliability. *Psychophysiology, 25,* 97–106.

Lovallo, W. R., Pincomb, G. A., & Wilson, M. F. (1986). Heart rate reactivity and type A behavior as modifiers of physiological response to active and passive coping. *Psychophysiology, 23*, 105–112.

Manuck, S. B., & Garland, F. N. (1980). Stability of individual differences in cardiovascular reactivity: A thirteen month follow-up. *Physiology and Behavior, 24*, 621–624.

Manuck, S. B., Kaplan, J. R., & Matthews, K. A. (1986). Behavioral antecedents of coronary heart disease and atherosclerosis. *Arteriosclerosis, 6*, 2–14.

Manuck, S. B., Kasprowicz, A. L., Monroe, S. B., Larkin, K. T., & Kaplan, J. R. (1989). Psychophysiologic reactivity as a dimension of individual differences. In N. Schneiderman, S. B. Weiss, & P. Kaufmann (Eds.), *Handbook of methods and measurements in cardiovascular behavioral medicine* (pp. 365–382). New York: Plenum.

Manuck, S. B., Kasprowicz, A. L., & Muldoon, M. F. (1990). Behaviorally-evoked cardiovascular reactivity and hypertension: Conceptual issues and potential associations. *Annals of Behavioral Medicine, 12*, 17–29.

Manuck, S. B., & Schaefer, D. C. (1978). Stability of individual differences in cardiovascular reactivity. *Physiology and Behavior, 21*, 675–678.

McKinney, M. E., Miner, M. H., Ruddel, H., McIlvain, H. E., Witte, H., Buell, J. C., Eliot, R. S., & Grant, L. B. (1985). The standardized mental stress protocol: Test–retest reliability and comparison with ambulatory blood pressure monitoring. *Psychophysiology, 22*, 453–463.

Myrtek, M. (1985). Adaptation effects and the stability of physiological responses to repeated testing. In A. Steptoe, H. Ruddel, & H. Neus (Eds.), *Clinical and methodological issues in cardiovascular psychophysiology* (pp. 93–106). Berlin: Springer-Verlag.

Nunnally, J. (1967). *Psychometric theory.* New York: McGraw-Hill.

O'Grady, K. E. (1983). A confirmatory maximum likelihood factor analysis of the WAIS-R. *Journal of Consulting and Clinical Psychology, 51*, 826–831.

Parati, G., Trazzi, S., Ravogli, A., Casadei, R., Omboni, S., & Mancia, G. (1991). Methodological problems in evaluation of cardiovascular effects of stress in humans. *Hypertension, 17*(Suppl. III), 50–55.

Pickering, T. G., & Gerin, W. (1990). Cardiovascular reactivity in the laboratory and the role of behavioral factors in hypertension: A critical review. *Annals of Behavioral Medicine, 12*, 3–16.

Rombouts, R. (1982). The reproducibility of cardiovascular reactions during cognitive tasks. *Activatas Nervosa Superior, Suppl. 3*(Pt. 2), 284–294.

Seraganian, P., Hanley, J. A., Hollander, B. J., Roskies, E., Smilga, C., Martin, N. D., Collu, R., & Oseasohn, R. (1985). Exaggerated psychophysiological reactivity: Issues in quantification and reliability. *Journal of Psychosomatic Research, 29*, 393–405.

Sharpley, C. F., Scuderi, C. S., & Heffernan, C. J. (1989). Reliability of heart rate reactivity to a psychological stressor. *Perceptual and Motor Skills, 68*, 319–322.

Sherwood, A., Turner, J. R., Light, K. C., & Blumenthal, J. A. (1990). Temporal stability of the hemodynamics of cardiovascular reactivity. *International Journal of Psychophysiology, 10,* 95–98.

Turner, J. R., Carroll, D., Sims, J., Hewitt, J. K., & Kelly, K. A. (1986). Temporal and intertask consistency of heart rate reactivity during active psychological challenge: A twin study. *Physiology and Behavior, 38,* 641–644.

van Egeren, L. F., & Sparrow, A. W. (1989). Laboratory stress testing to assess real-life cardiovascular reactivity. *Psychosomatic Medicine, 51,* 1–9.

CHAPTER 6

Habituation of Cardiovascular Reactivity to Psychological Stress: Evidence and Implications

Robert M. Kelsey

Research on cardiovascular reactivity to psychological stress has flourished in recent years, largely because of the notion that such reactivity may be involved in the development of cardiovascular diseases such as coronary heart disease and essential hypertension (Krantz & Manuck, 1984). Much of this research has concentrated on the magnitude of cardiovascular responses to acute stress rather than on patterns of cardiovascular responses to recurrent stress (i.e., repeated or chronic stress). Nevertheless, a systematic analysis of patterns of cardiovascular reactivity to recurrent psychological stress may be crucial for understanding how psychophysiological processes may contribute to the development of cardiovascular disease.

Consider, for example, three different patterns of cardiovascular reactivity, as illustrated in Figure 1, all of which yield the same overall magnitude of cardiovascular response to stress. *Pattern C* (constant) involves a moderate but persistent elevation of cardiovascular performance over time, whereas *pattern S* (sensitization) involves a linear in-

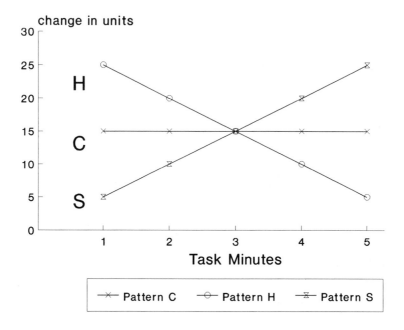

FIGURE 1. Three prototypical patterns of cardiovascular reactivity to stress.

crease in reactivity, and *pattern H* (habituation) involves a large initial response, which is followed by a rapid decline. These three cardiovascular response profiles may be associated with very different health outcomes. Although it is fairly easy to envision how pattern S could contribute to cardiovascular disease, it is more difficult to comprehend how pattern H could contribute to disease. Indeed, Dientsbier (1989) proposed that a pattern such as H may be associated with positive health outcomes. Such considerations underscore the importance of evaluating patterns of cardiovascular reactivity over time (Blascovich & Kelsey, 1990; Cacioppo & Tassinary, 1990).

In this chapter, I evaluate patterns of cardiovascular reactivity to recurrent psychological stress within the context of the dual process theory of habituation and sensitization (Groves & Thompson, 1970; Thompson, Berry, Rinaldi, & Berger, 1979). Two fundamental questions are addressed. Does cardiovascular reactivity to psychological stress habituate? If so, then how can it contribute to the development of cardiovascular disease?

Dual Process Theory

Habituation and sensitization are pervasive, fundamental forms of behavioral plasticity, which are evident in response systems ranging from the gill-withdrawal reflex in marine mollusks to the orienting reflex in humans (Groves & Thompson, 1970; Thompson et al., 1979). The dual process theory (Groves & Thompson, 1970) proposes that habituation and sensitization are independent processes that interact to determine the response to repeated stimulation. According to this theory, habituation is a decremental process that involves presynaptic depression of the interneurons in stimulus–response (S–R) pathways (i.e., the connections between receptor and effector organs). In contrast, sensitization is an incremental process that involves presynaptic facilitation of interneurons by modulatory state systems (i.e., arousal or activation systems), which determine the general degree of reactivity or sensitivity to stimulation.

According to the dual process theory (Groves & Thompson, 1970), repetition of an effective stimulus results in a response decrement or a response increment, depending on certain stimulus characteristics (e.g., frequency, intensity) and the state of the organism (i.e., level of arousal or excitability). The theory postulates that habituation increases with repeated stimulation, whereas sensitization increases initially but then decays. In either case, responding tends to return to initial levels after a respite from stimulation, a phenomenon known as spontaneous recovery. Further training tends to produce more habituation, less sensitization, and less subsequent spontaneous recovery. Indeed, extended training may produce habituation beyond the zero or asymptotic response level, an effect known as *below-zero habituation.*

Nevertheless, habituation may be disrupted by a change in stimulation; this dishabituation, in turn, tends to habituate with stimulus repetition. The theory also postulates that habituation and sensitization generalize across stimuli to the extent that common neural elements are activated by those stimuli; habituation generalizes to the extent that there is neural overlap in the activated S–R pathways, whereas sensitization generalizes to the extent that there is neural overlap in the activated state systems. Accordingly, dishabituation may result from insufficient generalization of habituation or sensitization or from an independent activation of state systems.

Cardiovascular Reactivity to Recurrent Stress

Given the ubiquitous nature of habituation and sensitization, it seems logical that these processes should contribute to changes in cardiovascular reactivity to recurrent stress. However, most research on habituation and sensitization has concentrated on repeated exposure to conditions involving sensory intake or passive coping rather than mental work or active coping. Because the latter conditions seem to elicit the greatest degree of β-adrenergic sympathetic cardiovascular activation (Krantz & Manuck, 1984; Obrist, 1981; Sherwood, Allen, Obrist, & Langer, 1986; Williams, 1986), it remains unclear whether habituation and sensitization contribute significantly to variations in cardiovascular reactivity to recurrent psychological stress.

A computer search of the literature for the past 15 years revealed little or no systematic analysis of cardiovascular habituation and sensitization to psychological stress in humans. Indeed, habituation of cardiovascular reactivity to stress has typically been considered a nuisance to be avoided or controlled rather than a phenomenon worthy of systematic investigation.

Research on Cardiac Reactivity

Nonetheless, studies that have evaluated patterns of cardiovascular reactivity over time have typically shown that cardiac reactivity peaks early during the initial presentation of a task, when task novelty is greatest, but declines with continued or repeated task exposure (Carroll, Cross, & Harris, 1990; Caroll, Turner, & Hellawell, 1986; Kelsey, 1991; Light & Obrist, 1980; Linden, 1987; Miller & Ditto, 1989a; Neus & von Eiff, 1985; Obrist, 1981; Sherwood et al., 1986; Turner, 1988). This sort of pattern has appeared during a variety of stressful tasks, ranging from reaction time tasks to mental arithmetic tasks. Moreover, several researchers have noted that cardiac reactivity declines significantly with repeated exposure to the same or similar stressors and that the effects of various task manipulations (e.g., difficulty, threat, and incentive manipulations) on cardiac performance often vary as a function of task repetition or task order (Elliott, 1969; Grossman & Svebak, 1987; Hastrup, Johnson, Hotchkiss, & Kraemer, 1986; Kelsey, 1991; Light & Obrist, 1980; Linden, 1987; Turner, 1988).

Previous studies in our laboratory (Kelsey, 1991; Kelsey & Katkin, 1991; Rousselle, Blascovich, Cerny, Kelsey, & Schiffert, 1988) demonstrated that cardiac reactivity to a difficult mental arithmetic task is most acute during the first minute of the task and declines rapidly over the remaining task minutes. The cardiac response profiles that are evoked by these tasks are remarkably consistent, emerging reliably in both men and women in every study we have conducted to date. Representative data are presented in Figure 2. Data in the top row are from undergraduate men in a study of electrodermal lability and myocardial reactivity to stress (Kelsey, 1991), whereas data in the bottom row are from undergraduate women in a study of cardiodynamic factors in Raynaud's disease (Kelsey & Katkin, 1991). In both studies, impedance cardiography and electrocardiography were used to assess cardiac performance during 5-min baseline and mental arithmetic task periods. The data represent changes from pretask baseline during a 5-min period of verbal serial subtractions by steps of 13. Three key measures are depicted in Figure 2: preejection period (an inverse index of myocardial contractile force), heart rate, and cardiac output. Despite individual differences in the magnitude of cardiac responses to stress, all groups show clear declines in cardiac reactivity over task minutes.

We also have observed declines in cardiac reactivity with repeated presentations of similar mental arithmetic tasks (Kelsey, 1991; Rousselle et al., 1988). For example, Rousselle et al. found that cardiac performance exceeded concurrent metabolic demand (as indexed by oxygen consumption) during the first presentation of a difficult mental arithmetic task, especially during the initial task minute. When a second mental arithmetic task was presented, however, no cardiac–somatic discrepancy appeared. These results suggest that as experience with a stressful task increases, cardiac performance declines to levels that match concurrent metabolic requirements.

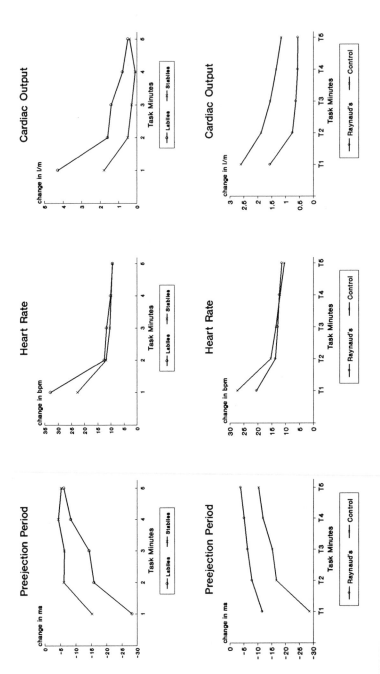

FIGURE 2. Mean preejection period (in milliseconds [ms]), heart rate (in beats per minute [bpm]), and cardiac output (in liters per minute [l/m]) reactivity (changes from baseline) during a 5-min period of mental arithmetic stress as a function of individual differences in electrodermal lability (top row; from "Electrodermal Lability and Myocardial Reactivity to Stress" by R. M. Kelsey, 1991, *Psychophysiology, 28*, 619–631; copyright 1991 by the Society for Psychophysiological Research; adapted by permission) and vasospastic symptoms (bottom row; from *International Perspectives on Self-Regulation and Health*, edited by J. G. Carlson and A. R. Seifert, 1991, New York: Plenum; copyright 1991 by Plenum Publishing Corporation; adapted by permission).

Research on Vascular Reactivity

Taken together, these observations suggest that prior experience with a stressor tends to attenuate β-adrenergic cardiac reactivity; that is, cardiac reactivity to stress tends to habituate. However, the pattern of habituation observed for cardiac measures does not necessarily hold for vascular measures such as peripheral vascular resistance, which may actually increase during stress (Carroll et al., 1990; Light & Obrist, 1980; Linden, 1987; Miller & Ditto, 1989a; Neus & von Eiff, 1985).

Recent studies by Carroll et al. (1990) and Miller and Ditto (1989a) examined patterns of cardiovascular reactivity to extended stressors, which lasted 16 min (Carroll et al., 1990) to 1 hr (Miller & Ditto, 1989a). In both cases, cardiac reactivity declined during the course of the task, whereas vascular resistance actually increased. Thus, cardiac reactivity followed a pattern consistent with habituation, whereas vascular reactivity followed a pattern more consistent with sensitization.

Although Carroll et al. (1990) and Miller and Ditto (1989a) interpreted these vascular response patterns in terms of autoregulatory processes, there are other possibilities. A rise in vascular resistance during stress may reflect a decrease in β-adrenergic vasodilation, which is consistent with an habituation process; alternatively, it may reflect an increase in α-adrenergic vasoconstriction, which is consistent with a sensitization process. Indeed, using α- and β-adrenergic antagonists, Miller and Ditto (1989b) demonstrated that the rise in vascular resistance during extended stress is mediated by peripheral adrenergic activity. In any case, differences in the patterns of cardiac and vascular reactivity to recurrent stress could have important implications for cardiovascular disease processes.

Recent Experimental Evidence

We recently conducted a study of cardiovascular reactivity to recurrent mental arithmetic stress to determine whether cardiovascular responses to psychological stress conform to principles of habituation and sensitization (Kelsey, Tomaka, & Leitten, 1991).

The experiment consisted of two 5-min task periods, each preceded by a 5-min baseline rest period. Ninety-seven undergraduate men were randomly assigned to one of five experimental conditions. During the first task period, four groups performed verbal mental arithmetic tasks of varying difficulty, which involved rapid serial subtractions from a four-digit number by steps of 1 ($n = 20$), 3 ($n = 23$), 7 ($n = 19$), or 13 ($n = 17$). Subjects were instructed to perform these tasks aloud as quickly and as accurately as possible. The fifth group ($n = 18$) rested quietly throughout this period. During the second task period, all five groups performed the same verbal mental arithmetic task, which consisted of rapid serial subtractions by steps of 7, starting from a new four-digit number.

Electrocardiographic (Lead II) and impedance cardiographic (IFM Model 304B) recordings were used to derive continuous measures of cardiac performance (cf. Kelsey & Guethlein, 1990). A continuous, non-invasive blood pressure monitor (Cortronic Model 7000) was used to record mean arterial pressure at the brachial artery. Mean arterial pressure was used in conjunction with cardiac output to calculate total peripheral resistance. Four key measures were evaluated: (a) heart rate, which is subject to sympathetic and parasympathetic influences; (b) preejection period, an inverse index of myocardial contractile force, upon which β-adrenergic sympathetic influences tend to predominate; (c) cardiac output, which reflects the interaction of cardiac rate and force, as well as stroke volume; and (d) total peripheral vascular resistance, which is subject to both α- and β-adrenergic influences (Newlin & Levenson, 1979; Obrist, 1981; Sherwood et al., 1990).

Delta scores for these cardiovascular measures (calculated by subtracting values for the last minute of the pretask baseline period from values for each task minute) were analyzed simultaneously in a set of multivariate trend analyses. The first analysis evaluated the effects of task difficulty and task repetition on cardiovascular reactivity in a 4 (Group) × 2 (Task) × 5 (Minute) mixed factorial design. The second analysis evaluated the effects of prior task exposure on cardiovascular reactivity during the second task period in a 5 (Group) × 5 (Minute) mixed factorial design. In addition to these analyses, task performance was evaluated in a multivariate analysis of the number of arithmetic responses and the number of arithmetic errors for each task minute.

Task Performance

The arithmetic performance data are presented in Figure 3. The groups differed as expected during the first task period. Subjects who counted backward by 1s had more responses and fewer errors than did subjects who counted backward by 3s, who in turn had more responses than did those who counted backward by 7s or 13s. All groups, including the "naive" control group (Group 5), performed about the same when counting backward by 7s during the second task period. Moreover, as the flatness of the response profiles suggests, there was little variation in arithmetic performance over time during either task period.

Cardiovascular Reactivity

The cardiovascular data are presented in Figure 4. In contrast to arithmetic performance, cardiovascular reactivity did not vary as a function of task difficulty; that is, there were no significant differences in cardiovascular reactivity among Groups 1–4.

As in prior studies, all three cardiac measures showed a large initial response followed by rapid decline during the first task period, a pattern that is consistent with habituation. The decrement in heart rate was more abrupt than that in preejection period, whereas cardiac output followed an intermediate pattern. There was some spontaneous recovery between task periods, but cardiac habituation clearly strengthened with task repetition. Moreover, during the second task period, the naive control group (Group 5) showed significantly greater cardiac reactivity than did the four "experienced" groups. These group differences indicate that the decline in cardiac reactivity over task periods in Groups 1–4 was not due to the general effects of time alone but rather to the specific effects of repeated exposure to stress.

In contrast to cardiac reactivity, vascular resistance showed a linear increase over task minutes. This result is consistent with those of Carroll et al. (1990) and Miller and Ditto (1989a) and adds to them by demonstrating a rise in vascular resistance over a much shorter period of time. Although vascular reactivity showed some recovery between task periods,

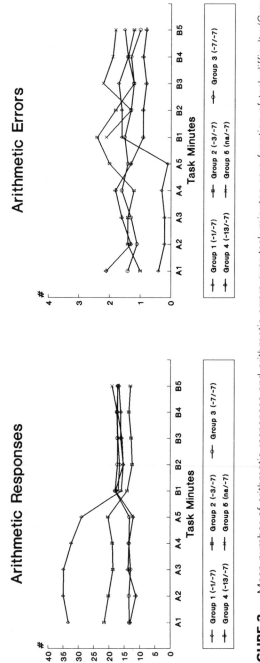

FIGURE 3. Mean number of arithmetic responses and arithmetic errors over task minutes as a function of task difficulty (Groups 1–5) and task repetition (Tasks A and B). Adapted from Kelsey, Tomaka, and Leitten (1991).

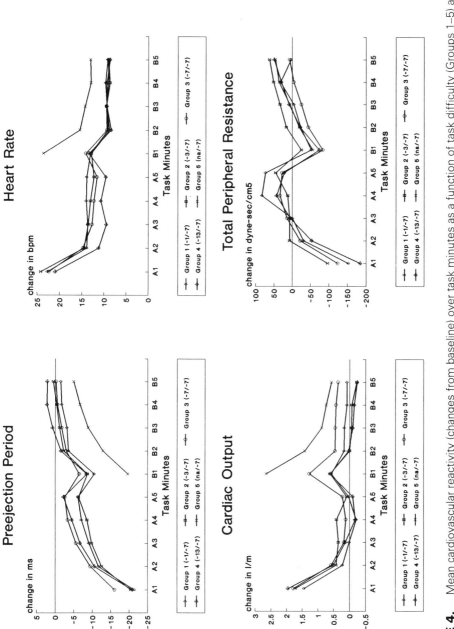

FIGURE 4. Mean cardiovascular reactivity (changes from baseline) over task minutes as a function of task difficulty (Groups 1–5) and task repetition (Tasks A and B). Adapted from Kelsey, Tomaka, and Leitten (1991).

the profile flattened with task repetition in Groups 1–4. However, vascular reactivity during the second task period in these four experienced groups did not differ significantly from that in the naive control group. Hence, unlike cardiac performance, vascular resistance did not vary reliably as a function of prior exposure to stress.

Given these results, it is tempting to explain the increase in vascular resistance during stress in terms of nonneural autoregulatory processes rather than neural habituation or sensitization processes. Such short-term autoregulatory processes are presumably triggered by elevations in cardiac output (Obrist, 1981). In the Kelsey et al. (1991) study, however, the naive and experienced groups showed similar vascular reactivity during the second task period despite significant differences in cardiac output reactivity. Furthermore, a combination of countervailing neural influences cannot be ruled out. Repeated exposure to stress may evoke a vascular response pattern that is ostensibly constant but that is actually determined by a shifting balance of underlying mechanisms. For example, the vascular response to stress may reflect an interaction of β-adrenergic vasodilation and α-adrenergic vasoconstriction, processes that may be subject to different degrees of habituation and sensitization.

Finally, as a comparison of the data in Figures 3 and 4 clearly suggests, the patterns of cardiovascular reactivity that were observed by Kelsey et al. (1991) were not attributable to variations in arithmetic task performance. Adjusting for variations in arithmetic performance had no appreciable impact on the observed variations in cardiovascular performance. So, with regard to the first question—Does cardiovascular reactivity to recurrent psychological stress habituate?—the answer appears to be *yes* for cardiac performance but *not necessarily* for vascular resistance.

Implications and Hypotheses

Although the chronic stress of daily life may elicit persistent, nonhabituating elevations in cardiovascular performance, it seems at least as likely that cardiovascular reactivity habituates to the routine demands and stress of everyday life, just as it seems to habituate in the laboratory. So, if cardiovascular responses to psychological stress habituate, then how can cardiovascular reactivity contribute to the development of cardio-vascular disease?

There are a several plausible mechanisms. Before presenting them, however, it may help to provide a theoretical model of cardiovascular reactivity to recurrent psychological stress.

Paradoxical Model of Habituation

The relationship between amount of stimulus exposure and degree of habituation may not be monotonic, as postulated originally in the dual process theory. For example, Stephenson and Siddle (1976) reported that the skin conductance response to a novel stimulus is enhanced, rather than reduced, after extended below-zero habituation training. Thompson et al. (1979) presented an intriguing model for this paradoxical below-zero habituation effect. Figure 5 presents a variant of this model for cardiac reactivity to stress.

In this simplified model, initial exposure to stressor A activates the S–R pathway that runs from processor A to the heart, which thereby triggers a cardiac response. Repeated exposure to this stressor results in a decrease in cardiac reactivity due to habituation of interneurons 1A and 2, as well as the SNS neuron (presynaptic depression). With prolonged or repeated exposure to stressor A, interneuron 1A remains depressed, which results in little or no activation of later neurons in the pathway; hence, interneuron 2 and the SNS neuron begin to recover.

Subsequent exposure to a new stressor, stressor B, activates a new S–R pathway that runs from processor B to the heart via interneuron 1B, interneuron 2, and the SNS neuron. Activation of the fresh interneuron 1B excites interneuron 2 and the SNS neuron, which restores the cardiac response if the latter neurons have recovered. In addition, the new stressor may activate a state system to sensitize the SNS neuron (presynaptic facilitation), which thereby enhances the cardiac response.

Plausible Pathophysiological Mechanisms

This model and related research may be used to derive the following potential pathophysiological mechanisms, which may contribute to the

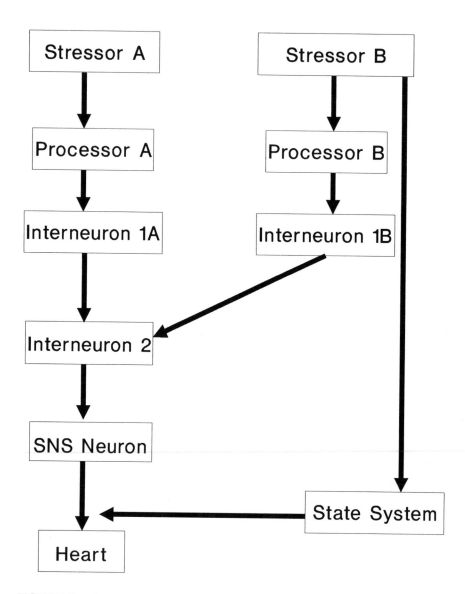

FIGURE 5. Paradoxical model of cardiac habituation to recurrent psychological stress. (SNS = sympathetic nervous system.)

development of cardiovascular disease despite, or even because of, cardiovascular habituation to recurrent stress.

First, cardiovascular reactivity may decline with repeated exposure to one stressor (habituation) but may increase drastically upon exposure to a new stressor (dishabituation), an effect with special relevance for relationships between acute and chronic stress. For example, Fleming, Baum, Davidson, Rectanus, and McArdle (1987) reported that people who are exposed to higher levels of chronic crowding stress exhibit greater cardiovascular reactivity to an acute mental stressor than do people who are exposed to lower levels of chronic stress.

Similar effects have been demonstrated for catecholamine responses to chronic intermittent (i.e., recurrent) stress in animals (McCarty, Horwatt, & Konarska, 1988). In relation to naive control animals, animals that have prior experience with a stressor exhibit reduced catecholamine reactivity to the familiar stressor but enhanced reactivity to a novel stressor (Konarska, Stewart, & McCarty, 1989a, 1989b; McCarty et al., 1988). Although repeated exposure to stress results in decreased catecholamine release, it also results in increased catecholamine synthesis, which may enhance the capacity to respond subsequently to novel stressors (McCarty et al., 1988). McCarty and colleagues suggested that these catecholamine responses reflect habituation and sensitization, as delineated by the dual process theory.

Furthermore, Majewski, Tung, and Rand (1981) demonstrated that epinephrine released from the adrenal medulla during stress can be absorbed by sympathetic nerve endings for subsequent release as a cotransmitter. Epinephrine released in this manner stimulates prejunctional β-adrenergic receptors to increase the discharge of sympathetic nerves, a process that is consistent with sensitization via presynaptic facilitation.

Second, Bassett and Cairncross (1977) have shown that habituation of the cortisol response to stress increases the risk of coronary vascular damage by endogenous inflammatory substances.

Third, there may be individual, gender, or racial differences in habituation and sensitization of cardiovascular responses to stress. Such differences may contribute to variations in the incidence of cardiovascular diseases among groups.

Implications for Stress Testing

In addition to implications for the development of cardiovascular disease and for the relationship between acute and chronic stress, the paradoxical model of cardiovascular adaptation to recurrent stress also has practical implications for the design of psychophysiological stress testing procedures and longitudinal research. If β-adrenergic cardiovascular reactivity to psychological stress is related to cardiovascular disease processes, as several investigators have proposed (e.g., Krantz & Manuck, 1984; Obrist, 1981), then tests that are designed to elicit β-adrenergic effects on the cardiovascular system may be useful in identifying individuals at risk for developing cardiovascular disease (cf. Krantz & Manuck, 1984; Neus & von Eiff, 1985; Obrist, 1981). The model in Figure 5 suggests that sympathetic effects on the heart should be greatest when a stressor is novel or unfamiliar but should diminish with repeated exposure to that stressor. Thus, psychophysiological stress testing protocols and longitudinal studies that entail repeated administrations of the same or similar tasks are likely to elicit less and less cardiovascular reactivity over time. However, the cardiovascular habituation model suggests that such declines in β-adrenergic cardiovascular reactivity to recurrent stress may be counteracted by (a) limiting the amount of exposure to a particular stressor (i.e., minimizing habituation), (b) increasing the amount of time between exposures to a stressor (i.e., maximizing spontaneous recovery), (c) presenting a new stressor that has relatively limited neural overlap with earlier stressors (i.e., maximizing dishabituation by minimizing generalization), or (d) extending the exposure to earlier stressors before presenting a novel stressor (i.e., maximizing dishabituation via paradoxical habituation).

Finally, the retest reliability and predictive validity of psychophysiological stress testing procedures are likely to vary as a function of cardiovascular adaptation to recurrent stress. It remains to be seen whether the initial, transient response or the subsequent, steady-state adaptation to stress is more predictive of later cardiovascular disease. Such issues emphasize the importance of evaluating patterns of cardiovascular reactivity to recurrent psychological stress.

References

Bassett, J. R., & Cairncross, K. D. (1977). Changes in the coronary vascular system following prolonged exposure to stress. *Pharmacology, Biochemistry and Behavior, 6,* 311–318.

Blascovich, J., & Kelsey, R. M. (1990). Using cardiovascular and electrodermal measures of arousal in social psychological research. *Review of Personality and Social Psychology, 11,* 45–73.

Cacioppo, J. T., & Tassinary, L. G. (1990). Psychophysiology and psychophysiological inference. In J. T. Cacioppo & L. G. Tassinary (Eds.), *Principles of psychophysiology: Physical, social, and inferential elements* (pp. 3–33). London: Cambridge University Press.

Carlson, J. G., & Seifert, A. R. (1991). *International perspectives on self-regulation and health.* New York: Plenum.

Carroll, D., Cross, G., & Harris, M. G. (1990). Physiological activity during a prolonged mental stress task: Evidence for a shift in the control of pressor reactions. *Journal of Psychophysiology, 4,* 261–269.

Carroll, D., Turner, J. R., & Hellawell, J. C. (1986). Heart rate and oxygen consumption during active psychological challenge: The effects of level of difficulty. *Psychophysiology, 23,* 174–181.

Dientsbier, R. A. (1989). Arousal and physiological toughness: Implications for mental and physical health. *Psychological Review, 96,* 84–100.

Elliott, R. (1969). Tonic heart rate: Experiments on the effects of collative variables lead to a hypothesis about its motivational significance. *Journal of Personality and Social Psychology, 12,* 211–228.

Fleming, I., Baum, A., Davidson, L. M., Rectanus, E., & McArdle, S. (1987). Chronic stress as a factor in physiologic reactivity to challenge. *Health Psychology, 6,* 221–237.

Grossman, P., & Svebak, S. (1987). Respiratory sinus arrhythmia as an index of parasympathetic cardiac control during active coping. *Psychophysiology, 24,* 228–235.

Groves, P. M., & Thompson, R. F. (1970). Habituation: A dual-process theory. *Psychological Review, 77,* 419–450.

Hastrup, J. L., Johnson, C. A., Hotchkiss, A. P., & Kraemer, D. L. (1986). Win some, lose some: Parental hypertension and heart rate change in an incentive versus response cost paradigm. *International Journal of Psychophysiology, 4,* 217–220.

Kelsey, R. M. (1991). Electrodermal lability and myocardial reactivity to stress. *Psychophysiology, 28,* 619–631.

Kelsey, R. M., & Guethlein, W. (1990). An evaluation of the ensemble averaged impedance cardiogram. *Psychophysiology, 27,* 24–33.

Kelsey, R. M., & Katkin, E. S. (1991). Environmental stress and myocardial reactivity:

Implications for Raynaud's disease. In J. G. Carlson & A. R. Seifert (Eds.), *International perspectives on self-regulation and health* (pp. 41–63). New York: Plenum.

Kelsey, R. M., Tomaka, J., & Leitten, C. L. (1991, October). *Patterns of cardiovascular reactivity to recurrent psychological stress.* Paper presented at the annual meeting of the Society for Psychophysiological Research, Chicago.

Konarska, M., Stewart, R. E., & McCarty, R. (1989a). Habituation of sympathetic–adrenal medullary responses following exposure to chronic intermittent stress. *Physiology and Behavior, 45,* 255–261.

Konarska, M., Stewart, R. E., & McCarty, R. (1989b). Sensitization of sympathetic–adrenal medullary responses to a novel stressor in chronically stressed laboratory rats. *Physiology and Behavior, 46,* 129–135.

Krantz, D. S., & Manuck, S. B. (1984). Acute psychophysiologic reactivity and risk for cardiovascular disease: A review and methodologic critique. *Psychological Bulletin, 96,* 435–464.

Light, K. C., & Obrist, P. A. (1980). Cardiovascular response to stress: Effects of opportunity to avoid, shock experience, and performance feedback. *Psychophysiology, 17,* 243–252.

Linden, W. (1987). Effect of noise distraction during mental arithmetic on phasic cardiovascular activity. *Psychophysiology, 24,* 328–333.

Majewski, H., Tung, L.-H., & Rand, M. J. (1981). Hypertension through adrenaline activation of prejunctional β-adrenoceptors. *Clinical and Experimental Pharmacology and Physiology, 8,* 463–468.

McCarty, R., Horwatt, K., & Konarska, M. (1988). Chronic stress and sympathetic–adrenal medullary responsiveness. *Social Science and Medicine, 26,* 333–341.

Miller, S. B., & Ditto, B. (1989a). Individual differences in heart rate and peripheral vascular responses to an extended aversive task. *Psychophysiology, 26,* 506–513.

Miller, S. B., & Ditto, B. (1989b). Hemodynamic patterns of response to extended active coping stress in offspring of hypertensives [Abstract]. *Psychophysiology, 26,* S3.

Neus, H., & von Eiff, A. W. (1985). Selected topics in the methodology of stress testing: Time course, gender and adaptation. In A. Steptoe, H. Ruddel, & H. Neus (Eds.), *Clinical and methodological issues in cardiovascular psychophysiology* (pp. 78–92). Berlin: Springer-Verlag.

Newlin, D. B., & Levenson, R. W. (1979). Pre-ejection period: Measuring beta-adrenergic influences upon the heart. *Psychophysiology, 16,* 546–553.

Obrist, P. A. (1981). *Cardiovascular psychophysiology: A perspective.* New York: Plenum.

Rousselle, J. G., Blascovich, J., Cerny, F. J., Kelsey, R. M., & Schiffert, J. H. (1988). Cardiorespiratory responses to a combination of aerobic exercise and mental arithmetic [Abstract]. *Psychophysiology, 25,* 477–478.

Sherwood, A., Allen, M. T., Fahrenberg, J., Kelsey, R. M., Lovallo, W. R., & van Doornen, L.

J. P. (1990). Committee report: Methodological guidelines for impedance cardiography. *Psychophysiology, 27,* 1–23.

Sherwood, A., Allen, M. T., Obrist, P. A., & Langer, A. W. (1986). Evaluation of beta-adrenergic influences on cardiovascular and metabolic adjustments to physical and psychological stress. *Psychophysiology, 23,* 89–104.

Stephenson, D., & Siddle, D. A. T. (1976). Effects of "below-zero" habituation on the electrodermal orienting response to a test stimulus. *Psychophysiology, 13,* 10–15.

Thompson, R. F., Berry, S. D., Rinaldi, P. C., & Berger, T. W. (1979). Habituation and the orienting reflex: The dual-process theory revisited. In H. D. Kimmel, E. H. van Olst, & J. F. Orlebeke (Eds.), *The orienting reflex in humans* (pp. 21–60). Hillsdale, NJ: Erlbaum.

Turner, J. R. (1988). Inter-task consistency: An integrative re-evaluation. *Psychophysiology, 25,* 235–238.

Williams, R. B., Jr. (1986). Patterns of reactivity and stress. In K. A. Matthews, S. M. Weiss, T. Detre, T. M. Dembroski, B. Falkner, S. B. Manuck, & R. B. Williams, Jr. (Eds.), *Handbook of stress, reactivity, and cardiovascular disease* (pp. 109–125). New York: Wiley.

PART FOUR

Technology

CHAPTER 7

Use of Impedance Cardiography in Cardiovascular Reactivity Research

Andrew Sherwood

T he aims of this chapter are twofold, and accordingly it is composed of two sections. The first section provides a methodological description of impedance cardiography as a noninvasive technique for measuring cardiac function, with special emphasis on cardiac output measurement. In describing the technique's fundamental principles, instrumentation, signal acquisition, and the derivation of cardiac performance indices, this section is written for the non–technically minded reader. Much of the material in this section is drawn from a committee report that outlined methodological guidelines for impedance cardiography, which is recommended to the reader who may plan to use the technique (Sherwood, Allen et al., 1990). The noninvasive and unobtrusive nature of cardiac output measurement by impedance cardiography makes it ideally suited for monitoring cardiovascular responses during exposure to

The preparation of this chapter was supported by National Institutes of Health grant HL38590. I thank Dot Faulkner for her secretarial assistance.

psychological stressors. The second section describes the growing impact of impedance cardiography in cardiovascular reactivity research, for which its use has proliferated over the last decade. Emerging evidence of individual differences and stressor differences in hemodynamic profiles is reviewed along with evidence of temporal stability, intertask consistency, and postural stability of hemodynamic response patterns. The aim of the second section is to show how documentation of the hemodynamic basis of blood pressure responses has impacted on our understanding of cardiovascular reactivity and its potential role in the etiology of hypertension.

Methodological Overview of Impedance Cardiography

Basic Principles of Impedance Cardiography

Impedance cardiography is a physiological measurement technique that relies on the fundamental principles of electrical conduction. For direct-current flow through parallel volume conductors, Ohm's law describes the relationship between resistance (R, measured in ohms), voltage (V, measured in volts), and current (I, measured in amperes) according to the equation $R = V/I$. Because direct current is harmful to biological tissues, impedance cardiography uses a high-frequency alternating current (>20 kHz), which is passed through the thorax. Resistance associated with alternating current is referred to as impedance (Z) and is also measured in ohms. In impedance cardiography, the thorax is viewed as an electrical volume conductor in which pulsatile blood flow can be quantified from observations of pulsatile impedance changes (delta Z). Pulsatile variations in impedance may originate from both systemic and pulmonary blood flow in the thorax, but studies have shown that aortic blood flow contributes 70–80% of the delta Z fluctuations (Ito, Yamakoshi, & Yamada, 1976; Thomsen, 1979). However, as is described later in this section, the electrical assumptions underlying stroke volume measurement by impedance cardiography are not upheld under close empirical scrutiny. In fact, the validity of blood flow measurements made using impedance cardiography has generally relied more on empirical evidence than on acceptance of the technique's theoretical principles. Nonetheless, the equations used to derive stroke volume are grounded in Ohm's law. The technically minded reader is referred to texts by Mohapatra (1981), Lamberts, Visser, and Zijlstra (1984), and Bernstein (1989) for a comprehensive description of electrical bioimpedance theory underlying impedance cardiography.

Instrumentation: Impedance Cardiographs

The defining characteristics of an impedance cardiograph are to provide an excitation current (normally 1–5 mA at a frequency of 20–100 kHz) and a means of recording the associated fluctuations in impedance. Because the first derivative of delta Z (dz/dt) is used in modern impedance cardiography, electronic differentiation circuitry to provide a direct dZ/dt output signal is also a necessary feature of an impedance cardiograph. There are a number of commercially available impedance cardiographs (e.g., Minnesota impedance cardiograph model 304B, Surcom, Inc., Minneapolis, MN; NCCOM-3 cardiovascular monitor, BoMed Medical Manufacturing, Ltd., Irvine, CA; tetrapolar high resolution impedance meter [THRIM], UFI, Inc., Morro Bay, CA). Of these, the Minnesota impedance cardiograph model 304B has been most widely used in research applications. This model uses a 4-mA constant-current source with a 100-kHz oscillator frequency and includes a light-emitting diode (LED) display of basal thoracic impedance (Z_0), with electrical outputs of Z_0, delta Z, and dZ/dt. The Minnesota model 340B also includes separate inputs for electrocardiogram (ECG) and phonocardiogram (heart sounds), with filtering and amplification of these signals. For a detailed example of the design of an impedance cardiograph, Qu, Zhang, Webster, and Tompkins (1986) provide a description that includes the circuit diagram of their custombuilt instrument.

Impedance Electrode Configurations

Band Electrodes

In 1966 Kubicek and colleagues first described a tetrapolar band electrode configuration, which has since been adopted in the majority of studies using the impedance technique for monitoring cardiovascular function (Kubicek, Karnegis, Patterson, Witsoe, & Mattson, 1966). The outer two *current electrodes* introduce the high-frequency excitation current, whereas the surface potential, which is proportional to impedance, is measured across the inner two *voltage electrodes*. Band electrodes typically consist of disposable strips of adhesive tape, approximately 2.5 cm wide, which have a thin strip (approximately 0.6 cm wide) of aluminum-coated Mylar that forms the electrode along the center of the tape. An electrode gel, such as an ultrasonic transmission gel, may be used to facilitate contact conduction and is advisable for subjects who have substantial body hair. A 10-min contact resistance stabilization period should be allowed to lapse before the onset of impedance measurements (Mohapatra, 1981).

Usual placement of the four band electrodes is illustrated in Figure 1. The upper and lower voltage electrodes are placed around the base of the neck and around the thorax at the level of the xiphisternal junction. The Kubicek stroke volume equation includes a constant (L) for the distance between voltage electrodes. L is usually computed as the mean distance (centimeters) between the voltage electrodes, measured over the sternum and over the spine. The outer current electrodes are placed at a minimum distance of 3 cm separation from the voltage electrodes to permit even distribution of current density emerging from the current electrodes. Thus, the usual placement of the current electrode bands, illustrated in Figure 1, is around the upper part of the neck and around the lower region of the rib cage. All four band electrodes are normally placed circumferentially around the respective body segments.

Variations in band electrode placements from those illustrated in Figure 1 have been reported. Kubicek et al. (1966) originally suggested that the lower voltage electrode should be placed 2 cm below the xiphisternal junction. On many individuals this would approximate placement over the xiphoid process, an anatomical landmark that has been used for lower voltage electrode placement in a number of studies (e.g., Edmunds, Godfrey, & Tooley, 1982; Ferrigno, Hickey, Liner, & Lungren, 1986; Miyamoto et al., 1983; Veigl & Judy, 1983). In view of evidence that variations in surface impedance reflect variations in blood content of proximal organs and vessels (Sakamoto, Muto, Kanai, & Iizuka, 1979), placement of the lower voltage electrode over the xiphisternal junction may be pref-

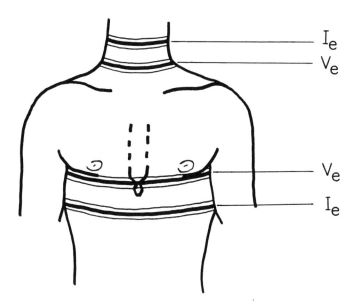

FIGURE 1. Band electrodes placement most typically reported. Voltage electrodes (V_e) are located around the base of the neck and around the chest at the level of the xiphisternal junction. Current electrodes (I_e) are located at least 3 cm distal to each voltage electrode. From "Committee Report: Methodological Guidelines for Impedance Cardiography" by A. Sherwood, M. T. Allen, J. Fahrenberg, R. M. Kelsey, W. R. Lovallo, and L. J. P. van-Doornen, 1990, *Psychophysiology, 27,* p. 5; copyright 1990 by the Society for Psychophysiological Research; reprinted by permission.

erable to lower placement, assuming that detection of blood flow in the heart and aorta is the objective of impedance cardiographic measurements. Variations in current electrode placements include placement of the upper current electrode across the forehead. Because the forehead placement meets the "at least 3 cm" rule, it is acceptable, especially for subjects with short necks.

Spot Electrodes
Band electrodes are sometimes experienced as being distressful or annoying, and women subjects may find the application of band electrodes unacceptable. Several investigators have explored the use of disposable ECG spot electrodes in impedance cardiography. For behavioral research,

minimizing the obtrusiveness of physiological monitoring procedures is desirable, so the possibility of using spot electrodes in impedance cardiography is of interest. Penney, Patwardhan, and Wheeler (1985) described a four–spot electrode configuration in which two electrodes were placed at the base of the neck and two on the left anteriolateral chest surface. Good correspondence between this configuration and the standard band configuration was found for the impedance signals recorded, but derived stroke volumes values showed considerable discrepancy. Qu et al. (1986) proposed a four–spot electrode array that exhibits enhanced signal-to-noise ratio characteristics. One current electrode is placed on the back of the neck over the fourth cervical vertebra, and the other is placed on the back over the ninth thoracic vertebra; whereas one voltage electrode is placed on the front of the neck, 4 cm above the clavicle, and the other is placed over the sternum at the fourth rib. Cardiac output values obtained using this spot electrode configuration showed a high correlation ($r_{78} = 0.90$) with those determined using the carbon dioxide (CO_2) rebreathing technique during treadmill exercise (Zhang et al., 1986). Two studies reported in the psychophysiology literature have compared the spot electrode configuration suggested by Qu et al. (1986) with the standard band configuration. Boomsma, deVries, and Orlebeke (1989) compared systolic time interval and stroke volume measures during a reaction time task and after bicycle exercise; they reported no differences for these measures between band and spot electrode methods. Although similar observations for systolic time intervals during graded bicycle exercise were found by Sherwood, Royal, Hutcheson, and Turner (1992), significant differnces between band and spot electrodes for stroke volume and cardiac output measurements were observed. A spot electrode configuration that incorporates eight electrodes in an arrangement that uses pairs of electrodes simulating the conventional tetrapolar band electrode configuration has also been used in several studies. The upper pair of voltage electrodes are placed as close as possible to the clavicles at the lateral aspect of the base of the neck, whereas the lower pair of voltage electrodes are placed perpendicular to the longitudinal plane of the sternum, lateral to the xiphoid process in the midaxillary line. The current electrodes are placed parallel to the voltage electrodes, with the upper pair 5 cm above the neck voltage electrodes and the lower pair 5 cm below the thoracic voltage electrodes. Encouraging results that have been reported using this configuration are summarized in a later section describing alternative stroke volume equations.

The available evidence suggests that spot electrodes may be used as an alternative to band electrodes in impedance cardiography. They offer convenience to the researcher and typically less discomfort to subjects. However, impedance cardiography is a technique that has gained credibility largely based on empirical support from validation studies comparing it with invasive techniques. Because the number of studies adopting the tetrapolar band configuration has now reached several hundred, the strengths and limitations of impedance cardiography using this methodology are well understood. In contrast, the number of studies reporting use of the various spot electrode configurations are relatively few, and there is some indication that not all of the measured parameters of cardiac function may be comparable with those recorded using band electrodes (Penney et al., 1985; Sherwood, Royal, Hutcheson, & Turner, 1992). This is not to say that spot electrodes are less suitable for impedance cardiography; in fact, as more methodological research is reported, a spot electrode configuration may arise as the accepted standard. In the interim, band electrodes remain the most widely accepted methodological approach.

Signals Recorded in Impedance Cardiography

ECG and Phonocardiogram (PCG)

The ECG is an integral part of signal acquisition in impedance cardiography. It is used for the accurate determination of heart rate, usually derived from the interval between successive R waves. It is also used to identify the onset of electromechanical systole (EMS), which is defined as the point of initiation of the Q wave (see Figure 2) and is necessary for the measurement of systolic time intervals. Most impedance cardiographs include ECG amplification circuitry, using input from either the impedance electrodes or separate ECG electrodes.

Recording of the PCG can provide useful backup information for the measurement of systolic time intervals. As can be seen in Figure 2,

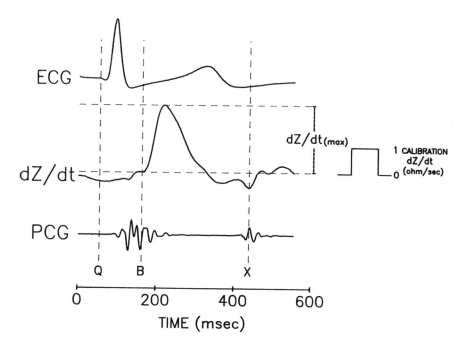

FIGURE 2. Electrocardiogram (ECG), first derivative of the pulsatile thoracic impedance signal (dZ/dt), and phonocardiogram (PCG) recorded during cardiac
systole. ECG Q wave onset (Q), dz/dt B point (B), and dZ/dt X point (X)
are depicted. Measurement of dZ/dt$_{(max)}$ is also illustrated as measured in
relation to the dZ/dt = 0 baseline. From "Committee Report: Methodological Guidelines for Impedance Cardiography" by A. Sherwood, M. T.
Allen, J. Fahrenberg, R. M. Kelsey, W. R. Lovallo, and L. J. P. vanDoornen,
1990, *Psychophysiology, 27*, p. 8; copyright 1990 by the Society for Psychophysiological Research; reprinted by permission.

the first and second heart sounds are usually well defined, with the onset
of the second heart sound indicating completion of EMS. Separate amplification and filtering circuitry for the PCG are included in some impedance cardiographs (e.g., Minnesota model 304B). The heart sounds mi-
crophone (e.g., Narco Biosystems 705-0016; Hewlett Packard 21050-A)
should be positioned over the upper part of the precordium at a location
providing optimal recordings of the initial high-frequency oscillations of
the aortic component of the second heart sound (Weissler, 1977).

Impedance Signals

The two most important signals requiring some means of display and storage in impedance cardiography are the ECG and impedance dZ/dt waveforms. These two signals, which may be considered to represent the impedance cardiogram, are illustrated in Figure 2. The dZ/dt signal is the first derivative of the delta Z signal, with the differentiation process performed electronically by the impedance cardiograph. Modern impedance cardiography uses the dZ/dt signal, making delta Z redundant because dZ/dt facilitates the measurement of systolic time intervals and stroke volume. The value of Z_0 during any given measurement period is necessary for stroke volume measurement, but because its magnitude of fluctuation is small within a given individual, digital rather than graphical display of Z_0 is more useful. Therefore, most impedance cardiographs provide a digital LED display of Z_0.

The waveform components that are normally identified from the impedance cardiogram to derive the various indices of cardiac function are illustrated in Figure 2. Q marks the onset of the ECG Q wave and defines the onset of EMS. B identifies the dZ/dt B point that occurs at the onset of the rapid upslope of dZ/dt and corresponds with the time of onset of left ventricular ejection. The B point has been shown to correspond with the onset of left ventricular ejection from simultaneous recordings of the impedance cardiogram with echocardiography (Petrovick, Kizakevich, Stacy, & Haak, 1980; Stern, Wolf, & Belz, 1985) and carotid pulse tracings (Sheps, Petrovick, Kizakevich, Wolfe, & Craige, 1982). When the breath is held, or at end-expiratory apnea, the B point normally falls on the $dZ/dt = 0$ axis, as shown in Figure 2. However, during normal breathing the B point often occurs above, and occasionally below, the $dZ/dt = 0$ axis. Furthermore, the B point may sometimes take the form of a subtle inflexion rather than a well-defined incisura. As a general guideline for identification, the B point may be viewed as the initiation of the rapid upstroke of the dZ/dt signal as it rises toward $dZ/dt_{(max)}$.

X marks the sharp, negatively deflecting notch in the dZ/dt waveform. It corresponds temporally with the second heart sound and denotes the completion of left ventricular ejection (Petrovick et al., 1980; Sheps et al., 1982). The X point is usually well defined and easily recognized.

$dZ/dt_{(max)}$ is the peak positive deflection of the dZ/dt signal and represents the maximum rate of change occurring in delta Z. Because delta Z actually shows a negative change with the ejection of blood from the left ventricle, $dZ/dt_{(max)}$ represents the peak negative rate of change in delta Z and is therefore sometimes referred to as $dZ/dt_{(min)}$. $dZ/dt_{(max)}$ has been found to correspond, both temporally and in terms of magnitude, with peak blood flow in the ascending aorta (Kubicek et al., 1974). The $dZ/dt_{(max)}$ value is measured in ohm/s as its absolute amplitude in relation to the $dZ/dt = 0$ baseline. Theoretical grounds have been proposed that suggest that it may be more appropriate to measure $dZ/dt_{(max)}$ in relation to the dZ/dt B point (Doerr, Miles, & Bassett Frey, 1981; Mohapatra, 1981). However, in a study that examined how measurement of $dZ/dt_{(max)}$ affects derived stroke volume accuracy, compared with thermodilution values in anesthetized dogs, empirical support for the measurement of $dZ/dt_{(max)}$ in relation to $dZ/dt = 0$ was reported (Sherwood, Carter, & Murphy, 1991).

Sampling and Processing Strategies

Manual Analysis of Cardiac Cycles Using a Chart Recorder
The ECG, PCG, and dZ/dt signals can be displayed on a chart recorder to provide a permanent record, although high paper speeds (100 mm/s) are required to provide adequate resolution for signal analysis. For manual analysis, cardiac cycles recorded during periods when the subject is relatively motionless should be selected to avoid the problem of movement artifact. Because respiration also affects the dZ/dt signal, recording of signals during voluntary breath holding has been used as one strategy to minimize noncardiac sources of impedance signal modulation (Denniston et al., 1976; Ebert, Eckberg, Vetrovec, & Cowley, 1984; Hill & Merrifield, 1976; Judy et al., 1969; Kobayashi et al., 1978). However, there is some evidence that cardiac performance during breath holding may not be representative of normal breathing (Andersen & Vik-Mo, 1984; Du-Quesnay, Stoute, & Hughson, 1987; Pigott & Spodick, 1971). In addition, the breath-holding strategy is undesirable for use in behavioral research because it is likely to interfere with the ongoing behavior under investigation. Sampling waveforms during normal breathing, but only at end-expiratory apnea, as indicated by some measurement of respiratory phase,

presents an alternative. Unfortunately, the latter strategy restricts the number of cardiac cycles available for analysis. To assure representative sampling, it may be preferable to analyze signals from all cardiac cycles occurring over several respiratory cycles and subsequently average derived cardiac performance indices. Using such a strategy is advocated by DeSouza and Panerai (1981), who recommend averaging approximately 60 cardiac cycles to produce a reliable averaged waveform. From a practical standpoint, however, manual analysis of such large numbers of cardiac cycles is far from convenient.

Computer-Assisted Analysis of the Impedance Cardiogram
The computer-based technique of ensemble averaging was first described for impedance cardiography applications by Kizakevich, Gollan, and McDermott (1976). This technique involves using the ECG R wave as a reference point for the synchronized averaging of both the ECG and dZ/dt signals over a number of consecutive cardiac cycles occurring during normal breathing. This procedure causes dZ/dt signals originating from cardiac events to be superimposed on each other, which causes them to be reinforced and become clearly defined in the resultant ensemble averaged waveform. At the same time, respiratory events of a natural lower frequency and random movement artifacts are effectively filtered from the ensemble averaged impedance cardiogram. Ensemble averaging of the impedance cardiogram has been documented to provide a reliable sampling strategy for the measurement of systolic time intervals and cardiac output during a variety of behavioral activities, including exercise (Miyamoto et al., 1981, 1982, 1983; Muzi et al., 1985; Muzi, Jeutter, & Smith, 1986; Sheps et al., 1982; Sherwood, Allen, Obrist, & Langer, 1986). Computer software designed for sampling and analysis of the impedance cardiogram, which has become widely available, is perhaps the most significant development responsible for growing interest in impedance cardiography, making the technique not only more reliable but also more practical and accessible to a variety of research applications. For cardiovascular reactivity research it has been especially beneficial because it precludes the need for behavioral disruption required by breath-holding sampling strategies.

Systolic Time Intervals and Contractility Measures

EMS may be measured using impedance cardiography as the interval from the onset of the Q wave of the ECG to the X point of the dZ/dt waveform. EMS is composed of two subintervals of interest: preejection period (*PEP*) and left ventricular ejection time (*LVET*). *PEP* is measured in milliseconds from ECG Q wave onset to the dZ/dt B point (see Figure 2). *LVET*, also measured in milliseconds, is the interval from the B point to the X point of the dZ/dt waveform (Figure 2). Impedance cardiographic measurement of systolic time intervals is considered more accurate than traditional techniques, which use ECG, peripheral pulse, and phonocardiographic signals that are prone to noise and movement artifacts (Balasubramanian, Mathew, Behl, Tewari, & Hoon, 1978; Colin & Timbal, 1982; Gollan, Kizakevich, & McDermott, 1978; Sheps et al., 1982).

PEP is a measure of myocardial contractility and is sensitive to mechanical preload and afterload factors, as well as sympathetic nervous system stimulation of the heart (Ahmed, Levinson, Schwartz, & Ettinger, 1972; Cousineau, de Champlain, & Lapointe, 1978). It is as an index of β-adrenergic stimulation of the heart that has been of particular interest to cardiovascular psychophysiologists (McCubbin, Richardson, Langer, Kizer, & Obrist, 1983; Newlin & Levenson, 1979; Obrist, Light, James, & Strogatz, 1987). *PEP* is mainly composed of isovolumic contraction time, which is the time during which the left ventricle contracts before its ejection of blood into the aorta. With augmented contractility, *PEP* becomes shorter; thus *PEP* is inversely related to contractility. When using *PEP* as an index of β-adrenergic activation, it is important to bear in mind the potential mechanical effects of cardiac loading factors. Increased preload increases contractility via the heterometric autoregulatory mechanism of Starling's law, thereby decreasing *PEP* independently of β-adrenergic activity. Conversely, increased afterload lengthens *PEP*. In the absence of altered preload and afterload, increased β-adrenergic activation may be tentatively inferred when *PEP* is shortened. However, *PEP* may decrease when heart rate increases, simply due to an overall reduction in EMS. In view of this problem, the *PEP:LVET* ratio has been proposed as a sensitive index of left ventricular function that is self-correcting for heart rate variations (Weissler, 1977). In support of its usefulness as a contractility measure, the $PEP:LVET$ ratio has been observed to show a significant inverse relationship to ejection fraction (Garrard, Weissler, & Dodge, 1970).

The Heather index is a measure of myocardial contractility that is unique to impedance cardiography (Heather, 1969). It is computed by dividing $dZ/dt_{(max)}$ (ohms per second) by the ECG Q wave to $dZ/dt_{(max)}$ time interval (seconds). The Heather index therefore combines two parameters that are affected by contractility in a way that should maximize sensitivity to contractility changes reflected in each of them. To standardize the Heather index across subjects, it has been suggested that correction for basal thoracic impedance (Z_0) should be applied and a corrected Heather index calculated as the ratio of $dZ/dt_{(max)}$ to Z_0 divided by the Q–Z interval (Kelsey, Guethlein, Eichler, Blascovich, & Katkin, 1987).

Stroke Volume and Cardiac Output Measurement

The Kubicek Equation

In 1966, Kubicek and colleagues proposed an equation for estimating left ventricular stroke volume using impedance cardiography, which became, and remains to the present day, the most widely used equation (Kubicek et al., 1966). This equation is described as follows:

$$SV = rho \cdot (L/Z_0)^2 \cdot LVET \cdot dZ/dt_{(max)}, \qquad (1)$$

where SV = stroke volume (milliliters), rho = blood resistivity (ohm · centimeters), L = distance between voltage electrodes (centimeters), Z_0 = basal thoracic impedance (ohms), $LVET$ = left ventricular ejection time (seconds), and $dZ/dt_{(max)}$ = maximum rate of change of dZ/dt during cardiac systole (ohms per second).

Thus, impedance cardiography permits the derivation of cardiac output (CO) by direct estimation of SV and measurement of heart rate (HR) ($CO = HR \times SV$), whereas traditional invasive techniques (e.g., Fick, dye/thermodilution) estimate CO directly. A distinct advantage of impedance cardiography, beyond its noninvasive character, is that the electrical signals needed to estimate SV and CO are continuously available, thereby permitting continuous measurement, unlike some of the traditional CO measurement methods that are restricted to discrete, intermittent measurement capabilities.

The Kubicek equation is based on the "forward extrapolation" method of estimating SV by impedance cardiography. When blood is ejected from the left ventricle into the aorta, a decrease in the delta Z signal is initially observed. The decrease in delta Z is assumed to be caused by an initial increase in aortic blood volume in the early ejection phase, which quickly subsides as blood flows through and out of this major vessel. As shown in Figure 3, the forward extrapolation method extends the initial maximum slope of delta Z, extrapolating through to the end of left ventricular ejection, to estimate delta Z'. The delta Z' value thereby estimates the total change (decrease) in delta Z that would have occurred if blood volume were not to flow through and out of the aorta as the ejection process proceeds. In other words, by forward extrapolation, it is assumed that the maximum slope of delta Z in early systole provides a measure of blood volume ejection rate and that this parameter remains constant throughout the ejection phase. Because it is cumbersome and relatively inaccurate to manually extrapolate the delta Z signal from a chart record, the delta Z signal is electronically differentiated by the impedance cardiograph to produce dZ/dt. As also shown in Figure 3, the peak of the dZ/dt signal, or $dZ/dt_{(max)}$, provides a far more convenient measure of the maximum initial change in delta Z. Thus, in the Kubicek equation, $dZ/dt_{(max)}$ is multiplied by $LVET$ (also more easily measured from the dZ/dt signal), which effectively incorporates the maximum estimated change in delta Z (delta Z') into the stroke volume estimate.

One of the assumptions underlying the forward extrapolation approach is that aortic blood flow rises to its maximum value almost instantaneously, remains constant throughout the ejection phase, and then instantaneously returns to zero flow at the end of ejection. Actual aortic blood flow velocity does not conform to such a rectangular profile, and there is some reverse flow at the end of ejection. The origin of the decrease in delta Z during the initial phase of ejection is also controversial. The assumption of the Kubicek equation is that delta Z decreases because of an increase in aortic blood volume, which facilitates electrical conduction

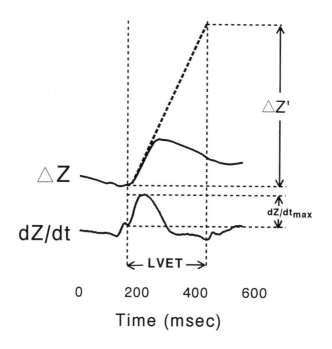

FIGURE 3. Schematic representation of the "forward extrapolation" method of estimating stroke volume. The maximum rate of change of delta Z (ΔZ) during
the initial left ventricular (LVET) ejection phase is extrapolated through to
the end of ejection, which thus provides an estimate of the total change
in delta Z ($\Delta Z'$), which would theoretically occur if the ejected blood did
not leave the aorta. Also shown is the electronically differentiated delta
Z signal (dZ/dt), which provides a more convenient means of measuring
the maximum initial change of delta Z ($dZ/dt_{(max)}$). Multiplying $dZ/dt_{(max)}$ by
LVET (as appears in the Kubicek stroke volume equation) yields delta Z'.

longitudinally through the thorax. An elegant series of experiments by
Lamberts et al. (1984) provided compelling evidence that blood cell orientation, in addition to volume change in the ascending aorta, is responsible for the decrease in delta Z. From both in vitro and in vivo experiments, Lamberts et al. showed that as blood flow accelerates, erythrocytes
become elongated in the direction of flow, thereby accentuating the con-
ducting cross-sectional plasma area in the aorta. These findings emphasize
again that the simple electrical principles providing the assumption for
SV measurement in impedance cardiography do not withstand empirical

scrutiny. Nonetheless, as previously noted, $dZ/dt_{(max)}$ magnitude has been found to correspond with peak blood flow velocity in the ascending aorta (Kubicek et al., 1974; Witsoe, Patterson, From, & Kubicek, 1969). It is perhaps the ability of impedance cardiography to measure aortic blood flow velocity and *LVET* that has led to its documented ability to measure relative changes in SV, whereas the validity of the absolute magnitude of such measures remains far more tenuous (Miller & Horvath, 1978; Sherwood, Allen et al., 1990).

Blood Resistivity Correction to the Kubicek Equation

The remaining components of the Kubicek equation have greater influence on the absolute magnitude of stroke volume rather than on relative change. This is particularly so for L and blood resistivity (*rho*). For *rho*, a fixed value of 150 ohm·cm, the average electrical resistivity of blood at 100 kHz was originally recommended by Kubicek et al. (1966). However, in attempts to improve *SV* estimation, the relationship between *rho* and hematocrit (HCT) has been described by equations arising from the results of bench experiments that measured the resistivity of blood samples of varying HCTs (Geddes & Sadler, 1973; Hill & Thompson, 1975; Mohapatra, Costeloe, & Hill, 1977; Mohapatra & Hill, 1975). Despite subtle variations, all of the equations describe a relationship whereby *rho* varies as a cur-vilinear function of HCT, with *rho* increasing as HCT rises. These findings suggest that individual *rho* values entered into the Kubicek equation, based on the individual's HCT, should improve the absolute accuracy of *SV* measurements. However, because HCTs do not vary substantially in healthy individuals, such corrections are likely to have significant impact only when impedance cardiography is applied in patients with abnormal HCTs. Moreover, a study that examined the relationship of HCT to *rho* in vivo suggests that the relationship between HCT and *rho* established by bench experiments may not be relevant in the context of impedance cardiography. Quail, Traugott, Porges, and White (1981) recorded the impedance cardiogram in conscious dogs in which electromagnetic flow probes had been surgically implanted around the aortic root. HCT was varied between 26% and 66%, whereas *rho* was derived by rearranging the Kubicek equation to make *rho* the subject of the equation and entering

SV from the electromagnetic flow probe measurements. The results of this study showed that *rho* remained relatively constant at an average value of 135 ohm·cm across the entire range of HCTs tested. Perhaps therefore not surprisingly, studies using HCT-corrected *rho* values in the Kubicek equation do not appear to estimate *SV* more accurately than those using a fixed *rho* (Mohapatra, 1981).

Accuracy of SV *and* CO *Measurements Using the Kubicek Equation*
The theoretical assumptions for impedance cardiographic measurement of *SV* using the Kubicek equation, as just discussed, do not hold up to careful scrutiny. Traditional invasive techniques for measuring *CO*, on the other hand, are more firmly grounded in their underlying theoretical principles. The controversial theoretical basis for impedance cardiography has meant that its acceptance has relied largely on validation studies comparing *CO*s with those simultaneously determined by traditional techniques. For an overview of the numerous validation studies that have been reported, the reader is referred to Kubicek, Witsoe, Patterson, and From (1969), Mohapatra (1981), Lamberts et al. (1984), Miller and Horvath (1978), and Porter and Swain (1987). These studies, which include comparisons using dye-dilution, thermodilution, Fick, CO_2 rebreathing, and nuclear ventriculography in humans, as well as these plus electromagnetic flow probe measurements in animals, have yielded some diversity in their findings. Correlations between impedance and reference *CO*s have ranged from 0.6 to greater than 0.9. The diversity of results may be partially attributable to variations in sampling and analysis strategies used with impedance cardiography. In addition, it is important to note that the traditional *CO* measurement techniques are themselves far from "gold standards." Indeed, several comparison studies have included comment that the reference technique appeared less precise than the impedance technique (e.g., Baker, Judy, Geddes, Langley, & Hill, 1971; Denniston et al., 1976).

Overall, the available evidence indicates that impedance cardiographic measurements accurately follow changes in *SV* and *CO* but that there may be unacceptably high (>10%) errors in individual cases. For group-averaged measures, impedance measurements of *SV* have generally been found to approximate the reference standards very well (error ranges = 0–9%). However, there has been a fairly consistent finding that the Kubicek equation tends to overestimate *SV*. Because of these limitations, impedance cardiography has been received with limited enthusiasm and much skepticism in the clinical arena, whereas the ability to operate around these limitations through appropriate experimental design has permitted a more enthusiastic reception for impedance cardiography in various research fields. The consensus of opinion continues to emphasize that relative change measures for *SV* and *CO* are more reliable than absolute values, and research questions should be formulated to use impedance cardiography within these constraints (Miller & Horvath, 1978; Sherwood, Allen et al., 1990).

Alternatives to the Kubicek Equation for Computing SV

Bernstein (1986a) described an alternative to the Kubicek equation that aimed to improve the absolute accuracy of *SV* measurements made using impedance cardiography. Several alterations from the Kubicek equations are evident. First, although the Kubicek equation uses a cylindrical model of the thorax, the Sramek-Bernstein equation is based on a model that views the thorax as a volume conductor that is geometrically similar to a frustum or truncated cone (Bernstein, 1986a; Sramek, 1981; Sramek, Rose, & Miyamoto, 1983). Second, in view of the findings of Quail et al. (1981), described earlier, *rho* is deleted from the equation. Third, the Sramek-Bernstein equation replaces *L* of the Kubicek equation with a value computed from body height, mathematically adjusted to estimate ideal body weight. Fourth, Bernstein (1986a) proposed that a body habitus correction factor (*delta*) be included, which is computed from the ratio of observed to ideal body weight multiplied by the "relative blood volume index," which adjusts for blood volume variations associated with deviations from ideal body weight. The resulting Sramek-Bernstein *SV* equation is described as follows:

$$SV = delta \cdot (0.17\ height)^3/4.2 \cdot LVET \cdot dZ/dt_{(max)}/Z_0. \qquad (2)$$

Studies that have adopted the Sramek-Bernstein equation have generally used a tetrapolar spot electrode configuration incorporating eight spot electrodes, as described earlier. Bernstein (1986b) reported a significant correlation ($r_{94} = 0.88$) between impedance CO values and those determined using thermodilution in a group of 17 critically ill patients. In a study of similar design, Appel, Kram, MacKabee, Fleming, and Shoe-maker (1986) found that impedance and thermodilution COs were significantly correlated ($r_{391} = 0.83$) in 16 critically ill patients. However, support for the Sramek-Bernstein equation is not uniformly positive. Less favorable findings were reported by De Mey and Enterling (1988), who found that the Kubicek and Sramek-Bernstein equations did not show agreement in the magnitude of SV responses to upright tilt. Furthermore, in the latter and other studies (e.g., Gotshall, Wood, & Miles, 1989), the Sramek-Bernstein equation has been found to overestimate absolute SV values to an even greater extent than the Kubicek equation, which brings into question whether it represents any improvement over the Kubicek equation. Although this question can only be resolved by further validation studies, improvement of the precision of SV estimation by impedance cardiography is ultimately likely to involve refinement of the Kubicek equation.

Computation of Total Peripheral Resistance

Mean arterial blood pressure (MBP) is the product of CO and the total peripheral resistance (TPR) of the systemic vasculature. If blood pressure and CO are measured simultaneously, it is possible to derive TPR according to the equation $TPR = MBP/CO$. Thus, impedance cardiography is a technique that permits assessment of the hemodynamic basis of blood pressure changes.

TPR is most often reported in units of dyne-s·cm^{-5}, derived as follows:

$$TPR \text{ (dynes-s·cm}^{-5}) = [MBP(\text{mmHg})/CO(\text{L/min})] \cdot 80. \tag{3}$$

Hemodynamic Response Patterns During Mental Stress

Background

Blood pressure and heart rate responses during exposure to psychological stressors have historically been the most widely studied measurement of cardiovascular reactivity. The relative ease of measuring these variables noninvasively largely accounts for why they have received so much attention. Measurement of CO, which permits the assessment of the hemodynamic basis of blood pressure responses, although of great interest, has been precluded by the risks associated with available measurement procedures. Notable exceptions are two very early studies, which perhaps mark the conception of the experimental investigation of cardiovascular reactivity. These studies not only used invasive procedures to measure CO but evaluated them as presenting the source of psychological stress (Hickman, Cargill, & Golden, 1948; Stead, Warren, Merrill, & Brannon, 1945). These studies demonstrated how the stress response that is associated with anxiety was characterized by a mobilization of the cardiovascular system, whereby blood pressure increased because of an increase in CO. The same response pattern was observed a decade later during exposure to a mental arithmetic task (Brod, Fencl, Hejl, & Jirka, 1959). In this widely cited study, CO was measured invasively using dye dilution, and forearm blood flow was also measured. The results demonstrated that the increased CO during stress appeared to be distributed to the skeletal muscle vasculature. This response is similar to the defense reaction, which has been documented in animals (Abrahams, Hilton, & Zbrozyna, 1960, 1964), and conforms to the sympathetically mediated fight–flight response first described by Cannon (1915). Although these early studies set the stage for cardiovascular reactivity research, systematic investigation of the stress response demanded measurement procedures that were minimally stressful, and preferably relatively unobtrusive, so that normal behavior would be minimally disturbed. In view of these concerns and the lack of availablity of reliable noninvasive CO measurement techniques, in addition to ethical issues surrounding the use of risky procedures in healthy subjects, studies reporting hemodynamic responses during psychological stress in humans have been rare until recently. The situation was changed when the technique of impedance cardiography gained recognition in the late 1970s for its use in furthering cardiovascular psychophysiology research (Miller & Horvath, 1978). The research described in the remainder of this chapter shares the common methodological approach of investigating hemodynamic responses during stress by using impedance cardiography to measure CO.

Stressor Differences in Hemodynamic Responses Patterns

Over the past 25 years, a wide variety of tasks, each construed as con-stituting some element of psychological stress, have been reported in the cardiovascular reactivity research literature. A number of different tasks tend to elicit flight–flight cardiovascular mobilization that is mediated by the sympathetic nervous system. Obrist (1976) coined the now widely used term "active coping" to describe the behavioral challenges that tend to elicit such responses in humans. Such tasks typically demand active engagement of some behavioral skill and involve either a specified or implied objective for successful performance on the task. In his own research, aversive reaction time tasks involving threat of shock were extensively used to study the active coping response (Obrist, 1981). Var-ious other laboratory tasks, including appetitive reaction time tasks (Light & Obrist, 1983), mental arithmetic (Brod et al., 1959), and video games (Turner, Carroll, & Courtney, 1983), as well as real-life stressors such as public speaking (Gliner, Bunnell, & Horvath, 1982), generally tend to pro-duce somewhat similar responses. Such tasks appear to evoke sympa-thetic nervous system responses that stimulate cardiac and vascular β-adrenergic receptors. The similarity of the active coping stress response to the mobilization of the cardiovascular system during exercise is illus-trated in Figure 4, in which CO and vascular resistance responses during an aversive reaction time task and during bicycle exercise are compared. This illustration is based on data from a study reported by Sherwood et al. (1986), in which subjects were tested once after saline infusion and once after intravenous infusion of 4 mg propranolol to block β-adrenerg-ically mediated responses. As can be seen from Figure 4, after beta block-ade, the increase in CO and decrease in TPR during the psychological challenge were abolished, whereas the similar responses associated with physical exertion were essentially unaffected. In fact, because TPR in-creased during the reaction time task following beta blockade, blood pressure increases associated with the task prevailed both with and with-out beta blockade. Thus, only by monitoring the underlying hemodynamic determinants of the pressor response, in terms of CO and TPR adjust-ments, does the role of the β-adrenergic mechanisms of the stress re-sponse become clearly evident.

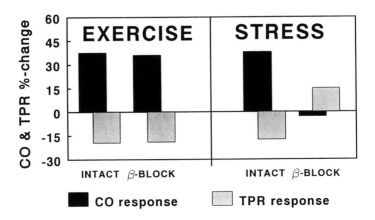

FIGURE 4. Mean percentage of change from resting baseline for cardiac output (CO) and total peripheral resistance (TPR) during 25-W bicycle exercise (EX-ERCISE) and during a shock-avoidance reaction time task (STRESS) in 5 healthy young men. Responses are shown with innervations intact (IN-TACT) and after β-adrenergic blockade (β-BLOCK) by intravenous injection of 4 mg propranolol and demonstrate that the hemodynamically similar responses that are associated with the two tasks are the result of different mechanisms. From "Evaluation of Beta-Adrenergic Influences on Cardio-vascular and Metabolic Adjustments to Physical and Psychological Stress" by A. Sherwood, M. T. Allen, P. A. Obrist, and A. W. Langer, 1986, *Psychophysiology, 23,* p. 99; copyright 1986 by the Society for Psychophys-iological Research; adapted by permission.

In contrast to a pattern resembling the fight–flight cardiovascular response, other tasks that may involve passive coping or passive sensory intake and tasks demanding vigilance and/or eliciting frustration are more often associated with sympathetic activation leading to pressor responses mediated by the vasoconstrictive action of α-adrenergic receptor stimu-lation. The cold pressor test, which involves application of iced water to some body part, usually the hand or foot, is the most widely studied stressor in this general category (Peckerman et al., 1991). The response is hemodynamically the opposite of that previously described for the aversive reaction time task, with increased *TPR* accounting entirely for the pressor response and *CO* remaining unchanged. Most other tasks can be conveniently viewed as falling onto a spectrum bounded by these two hemodynamic response profiles. To illustrate this point, systolic blood pressure (SBP), diastolic blood pressure (DBP), *CO*, and *TPR* responses during five tasks are shown in Figure 5, in terms of percentage of change from resting baseline levels. The five tasks are representative of the kinds of stressors used in laboratory reactivity testing. The mental arithmetic task required subjects to solve simple subtraction problems presented on a computer video display, with task difficulty kept constant across sub-

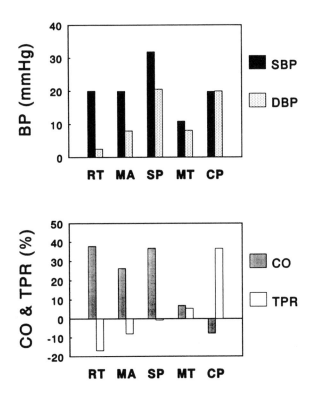

FIGURE 5. Hemodynamic response patterns in terms of mean change from resting baseline for systolic blood pressure (SBP), diastolic blood pressure (DBP), cardiac output (CO), and total peripheral resistance (TPR) in 20 healthy young men during exposure to five commonly used laboratory stressors: reaction time task (RT), mental arithmetic (MA), simulated public speaking (SP), mirror trace (MT), and a forehead cold pressor (CP). From "Cardiovascular Reactivity Assessment: Effects of Choice of Difficulty on Laboratory Task Responses" by A. Sherwood, M. R. Davis, C. A. Dolan, and K. C. Light, 1992, *International Journal of Psychophysiology, 12,* p. 92; copyright 1992 by Elsevier Science Publishers; adapted by permission.

jects by automatic adjustment of problem difficulty according to performance. The reaction time task required subjects to simply press a key as quickly as possible whenever they heard a loud tone, ostensibly to avoid the possibility of mild electric shock to the leg. The speech stressor task involved oral presentation of an article that subjects had previously read, while three judges would view and evaluate their performance on a video monitor. The mirror trace task required subjects to simply trace, at their own speed, using a computer mouse, a shape displayed on a computer monitor, with a line generated on the screen representing the mirror-image of mouse movements. Finally, the cold pressor task required subjects to passively tolerate an ice-pack held against their forehead. Subjects in this study, which is described in more detail by Sherwood, Davis, Dolan, and Light (1992), were 20 healthy young adult men who were tested on all five tasks.

Individual Differences in Hemodynamic Response Patterns

Spectrum of Response Patterns

Although specific stressors can be characterized as tending to elicit certain hemodynamic response patterns, the individual differences in such responses for a given stressor can vary dramatically. As a consequence, apparently similar cardiovascular responses to a stressor in terms of blood pressure can be associated with very different underlying hemodynamic mechanisms. Brod et al. (1959) first noted such individual differences in their original description of hemodynamic responses during a mental arithmetic stressor. Of the 17 subjects tested, 13 showed the classic fight–flight response pattern, with increased blood pressure due to increased CO and with TPR falling in most of them; whereas in the remaining 4 subjects, TPR increased and CO fell during mental arithmetic. The importance of hemodynamic measurements in understanding individual differences in the stress response is emphasized by a striking example of two contrasting individuals illustrated in Figure 6. The 2 subjects, A and B, were both healthy young men who participated in a reactivity study of 60 healthy young men, described by Sherwood, Royal, and Light (1993). These 2 subjects showed identical resting hemodynamic profiles, with $SBP = 131$ mmHg, $DBP = 76$ mmHg, $CO = 7.5$ L/min, and $TPR = 1,000$

dyne-s·cm^{-5} for both subjects. As shown in Figure 6, the 2 subjects remained indistinguishable when assessed by their blood pressure responses during a mental arithmetic task. However, upon examining their *CO* and vascular resistance responses, also shown in Figure 2, it becomes clear that these 2 subjects showed very different cardiovascular responses to the task. Subject A displayed a response similar to the fight–flight response described earlier, with *CO* increasing and vascular resistance decreasing. This response was probably mediated predominantly via β-adrenergic receptors. In contrast, to the same mental arithmetic task, Subject B showed an increase in vascular resistance and essentially no change in *CO*. Presumably, α-adrenergic receptor activity was more in-

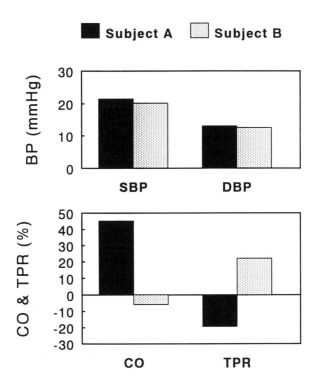

FIGURE 6. Hemodynamic response patterns in terms of change from resting baseline for systolic blood pressure (SBP), diastolic blood pressure (DBP), cardiac output (CO), and total peripheral resistance (TPR) in 2 subjects (A and B) during mental arithmetic task performance.

volved during Subject B's exposure to the stressor. This illustration again underscores the importance of examining the hemodynamic mechanisms underlying blood pressure responses in cardiovascular reactivity research. Observations of this kind have led to an extension of descriptive categories in reactivity research from "high" versus "low" or "hot" versus "cold" reactors, referring to the magnitude of blood pressure responses, to "myocardial" and "vascular" reactors, referring to the predominant hemodynamic mechanism underlying the blood pressure response. Of course, such categorizations serve descriptive convenience better than accurate portrayal of individual differences, which rarely conform to the extremes observed in Subjects A and B in Figure 6.

Responses in Borderline Hypertensives
There is growing evidence that individuals who may be grouped according to common characteristics show similar patterns of cardiovascular reactivity. Such evidence has been of particular interest in relation to groups that differ in risk for hypertensive disease, which promises to help reveal pathological mechanisms by which cardiovascular reactivity may be implicated in the etiology of hypertension (Manuck, Kasprowicz, & Muldoon, 1990). For example, a number of studies have reported that borderline hypertensives show greater blood pressure responses during active, but not passive, coping tasks (see Fredrikson & Matthews, 1990). As might be expected, the excessive pressor responses seen in borderline hypertensives are fight–flight patterns, which are associated with greater increases in CO responsible for the exaggerated blood pressure responses (Sherwood et al., 1993). Given that borderline hypertensives are at significant risk for developing established hypertension, there has been much speculation that the hyperkinetic circulatory state associated with increased sympathetic drive and abnormally high CO levels may trigger autoregulatory reflexes that ultimately increase vascular resistance due to vascular hypertrophy, which results in established hypertension (Julius, 1981). In other words, the excessive CO reactivity observed in borderline hypertensives suggests that excessive CO increases during stress may be more deleterious than the magnitude of blood pressure responses.

Race and Gender Differences in Responses

There is also growing evidence that a tendency to exhibit a given hemo-dynamic response pattern may differ according to race. Black men generally appear to exhibit greater vascular tone during exposure to various stressors. Anderson and colleagues observed that increases in forearm vascular resistance were greater in 10 Black versus 10 White young adult men during a forehead cold pressor test, a task that, as previously mentioned, is mediated by stimulation of vascular α-adrenergic receptors (Anderson, Lane, Muranaka, Williams, & Houseworth, 1988). Treiber and associates reported that *TPR* increased more in Black boys and young adults to a similar forehead cold pressor challenge than in White subjects (Treiber et al., 1990). Light and Sherwood (1990) observed that 20 young Black men showed lesser decreases in *TPR* than did 20 age-matched White men during a competitive reaction time task, an active coping task that is associated with β-adrenergically mediated vasodilation. This racial group difference was converted to a greater increase in *TPR* for the Black subjects when the task was repeated after β-receptor blockade with pro-pranolol. Collectively, these observations suggest that among men, Blacks tend to maintain greater vascular tone during stress-related sympathetic nervous system activation than do Whites, regardless of whether the task generally evokes increases or decreases in vascular resistance. It is of note that, although these differences in hemodynamic responses have been observed consistently for Black versus White men, studies describing only observations of the magnitude of blood pressure responses have reported inconsistent findings for racial differences (cf. Fredrikson, 1986; Light, Obrist, Sherwood, James, & Strogatz, 1987). It is well known that there is a significantly greater prevalence of essential hypertension among Black men than among White men (Akinkugbe, 1985; Roberts & Rowland, 1981). Therefore, in contrast to the conclusions suggested by the observations described earlier for borderline hypertensives, the observations that Black men show a propensity to exhibit greater vascular contributions to stress-induced pressor responses suggest that vascular hyper-reactivity may be a pathophysiological marker for hypertension. These conflicting conclusions suggest that postulating hypothetical mechanisms implicating stress reactivity in the etiology of hypertension may be of limited value and underscore the need for longitudinal data to clarify the issue (Manuck et al., 1990).

Gender is also associated with differential prevalence of hypertension. Women show lower average blood pressures and lesser prevalence of hypertension than do men until approximately age 50, when this trend reverses (U.S. Bureau of the Census, 1987). Although differences between men and women in blood pressure responses during stress have been observed (Saab, 1989; Stoney, Davis, & Matthews, 1987), only one published report has evaluated hemodynamic response patterns (Girdler, Turner, Sherwood, & Light, 1990). In the latter study, women exhibited greater CO increases, whereas men showed greater vascular resistance responses across a series of stressful tasks. However, it is not clear how representative these observations may be of gender differences in general because the study tested only a small sample ($n = 31$) of predominantly White college graduate students. Nonetheless, the observations by Girdler et al. (1990) are provocative and emphasize the need for further evaluation of whether gender is a factor predisposing to specific hemodynamic reactivity patterns.

Stability of Hemodynamic Responses

Temporal stability and intertask consistency of stress responses are two individual-difference dimensions that have been studied to ascertain whether cardiovascular reactivity exhibits the characteristics of an idiosyncratic response (Manuck et al., 1990). These dimensions are of particular importance to psychosomatic theories of disease development because such consistency is a prerequisite if reactivity is to be viewed as a behavioral trait and stress responses are to be implicated in the disease process. Thus, if exaggerated cardiovascular responses are indeed of etiological significance, it is reasonable to argue that a given individual should react in the same way to the same challenge met at different times and should react similarly to other, different challenges.

Temporal Stability

Measures of temporal stability have been reported most frequently as simple correlation coefficients that depict the degree of correspondence of reactivity assessed at an initial laboratory test session with that at a subsequent test session. A number of investigators have reported temporal stability of blood pressure responses to behavioral challenges (e.g., Allen, Sherwood, Obrist, Crowell, & Grange, 1987; Lovallo, Pincomb, & Wilson, 1986; Manuck & Garland, 1980; Manuck & Shaefer, 1978; Matthews, Rakaczky, Stoney, & Manuck, 1987; van Egeren & Sparrow, 1989). The general finding from these studies has been that SBP responses show significant test–retest correlations over weeks to several years, whereas DBP responses show much weaker, often nonsignificant correlations. There are relatively few reports regarding the temporal stability of hemodynamic response patterns. Myrtek (1985) reported statistically stable CO responses in young college men for a reaction time task, a number-sequencing cognitive test, and a cold pressor test over a 1-week interval. Similar findings, reported in terms of correlation coefficients, were observed over a 3-month test–retest interval in older men for a reaction time task ($r = 0.43$) and video game ($r = 0.58$) (McKinney et al., 1985). In contrast, Fahrenberg and colleagues reported nonsignificant test–retest correlations for CO responses to mental arithmetic and cold pressor tests administered to young adult men on four occasions: at initial testing and subsequently after 3 weeks, 3 months, and 1 year (Fahrenberg, Schneider, Foerester, Myrtek, & Muller, 1985). In a more recent report, 13 middle-aged type A men were tested twice on a competitive reaction time task over a 3-month interval (Sherwood, Turner, Light, & Blumenthal, 1990). Test–retest correlations were significant for SBP ($r = 0.67$), CO ($r = 0.81$), and TPR ($r = 0.68$) but not for DBP ($r = 0.31$). Finally, in 39 college students tested over a 4-week interval on a mental arithmetic and a mirror tracing task, test–retest correlations were significant, although sometimes only marginally so, for blood pressure, cardiac, and vascular responses (Kasprowicz, Manuck, Malkoff, & Krantz, 1990). However, in post hoc analyses of their data, Kasprowicz et al. identified subgroups of clearly defined cardiac and vascular reactors according to task responses at initial testing. These subgroups of individuals displayed impressive temporal stability of their hemodynamic response patterns at follow-up testing. It is not readily clear why there is some discrepency in the observations of temporal consistency from the five available studies. One possibility that is suggested by careful scrutiny of the observations made in these studies is that differences may be due to differences in tasks, with those tasks that exhibit the most response habituation over time associated with the weakest evidence of temporal stability. Despite such potential confounds, the weight of evidence supports the conclusion that hemodynamic response patterns during mental stress generally appear to be quite stable over time.

Intertask Consistency

Although considerable supportive evidence of intertask consistency has been documented for blood pressure responses (see Sherwood & Turner, 1992), only three such reports have also examined *CO* and *TPR* responses. Sherwood, Dolan, and Light (1990) assessed hemodynamic responses to active and passive coping stressors in a sample of 90 healthy young college men. They found that reaction time tasks, which demand active coping responses, tended to raise blood pressure due primarily to augmented *CO*, whereas *TPR* fell. During passive coping situations, which included passive participation with a partner in a reaction time task and exposure to an emotionally arousing film, *CO* also tended to increase, but so too did *TPR*, thereby raising blood pressure by their synergistic effects. Despite the variation in hemodynamic patterns that are associated with the different kinds of stressors, intertask correlations for SBP, DBP, *CO*, and *TPR* during the active and passive coping stressors were significant ($p < .01$) in 39 of 40 comparisons made. The consistency of hemodynamic response patterning suggested by these correlations was further explored by post hoc classification of 30 myocardial reactors (pressor responses to increased *CO*) and 31 vascular reactors (pressor responses associated with vascular resistance increase), who were defined according to their responses during a competitive task. The contrasting hemodynamic response patterns exhibited by the two groups was preserved across other active and passive coping stressors, which suggests that the hemodynamic basis of reactivity is an individual characteristic only partially modified by the coping demands of a situation. Kasprowicz et al. (1990), as noted in the previous section on temporal stability, examined the responses of 39 subjects to mental arithmetic and a mirror tracing task on two occasions, 4 weeks apart. Modest, but significant, associations were found for blood pressure responses across tasks on both occasions of testing. However, *CO* and *TPR* responses were found to evidence significant intertask consistency only for the second test session; with no explanation readily apparent for this discrepancy. In the third existing report, the intertask consistency of hemodynamic responses of 36 subjects during four psychological stress conditions (mental arithmetic, reaction time, active speech, and passive speech) was examined (Turner, Sherwood, & Light, 1991). For SBP, all six of the possible intertask correlations were significant ($p < .01$; $rs = 0.49–0.80$), whereas only three of the six were significant for DBP ($rs = 0.28–0.66$). Basically similar findings were found for *CO* and *TPR*, with both showing five out of six significant correlations; the coefficients ranged from 0.37 to 0.75 for *CO* and from 0.38 to 0.76 for *TPR*. Evidence is thus accumulating that the underlying hemodynamic responses to psychological stressors show intertask consistency comparable to that for blood pressure responses.

Postural Stability

It is well known that the resting hemodynamic profile of the standing posture differs considerably from that of the seated posture (Turjanmaa, 1989). However, laboratory-based cardiovascular reactivity testing has been conducted almost universally while subjects are seated. The possibility that hemodynamic response patterns that are characteristic of given stressors and individual hemodynamic response predispositions may be different in the standing versus sitting posture was evaluated in a recent study (Sherwood & Turner, 1993). A highly standardized, computer-controlled mental arithmetic task was used as the stress task in the study. Twenty healthy young adult men were tested four times on the mental arithmetic task, twice while seated and twice while standing. As reported in previous studies that evaluated orthostatic influences on resting blood pressure, the standing compared with seated posture was associated with an increase in DBP, whereas SBP tended to fall slightly. Underlying the alteration in blood pressure, there was a fall in *CO* and a rise in vascular resistance at rest in the standing posture, changes that are also consistent with existing evidence (Julius, 1988; Rushmer, 1976;

Tell, Prineas, & Gomez-Marin, 1988). In the seated posture, the response to mental arithmetic was similar to that previously reported for this task: SBP and DBP were elevated, CO increased, and vascular resistance showed relatively little change (see Table 1). In the standing posture, the blood pressure responses to the same mental arithmetic task were only minimally altered, with an equivalent response seen for DBP and with SBP tending to rise more than in the seated posture. In sharp contrast, the hemodynamic basis of blood pressure responses was reversed in the standing posture, with an increase in TPR responsible for the pressor response, whereas CO showed no significant change (Table 1). The issue of postural stability of individual differences in cardiovascular responses was addressed by correlational analyses. The correlations for all cardio-vascular response measures during repeated task exposure in the same posture were positive, significant, and comparable in magnitude. Corre-lations comparing cardiovascular responses across postures are pre-sented in Table 2. Generally positive, but nonsignificant, correlations were found for blood pressure, which indicates relatively poor stability of the blood pressure response from sitting to standing posture. In contrast, the correlations for the underlying CO and TPR responses were positive and

TABLE 1

Mean ($\pm SD$) Hemodynamic Responses (Task Minus Corresponding Posture Baseline) During Performance on a Mental Arithmetic (MA) Task in a Sitting Posture Compared With a Standing Posture in 20 Healthy Young Men

Measure	Sitting MA		Standing MA		$F(1, 19)$	p
	M	SD	M	SD		
SBP (mmHg)	11.1	6.4**	15.2	5.5**	6.36	<.05
DBP (mmHg)	7.4	4.7**	8.8	5.1**	1.48	ns
CO (L/min)	0.42	0.9*	0.12	0.8	7.42	<.025
TPR (dyne-s · cm⁻⁵)	51	123	152	178**	10.98	<.005

Note. SBP = total systolic blood pressure; DBP = diastolic blood pressure; CO = cardiac output; TPR = total peripheral resistance. F and associated p values summarize results of an analysis of variance that compared postures. From "Postural Stability of Hemodynamic Re-sponses During Mental Challenge" by A. Sherwood and J. R. Turner, 1993, Psychophysiology, 30; copyright 1993 by the Society for Psychophysiological Research; adapted by permission. *p < .05, significant change compared with baseline. **p < .01, significant compared with baseline.

TABLE 2

Pearson Product–Moment Correlations (r) and Associated p Values for Hemodynamic Responses (Task Minus Corresponding Posture Baseline) During a Mental Arithmetic Task for Sitting Posture Compared With Standing Posture in 20 Healthy Young Men

Measure	Pearson r	p
SBP (mmHg)	0.265	ns
DBP (mmHg)	0.423	ns
CO (L/min)	0.850	<.0001
TPR (dyne-s · cm^{-5})	0.646	<.005

Note. SBP = systolic blood pressure; DBP = diastolic blood pressure; CO = cardiac output; TPR = total peripheral resistance. From "Postural Stability of Hemodynamic Responses During Mental Challenge" by A. Sherwood and J. R. Turner, 1993, *Psychophysiology, 30;* copyright 1993 by the Society for Psychophysiological Research; adapted by permission.

significant (see Table 2). This preliminary evidence suggests that the hemodynamic response mechanisms of cardiovascular activation during mental challenge may be more stable across postures than the associated blood pressure responses.

Summary and Future Directions

The addition of impedance cardiography to standard blood pressure monitoring during reactivity assessment has revealed that (a) different stressors may increase blood pressure due to quite different hemodynamic mechanisms and (b) individuals may differ quite dramatically in terms of the hemodynamic mechanisms responsible for increasing their blood pressure when exposed to a given stressor. These observations have been of particular interest in relation to psychosomatic theories of cardiovascular disease, whereby individual predispositions to respond to stress may be a marker for increased risk of such slowly developing conditions as hypertension. In this regard, evidence that groups of individuals at higher risk for hypertension, such as borderline hypertensives and Black Americans who appear to exhibit cardiovascular reactivity patterns that differ from lower risk groups, has provoked much speculation about potential pathophysiological processes. Theories have been postulated suggesting that specific hemodynamic response patterns during stress may not only be a marker, but when frequently evoked, themselves contribute to long-term structural alterations of the cardiovascular system that are the basis of hypertensive disease.

Cardiovascular responses to psychological stress should exhibit the characteristics of stable individual traits if they are to be viewed as playing a role in the development of hypertension (Manuck et al., 1990). The emerging evidence, as reviewed in this chapter, indicates that individual hemodynamic response patterns persist over time and are only partially modified by the demands of different stressors. Nonetheless, it is important to remember that if cardiovascular reactivity is a behavioral trait directly implicated in disease processes, it is in the realm of real-life stress where its expression must take its toll. However, there is a lack of compelling evidence for generalization of blood pressure responses from laboratory to real-life situations, which has been a source of criticism for the reactivity hypothesis of hypertension (Pickering & Gerin, 1990). Preliminary evidence, as described in this chapter, suggests that individual differences in the *CO* and *TPR* responses during mental stress may be preserved even when posture is altered, whereas blood pressure responses appear to be less robust. The possibility that cardiovascular reactivity assessed according to hemodynamic response patterns may show a greater degree of consistency from laboratory to real-life stress has yet to be examined. Recent technological advances now make it possible to develop a viable ambulatory impedance cardiograph that, when coupled with an ambulatory blood pressure monitor, will permit 24-hr monitoring of hemodynamic response patterns during the events of daily life. The realization of this methodology promises to further our understanding of the nature and impact of cardiovascular responses during real-life stress and thereby help to define the significance of the cardiovascular reactivity concept.

References

Abrahams, V. C., Hilton, S. M., & Zbrozyna, A. W. (1960). Active muscle vasodilitation produced by stimulation of the brain stem: Its significance in the defence reaction. *Journal of Physiology, 154,* 491–513.

Abrahams, V. C., Hilton, S. M., & Zbrozyna, A. W. (1964). The role of active muscle vasodilation in the alerting stage of the defence reaction. *Journal of Physiology, 171,* 189–202.

Ahmed, S. S., Levinson, G. E., Schwartz, C. J., & Ettinger, P. O. (1972). Systolic time intervals as measures of the contractile state of the left ventricular myocardium in man. *Circulation, 46*, 559–571.

Akinkugbe, O. O. (1985). World epidemiology of hypertension in blacks. In W. D. Hall, E. Saunders, & N. B. Shulman (Eds.), *Hypertension in blacks: Epidemiology, pathophysiology, and treatment* (pp. 3–16). Chicago: Yearbook Publishers.

Allen, M. T., Sherwood, A., Obrist, P. A., Crowell, M. D., & Grange, L. A. (1987). Stability of cardiovascular reactivity to laboratory stressors: A 2 1/2 year follow-up. *Journal of Psychosomatic Research, 31*, 639–645.

Andersen, K., & Vik-Mo, H. (1984). Effects of spontaneous respiration on left ventricular function assessed by echocardiography. *Circulation, 69*, 874–879.

Anderson, N. B., Lane, J. D., Muranaka, H., Williams, R. B., Jr., & Houseworth, S. A. (1988). Racial differences in cardiovascular reactivity to mental arithmetic. *International Journal of Psychophysiology, 6*, 161–164.

Appel, P. L., Kram, H. B., MacKabee, J., Fleming, A. W., & Shoemaker, W. C. (1986). Comparison of measurements of cardiac output by bioimpedance and thermodilution in severely ill surgical patients. *Critical Care Medicine, 14*, 933–935.

Baker, L. E., Judy, W. V., Geddes, L. E., Langley, F. M., & Hill, D. W. (1971). The measurement of cardiac output by means of electrical impedance. *Cardiovascular Research Center Bulletin, 9*, 135–145.

Balasubramanian, V., Mathew, O. P., Behl, A., Tewari, S. C., & Hoon, R. S. (1978). Electrical impedance cardiogram in derivation of systolic time intervals. *British Heart Journal, 40*, 268–275.

Bernstein, D. P. (1986a). A new stroke volume equation for thoracic electrical bioimpedance: Theory and rationale. *Critical Care Medicine, 14*, 904–909.

Bernstein, D. P. (1986b). Continuous noninvasive real-time monitoring of stroke volume and cardiac output by thoracic electrical bioimpedance. *Critical Care Medicine, 14*, 898–901.

Bernstein, D. P. (1989). Noninvasive cardiac output measurement. In W. C. Shoemaker, S. Ayres, A. Grenvik, P. R. Holbrook, & W. L. Thompson (Eds.), *Textbook of critical care* (pp. 159–185). Philadelphia: W. B. Saunders.

Boomsma, D. I., deVries, J., & Orlebeke, J. F. (1989). Comparison of spot and band impedance cardiogram electrodes across different tasks. *Psychophysiology, 26*, 695–699.

Brod, J., Fencl, V., Hejl, Z., & Jirka, J. (1959). Circulatory changes underlying blood pressure elevation during acute emotional stress (mental arithmetic) in normotensive and hypertensive subjects. *Clinical Science, 18*, 269–279.

Cannon, W. B. (1915). *Bodily changes in pain, hunger, fear and rage.* New York: Appleton.

Colin, J., & Timbal, J. (1982). Measurement of systolic time intervals by electrical plethysmography: Validation with invasive and noninvasive methods. *Aviation, Space, and Environmental Medicine, 53*, 62–68.

Cousineau, D., de Champlain, J., & Lapointe, L. (1978). Circulating catecholamines and systolic time intervals in labile and sustained hypertension. *Clinical Science and Molecular Medicine, 55,* 65s–68s.

De Mey, C., & Enterling, D. (1988). Noninvasive assessment of cardiac performance by impedance cardiography: Disagreement between two equations to estimate stroke volume. *Aviation, Space, and Environmental Medicine, 59,* 57–62.

Denniston, J. C., Maher, J. T., Reeves, J. T., Cruz, J. C., Cymerman, A., & Grover, R. F. (1976). Measurement of cardiac output by electrical impedance at rest and during exercise. *Journal of Applied Physiology, 40,* 91–95.

DeSouza, W. M., & Panerai, R. B. (1981). Variability of thoracic impedance cardiograms in man. *Medical and Biological Engineering and Computing, 19,* 411–415.

Doerr, B. M., Miles, D. S., & Bassett Frey, M. A. (1981). Influence of respiration on stroke volume determined by impedance cardiography. *Aviation, Space and Environmental Medicine, 52,* 394–398.

DuQuesnay, M. C., Stoute, G. J., & Hughson, R. L. (1987). Cardiac output in exercise by impedance cardiography during breath holding and normal breathing. *Journal of Applied Physiology, 62,* 101–107.

Ebert, T. J., Eckberg, D. L., Vetrovec, G. M., & Cowley, M. J. (1984). Impedance cardiograms reliably estimate beat-by-beat changes of left ventricular stroke volume in humans. *Cardiovascular Research, 18,* 354–360.

Edmunds, A. T., Godfrey, S., & Tooley, M. (1982). Cardiac output measured by transthoracic impedance cardiography at rest, during exercise, and various lung volumes. *Clinical Science, 63,* 107–113.

Fahrenberg, J., Schneider, H.-J., Foerester, F., Myrtek, M., & Muller, W. (1985). The quantification of cardiovascular reactivity in longitudinal studies. In A. Steptoe, H. Ruddel, & H. Neus (Eds.), *Clinical and methodological issues in cardiovascular psychophysiology* (pp. 107–120). Berlin: Springer-Verlag.

Ferrigno, M., Hickey, D. D., Liner, M. H., & Lundgren, C. E. (1986). Cardiac performance in humans during breath holding. *Journal of Applied Physiology, 60,* 1871–1877.

Fredrikson, M. (1986). Racial differences in reactivity to behavioral challenge in essential hypertension. *Journal of Hypertension, 4,* 325–331.

Fredrikson, M., & Matthews, K. A. (1990). Cardiovascular responses to behavioral stress and hypertension: A meta-analytic review. *Annals of Behavioral Medicine, 12,* 30–39.

Garrard, C. L., Jr., Weissler, A. M., & Dodge, H. T. (1970). The relationship of alterations in systolic time intervals to ejection fraction in patients with cardiac disease. *Circulation, 42,* 455–462.

Geddes, L. A., & Sadler, C. (1973). The specific resistance of blood at body temperature. *Medical and Biological Engineering, 11,* 335–339.

Girdler, S. S., Turner, J. R., Sherwood, A., & Light, K. C. (1990). Gender differences in blood pressure control during a variety of behavioral stressors. *Psychosomatic Medicine, 52*, 571–591.

Gliner, J. A., Bunnell, D. E., & Horvath, S. M. (1982). Hemodynamic and metabolic changes prior to speech performance. *Physiological Psychology, 10*, 108–113.

Gollan, F., Kizakevich, P.N., & McDermott, J. (1978). Continuous electrode monitoring of systolic time intervals during exercise. *British Heart Journal, 40*, 1390–1396.

Gotshall, R. W., Wood, V. C., & Miles, D. S. (1989). Comparison of two impedance cardiographic techniques for measuring cardiac output. *Annals of Biomedical Engineering, 17*, 495–505.

Heather, L. W. (1969). A comparison of cardiac output values by the impedance cardiograph and dye dilution techniques in cardiac patients. In W. G. Kubicek, D. A. Witsoe, R. P. Patterson, & A. H. L. From (Eds.), *Development and evaluation of an impedance cardiographic system to measure cardiac output and other cardiac parameters* (NASA CR-101965, pp. 247–258). Houston, TX: National Aeronautics and Space Administration.

Hickman, J. B., Cargill, W. H., & Golden, A. (1948). Cardiovascular reactions to emotional stimuli: Effect on the cardiac output, arterio-venous oxygen difference, arterial pressure and peripheral resistance. *Journal of Clinical Investigation, 27*, 290–298.

Hill, D. W., & Merrifield, A. J. (1976). Left ventricular ejection and the Heather index measured by noninvasive methods during postural changes in man. *Acta Anaesthesiologica Scandinavica, 20*, 313–320.

Hill, D. W., & Thompson, F. D. (1975). The importance of blood resistivity in the measurement of cardiac output by the thoracic impedance method. *Medical and Biological Engineering, 13*, 187–191.

Ito, H., Yamakoshi, K., & Yamada, A. (1976). Physiological and fluid-dynamic investigations of the transthoracic impedance plethysmography method for measuring cardiac output: Part II. *Medical and Biological Engineering and Computation, 14*, 373–381.

Judy, W. V., Langley, F. M., McCowen, K. D., Stinnett, D. M., Baker, L. E., & Johnson, P. C. (1969). Comparative evaluation of the thoracic impedance and isotope dilution methods for measuring cardiac output. In W. G. Kubicek, D. A. Witsoe, R. P. Patterson, & A. H. L. From (Eds.), *Development and evaluation of an impedance cardiographic system to measure cardiac output and other cardiac parameters* (NASA-CR-101965, pp. 296–300). Houston, TX: National Aeronautics and Space Administration.

Julius, S. (1981). The psychophysiology of borderline hypertension. In H. Weiner, M. A. Hofer, & A. J. Stunkard (Eds.), *Brain, behavior and bodily disease* (pp. 293–303). New York: Raven Press.

Julius, S. (1988). The blood pressure seeking properties of the central nervous system. *Journal of Hypertension, 6*, 177–185.

Kasprowicz, A. L., Manuck, S. B., Malkoff, S. B., & Krantz, D. A. (1990). Individual differences in behaviorally evoked cardiovascular response: Temporal stability and hemodynamic patterning. *Psychophysiology, 27*, 605–619.

Kelsey, R. M., Guethlein, W., Eichler, S., Blascovich, J. J., & Katkin, E. S. (1987). An evaluation of ensemble-averaged impedance cardiographic measures of myocardial performance [Abstract]. *Psychophysiology, 24*, 595.

Kizakevich, P. N., Gollan, F., & McDermott, J. (1976). An automated system for systolic time interval analysis. *Proceedings of the Digital Equipment Users Society, 2*, 795–798.

Kobayashi, Y., Andoh, Y., Fujinami, T., Nakayama, K., Takada, K., Takeuchi, T., & Okamoto, M. (1978). Impedance cardiography for estimating cardiac output during submaximal and maximal work. *Journal of Applied Physiology, 45*, 459–462.

Kubicek, W. G., Karnegis, J. N., Patterson, R. P., Witsoe, D. A. & Mattson, R. H. (1966). Development and evaluation of an impedance cardiograph system. *Aerospace Medicine, 37*, 1208–1212.

Kubicek, W. G., Kottke, F. J., Ramos, M. U., Patterson, R. P., Witsoe, D. A., Labree, J. W., Remole, W., Layman, T. E., Schoening, H., & Garamella, J. T. (1974). The Minnesota impedance cardiograph—theory and applications. *Biomedical Engineering, 9*, 410–416.

Kubicek, W. G., Witsoe, D. A., Patterson, R. P., & From, A. H. L. (Eds.). (1969). *Development and evaluation of an impedance cardiographic system to measure cardiac output and other cardiac parameters* (NASA-CR-101965). Houston, TX: National Aeronautics and Space Administration.

Lamberts, R., Visser, K. R., & Zijlstra, W. G. (1984). *Impedance cardiography.* Assen, The Netherlands: Van Gorcum.

Light, K. C., & Obrist, P. A. (1983). Task difficulty, heart rate reactivity, and cardiovascular responses to an appetitive reaction time task. *Psychophysiology, 20*, 301–312.

Light, K. C., Obrist, P. A., Sherwood, A., James, S. A., & Strogatz, D. S. (1987). Effects of race and marginally elevated blood pressure on cardiovascular responses to stress in young men. *Hypertension, 10*, 555–563.

Light, K. C., & Sherwood, A. (1990). Race, borderline hypertension and hemodynamic responses to behavioral stress before and after beta-adrenergic blockade. *Health Psychology, 8*, 577–595.

Lovallo, W. R., Pincomb, G. A., & Wilson, M. F. (1986). Heart rate reactivity and type A behavior as modifiers of physiological response to active and passive coping. *Psychophysiology, 23*, 105–112.

Manuck, S. B., & Garland, F. N. (1980). Stability of individual differences in cardiovascular reactivity: A thirteen-month follow-up. *Physiology and Behavior, 24*, 621–624.

Manuck, S. B., Kasprowicz, A. L., & Muldoon, M. F. (1990). Behaviorally-evoked cardiovascular reactivity and hypertension: Conceptual issues and potential associations. *Annals of Behavioral Medicine, 12,* 17–29.

Manuck, S. B., & Shaefer, D. C. (1978). Stability of individual differences in cardiovascular reactivity. *Physiology and Behavior, 21,* 675–678.

Matthews, K. A., Rakaczky, C. J., Stoney, C. M., & Manuck, S. B. (1987). Are cardiovascular responses to behavioral stressors a stable individual difference variable in childhood? *Psychophysiology, 24,* 464–473.

McCubbin, J. A., Richardson, J. E., Langer, A. W., Kizer, J. S., & Obrist, P. A. (1983). Sympathetic neuronal function and left ventricular performance during behavioral stress in humans: The relationship between plasma catecholamines and systolic time intervals. *Psychophysiology, 20,* 102–110.

McKinney, M. E., Miner, M. H., Ruddel, H., McIlvain, H. E., Witte, H., Buell, J. C., Elliot, R. S., & Grant, L. B. (1985). The standardized mental stress protocol: Test–retest reliability and comparison with ambulatory blood pressure monitoring. *Psychophysiology, 22,* 453–463.

Miller, J. C., & Horvath, S. M. (1978). Impedance cardiography. *Psychophysiology, 15,* 80–91.

Miyamoto, Y., Higuchi, J., Abe, Y., Hiura, T., Nakazono, Y., & Mikami, T. (1983). Dynamics of cardiac output and systolic time intervals in supine and upright exercise. *Journal of Applied Physiology, 55,* 1674–1681.

Miyamoto, Y., Takahashi, M., Tamura, T., Nakamura, T., Hiura, T., & Mikami, M. (1981). Continuous determination of cardiac output during exercise by the use of impedance plethysmography. *Medical and Biological Engineering and Computing, 19,* 638–644.

Miyamoto, Y., Tamura, T., Hiura, T., Nakamura, T., Higuchi, J., & Mikami, T. (1982). The dynamic response of the cardiopulmonary parameters to passive head-up tilt. *Japanese Journal of Physiology, 32,* 245–258.

Mohapatra, S. N. (1981). *Non-invasive cardiovascular monitoring by electrical impedance technique.* London: Pittman Medical.

Mohapatra, S. N., Costeloe, K. L., & Hill, D. W. (1977). Blood resistivity and its implications for the calculation of cardiac output by the thoracic electrical impedance technique. *Intensive Care Medicine, 3,* 63–67.

Mohapatra, S. N., & Hill, D. W. (1975). The changes in blood resistivity with hematocrit and temperature. *European Journal of Intensive Care Medicine, 1,* 153–162.

Muzi, M., Ebert, T. J., Tristani, F. E., Jeutter, D. C., Barney, J. A., & Smith, J. J. (1985). Determination of cardiac output using ensemble-averaged impedance cardiograms. *Journal of Applied Physiology, 58,* 200–205.

Muzi, M., Jeutter, D. C., & Smith, J. J. (1986). Computer-automated impedance-derived cardiac indexes. *IEEE Transactions on Biomedical Engineering, BME-33,* 42–47.

Myrtek, M. (1985). Adaptation effects and the stability of physiological responses to repeated testing. In A. Steptoe, H. Ruddel, & H. Neus (Eds.), *Clinical and methodological issues in cardiovascular psychophysiology* (pp. 93–106). Berlin: Springer-Verlag.

Newlin, D. B., & Levenson, R. W. (1979). Pre-ejection period: Measuring beta-adrenergic influences upon the heart. *Psychophysiology, 16,* 546–553.

Obrist, P. A. (1976). The cardiovascular–behavioral interaction—as it appears today. *Psychophysiology, 13,* 95–107.

Obrist, P. A. (1981). *Cardiovascular psychophysiology: A perspective.* New York: Plenum.

Obrist, P. A., Light, K. C., James, S. A., & Strogatz, D. S. (1987). Cardiovascular responses to stress: I. Measures of myocardial response and relationships to high resting systolic pressure and parental hypertension. *Psychophysiology, 24,* 65–78.

Peckerman, A., Saab, P. G., McCabe, P. M., Skyler, J. S., Winters, R. W., Llabre, M. M., & Schneiderman, N. (1991). Blood pressure reactivity and the perception of pain during the forehead cold pressor test. *Psychophysiology, 28,* 485–495.

Penney, B. C., Patwardhan, N. A., & Wheeler, H. B. (1985). Simplified electrode array for impedance cardiography. *Medical and Biological Engineering and Computing, 23,* 1–7.

Petrovick, M. L., Kizakevich, P. N., Stacy, R. W., & Haak, E. D. (1980). A comprehensive cardiac exercise stress processor for environmental health effects studies. *Journal of Medical Systems, 4,* 137–150.

Pickering, T. G., & Gerin, W. (1990). Cardiovascular reactivity in the laboratory and the role of behavioral factors in hypertension: A critical review. *Annals of Behavioral Medicine, 12,* 3–16.

Pigott, V. M., & Spodick, D. H. (1971). Effects of normal breathing and expiratory apnea on duration of the phases of cardiac systole. *American Heart Journal, 82,* 786–793.

Porter, J. M., & Swain, I. D. (1987). Measurement of cardiac output by electrical impedance plethysmography. *Journal of Biomedical Engineering, 9,* 222–231.

Qu, M., Zhang, Y., Webster, J. G., & Tompkins, W. J. (1986). Motion artifact from spot and band electrodes during impedance cardiography. *IEEE Transactions on Biomedical Engineering, BME-33,* 1029–1036.

Quail, A. W., Traugott, F. M., Porges, W. L., & White, S. W. (1981). Thoracic resistivity for stroke volume calculation in impedance cardiography. *Journal of Applied Physiology, 50,* 191–195.

Roberts, J., & Rowland, M. (1981). *Hypertension in adults 25–74 years of age: United States 1971–75* (DHEW Publication No. PHS 81-1671). Vital and health statistics (Series 11, No. 221). Washington, DC: U.S. Government Printing Office.

Rushmer, R. F. (1976). *Cardiovascular dynamics* (4th ed.). Philadelphia: W. B. Saunders.

Saab, P. G. (1989). Cardiovascular and neuroendocrine responses to challenge in males and females. In N. Schneiderman, S. M. Weiss, & P. G. Kaufmann (Eds.), *Handbook of research methods in cardiovascular behavioral medicine* (pp. 453–481). New York: Plenum.

Sakamoto, K., Muto, K., Kanai, H., & Iizuka, M. (1979). Problems of impedance cardiography. *Medical and Biological Engineering and Computing, 17*, 697–709.

Sheps, D. S., Petrovick, M. L., Kizakevich, P. N., Wolfe, C., & Craige, E. (1982). Continuous noninvasive monitoring of left ventricular function during exercise by thoracic impedance cardiography—automated derivation of systolic time intervals. *American Heart Journal, 103*, 519–524.

Sherwood, A., Allen, M. T., Fahrenberg, J., Kelsey, R. M., Lovallo, W. R., & vanDoornen, L. J. P. (1990). Committee report: Methodological guidelines for impedance cardiography. *Psychophysiology, 27*, 1–23.

Sherwood, A., Allen, M. T., Obrist, P. A., & Langer, A. W. (1986). Evaluation of beta-adrenergic influences on cardiovascular and metabolic adjustments to physical and psychological stress. *Psychophysiology, 23*, 89–104.

Sherwood, A., Carter, L. S., Jr., & Murphy, C. A. (1991). Cardiac output by impedance cardiography: Two alternative methodologies compared with thermodilution. *Aviation, Space, and Environmental Medicine, 62*, 116–122.

Sherwood, A., Davis, M. R., Dolan, C. A., & Light, K. C. (1992). Cardiovascular reactivity assessment: Effects of choice of difficulty on laboratory task responses. *International Journal of Psychophysiology, 12*, 87–94.

Sherwood, A., Dolan, C., & Light, K. C. (1990). Hemodynamics of blood pressure responses during active and passive coping. *Psychophysiology, 27*, 656–668.

Sherwood, A., Royal, S. A., Hutcheson, J. S., & Turner, J. R. (1992). Comparison of impedance cardiographic measurements using band and spot electrodes. *Psychophysiology, 29*, 734–741.

Sherwood, A., Royal, S. A., & Light, K. C. (1993). Laboratory reactivity assessment: Effects of casual blood pressure status and choice of task difficulty. *International Journal of Psychophysiology, 14*, 81–95.

Sherwood, A., & Turner, J. R. (1992). A conceptual and methodological overview of cardiovascular reactivity research. In J. R. Turner, A. Sherwood, & K. C. Light (Eds.), *Individual differences in cardiovascular response to stress* (pp. 3–27). New York: Plenum.

Sherwood, A., & Turner, J. R. (1993). Postural stability of hemodynamic responses during mental challenge. *Psychophysiology, 30*.

Sherwood, A., Turner, J. R., Light, K. C., & Blumenthal, J. A. (1990). Temporal stability of the hemodynamics of cardiovascular reactivity. *International Journal of Psychophysiology, 10*, 95–98.

Sramek, B. B. (1981). Noninvasive technique for measurement of cardiac output by means of electrical impedance. *Proceedings of the Fifth International Conference on Electrical Bioimpedance* (pp. 39–42). Tokyo, Japan.

Sramek, B. B., Rose, D. M., & Miyamoto, A. (1983). Stroke volume equation with a linear base impedance model and its accuracy as compared to thermodilution and magnetic flowmeter techniques in humans and animals. *Proceedings of the Sixth International Conference on Electrical Bioimpedance* (p. 38). Zadar, Yugoslavia.

Stead, E. A., Warren, J. V., Merrill, A. J., & Brannon, E. S. (1945). The cardiac output in male subjects as measured by the technique of atrial catheterization: Normal values with observation on the effects of anxiety and tilting. *Journal of Clinical Investigation, 24,* 326–331.

Stern, H. C., Wolf, G. K., & Belz, G. G. (1985). Comparative measurements of left ventricular ejection time by mechano-, echo- and electrical impedance cardiography. *Drug Research, 35,* 1582–1586.

Stoney, S. M., Davis, M. C., & Matthews, K. A. (1987). Sex differences in physiological responses to stress and in coronary heart disease: A causal link? *Psychophysiology, 24,* 127–131.

Tell, G. S., Prineas, R. J., & Gomez-Marin, O. (1988). Postural changes in blood pressure and pulse rate among Black adolescents and White adolescents: The Minneapolis children's blood pressure study. *American Journal of Epidemiology, 128,* 360–369.

Thomsen, A. (1979). Impedance cardiography: Is the output from the right or left ventricle measured? *Intensive Care Medicine, 5,* 206.

Treiber, F. A., Musante, L., Braden, D., Arensman, F., Strong, W. B., Levy, M., & Leverett, S. (1990). Racial differences in hemodynamic responses to the cold face stimulus in children and adults. *Psychosomatic Medicine, 52,* 286–296.

Turjanmaa, V. (1989). Determination of blood pressure level and changes in physiological situations: Comparisons of the standard cuff method with direct intra-arterial recording. *Clinical Physiology, 9,* 373–387.

Turner, J. R., Carroll, D., & Courtney, H. (1983). Cardiac and metabolic responses to "Space Invaders": An instance of metabolically-exaggerated cardiac adjustment? *Psychophysiology, 20,* 544–549.

Turner, J. R., Sherwood, A., & Light, K. C. (1991). Generalization of cardiovascular response: Supportive evidence for the reactivity hypothesis. *International Journal of Psychophysiology, 11,* 207–212.

U.S. Bureau of the Census. (1987). *Statistical Abstract of the United States: 1988* (108th ed.), Washington, DC: U.S. Government Printing Office.

van Egeren, L. F., & Sparrow, A. W. (1989). Laboratory stress testing to assess real life cardiovascular reactivity. *Psychosomatic Medicine, 51,* 1–9.

Veigl, V. L., & Judy, W. V. (1983). Reproducibility of hemodynamic measurements by impedance cardiography. *Cardiovascular Research, 17,* 728–734.

Weissler, A. M. (1977). Current concepts in cardiology: Systolic time intervals. *New England Journal of Medicine, 296,* 321–324.

Witsoe, D. A., Patterson, R. P., From, A. H. L., & Kubicek, W. G. (1969). Evaluation of impedance cardiographic techniques for measuring relative changes in cardiac output by simultaneous comparison with indicator dilution and electromagnetic flowmeter. In W. G. Kubicek, D. A. Witsoe, R. P. Patterson, & A. H. L. From (Eds.), *Development and evaluation of an impedance cardiographic system to measure cardiac output and other cardiac parameters* (NASA-CR-101965 pp. 330–355). Houston, TX: National Aeronautics and Space Administration.

Zhang, Y., Qu, M., Webster, J. G., Tompkins, W. J., Ward, B. A., & Bassett, D. R. (1986). Cardiac output monitoring by impedance cardiography during treadmill exercise. *IEEE Transactions on Biomedical Engineering, BME-33*, 1037–1042.

CHAPTER 8

Use of Ambulatory Monitoring of Left Ventricular Function With the VEST

David S. Kayden and John W. Burns

I schemic myocardial syndromes were first associated with chest pain and patterns of characteristic electrocardiographic (ECG) ST segment changes. Myocardial ischemia has more recently been demonstrated to occur in the absence of chest pain, that is, during so-called "silent ischemia" (Gottlieb et al., 1988; Gottlieb, Weisfeldt, Ouyang, Mellits, & Gerstenblith, 1986; Nademanbee et al., 1987).

Significant regional and global left ventricular dysfunction has been demonstrated to precede clinical symptoms and ST changes during myocardial ischemia (Borer et al., 1979; Newman, Rerych, Upton, Sabiston, & Jones, 1980; Shah, Pichler, Berman, Singh, & Swan, 1980). Animal and clinical studies have suggested that measures of regional and global left ventricular function may thus be more accurate and sensitive for myocardial ischemia than either clinical symptoms or ECG changes (Grover-McKay, Matsuzaki, & Ross, 1987; Hung, Goris, Nash, Kraemer, & DeBusk, 1984). This difference in sensitivity may be most significant during mental stress (e.g., Rozanski et al., 1988).

Ambulatory Holter monitoring has been used to study the incidence, frequency, and duration of myocardial ischemic episodes over long periods of time. The use of radionuclide techniques to detect and quantify myocardial ischemia by measures of regional and global left ventricular function has been obtained generally for relatively short periods of time during laboratory stress testing. However, a recently developed technique continuously monitors left ventricular ejection fraction over prolonged periods in ambulatory patients (Wilson et al., 1983). This technique uses standard principles of radionuclide ventriculography. It provides physiological data that are useful in the evaluation and treatment of patients with both silent and symptomatic myocardial ischemia.

Technical Aspects

Instrumentation

The *VEST* is an ambulatory left ventricular function monitoring device. It was initially described by Wilson et al. (1983). The VEST consists of several components: a nonimaging gamma detector, a semirigid plastic vestlike garment to support the detector in a stable position over the heart, a microprocessor, and a modified Holter-type cassette recorder to record the data. The total system weighs approximately 5 pounds ($\sim$2.3 kg).

The nuclear data consist of sequential ECG gated gamma counts of left ventricular blood pool activity sampled 32 times per second. These data, as well as two-channel ECG and timing information, are simultaneously recorded on the Holter cassette tape.

Technique

The VEST detector is positioned using a gamma camera. A standard gated equilibrium radionuclide angiocardiographic study is initially obtained to calculate the baseline ejection fraction and to position the detector over the left ventricle. ECG leads for the two-channel ECG are placed on the chest so as not to interfere with the detection of blood pool activity.

Baseline data are initially obtained for 5–10 min at rest. Patients are then asked to keep a detailed log of all activities including changes in position (sitting to standing, walking, etc.), eating, and symptoms during monitoring. They are asked to refrain from performing maneuvers that could potentially change the relative position of the detector with respect to the heart (i.e., lying down). At the conclusion of the monitoring period, gamma camera images are obtained to document the final position of the detector. This confirms that any observed changes in the ejection fraction are real and not due to positioning.

Patients can be monitored for 4–6 hr with this technique. Monitoring can be continued for longer periods with additional radionuclide injection.

Data Analysis

The cassette tape with the data are read into a dedicated computer (IBM RT). The radionuclide data, gated with the ECG, are summed for 15–30 s. The left ventricular ejection fraction, decay-corrected relative end-systolic and end-diastolic volumes, heart rate, and ST segment changes are calculated for the entire monitoring period. End-diastolic volume is considered 100% at the beginning of a study and is expressed relative to this initial value throughout a study; systolic volume is also expressed relative to end-diastolic volume. These data can be graphically displayed in a trended format over various time periods depending on the individual interest of the study (Figure 1).

Clinical Application

Validation

Left ventricular function measured by the VEST has correlated well with measurements obtained with a standard gamma camera. Tamaki et al. (1988) and Yang, Bairey, Berman, Nichols, and Odom-Mayron (1991) have separately compared the left ventricular ejection fraction measured by the VEST and a standard gamma camera at rest ($r = 0.92$) and during upright bicycle exercise ($r = 0.86$–0.90).

The normal resting variability of the ejection fraction measured by the VEST, expressed as the standard deviation of serial measurements rest, has been reported to be 0.021 (Tamaki et al., 1988; Kayden, Wackers, & Zaret, 1990). Thus, significant left ventricular dysfunction as measured

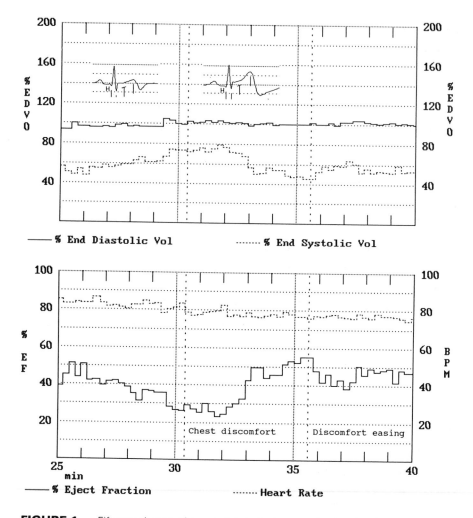

FIGURE 1. Fifteen minutes of trended data during an episode of angina. The relative end-diastolic and end-systolic volumes are shown in the upper panel, and the heart rate and ejection fraction are shown in the lower panel. One-minute time marks are indicated along the horizontal axis. The onset of angina occurred just after Min 30 and ended just before Min 36 (as indicated by the vertical dotted lines). There is a decrease in ejection fraction from 0.40 to 0.27 during this episode of angina. The decrease in ejection fraction preceded the onset of angina. There is a slight increase in end-diastolic volume and a major increase in end-systolic volume during the time when ejection fraction is reduced, which reflects decreased left ventricular systolic performance. The inset shows a representative electrocardiographic QRS complex at baseline and during angina, for which there is 1.5 mm of ST segment elevation.

by the VEST is considered to be a decrease in the ejection fraction that exceeds 0.05 ejection-fraction units (two standard deviations). The decrease in left ventricular function must persist for at least 1 min to be considered significant. These guidelines are similar to those used for exercise radionuclide ventriculography with respect to ejection fraction and similar to Holter monitoring with respect to the duration of abnormality required to diagnose myocardial ischemia. During validation studies, normal subjects have not demonstrated decreases in the ejection fraction of this magnitude at rest or with activity. It should be noted, however, that decreases in the ejection fraction of this magnitude can be provoked in normal subjects by measures such as exposure to cold or by mental stress.

The period of balloon occlusion during angioplasty represents a human model of transient myocardial ischemia caused by an acute reduction in coronary blood flow (Serruys et al., 1984; Wohlgelernter et al., 1986). We studied 18 balloon inflations in 12 patients with normal or near-normal left ventricular function who were undergoing angioplasty of the left anterior descending coronary artery (Kayden et al., 1991). In 17 of the 18 inflations, the left ventricular ejection fraction (EF) decreased by greater than 0.10 EF units. The mean ejection fraction decreased from 0.53 ± 0.08 to 0.28 ± 0.11 at peak inflation. This occurred with a minimal increase in left ventricular end-diastolic volume ($4 \pm 3\%$) and a significant increase in end-systolic volume ($69 \pm 43\%$), which represents severe systolic dysfunction. Clinically, angina occurred in only 10 of the 18 inflations, and ECG changes occurred in 7 of the 18 inflations. The onset of left ventricular dysfunction occurred within 15 s of the onset of balloon inflation. When present, ECG ST segment changes occurred 18 ± 7 s after balloon inflation, and chest pain occurred 41 ± 8 s after inflation.

The results of this study indicate that profound reductions in the ejection fraction can be demonstrated in the absence of chest pain and ischemic ECG ST segment changes. These data confirm the validity of applying this technology to the general study of coronary artery disease and demonstrate the potential of this technology for the study of silent ischemia.

Ambulatory Left Ventricular Function

Normal Subjects

Left ventricular function normally varies during routine activity. The response of normal subjects to a variety of physiological activities was reported by Tamaki et al. (1987). Standing caused an increase in the ejection fraction of 0.03 ± 0.04, with a concomitant decrease in left ventricular end-diastolic volume of 10.9 ± 4.7%. During walking, the ejection fraction increased by 0.10 ± 0.05 and end-diastolic volume increased by 7.8 ± 3.5%. The climbing of stairs resulted in an increase in the ejection fraction of 0.18 ± 0.09 and an increase in end-diastolic volume of 12.8 ± 4.3%. Serial measurements during graded upright exercise (bicycle or treadmill) demonstrated a rapid rise in the ejection fraction during the early stages of exercise with an associated increase in end-diastolic volume and a marked decrease in end-systolic volume. At the later stages of exercise, there was little change in the ejection fraction, although heart rate and systolic blood pressure continued to rise. Immediately after exercise, end-diastolic and end-systolic volumes decreased, but the ejection fraction increased before returning to baseline values.

Coronary Artery Disease

In contrast to the responses observed in normal subjects, patients with coronary artery disease have manifested significant abnormality in left ventricular ejection fraction responses under a variety of conditions. Although abnormal left ventricular function can be induced with provocative maneuvers, many episodes of dysfunction have been recorded at rest or with routine activity, often with minimal associated increases in heart rate. Most of the episodes of left ventricular dysfunction have been clinically silent, and a majority have occurred without associated ECG ST segment changes.

Tamaki et al. (1988) monitored 39 patients with known coronary artery disease for a mean of 2.6 ± 1.3 hr with the VEST. Patients with coronary artery disease as a group had significantly less increase in the ejection fraction during walking or the climbing of stairs than did a group of 12 normal volunteers. There were 36 episodes of transiently decreased ejection fraction documented in 16 patients. Two thirds of these episodes were both painless and without associated ECG changes. Decreases in the ejection fraction preceded both ECG changes and chest pain. These data suggest that transient myocardial ischemia, as demonstrated by left ventricular dysfunction, may occur unrecognized by standard Holter monitor recording.

Clinical Use After Myocardial Infarction

To assess the clinical relevance of transient left ventricular dysfunction that occurs during routine activity after myocardial infarction (MI), we prospectively monitored 33 thrombolytic patients at the time of hospital discharge with the VEST (Kayden, Wackers, & Zaret, 1990). Twelve patients demonstrated 19 episodes of transient left ventricular dysfunction with no significant change in heart rate during an average of 187 ± 56 min of monitoring. All but 2 episodes occurred while the patients were sitting; 1 episode was clearly related to emotional stress. There were no clinically significant differences between the group of patients with and without these episodes. At follow-up (19.2 ± 5.4 months), cardiac events (defined as unstable angina requiring hospitalization or intervention, MI, or death) occurred in 8 of the 12 patients with, but in only 3 of the 21 patients without, episodes of left ventricular dysfunction ($p < .01$).

Breisblatt et al. (1988) combined VEST monitoring with provocative stimuli in the post-MI patient and compared these results with those of thallium-201 stress scintigraphy. The provocative stimuli included exercise treadmill, mental stress, cold pressor, and isometric stress tests. In this study, 56 episodes of left ventricular dysfunction occurred in 23 of the 35 patients who were studied. Twenty-two events occurred during exercise, and 13 occurred during mental stress; 75% of the episodes were clinically silent, and only 39% were associated with ECG ST segment abnormalities. Eighteen of the 20 patients with ischemic thallium-201 scintigraphic responses demonstrated decreases in the ejection fraction during exercise with the VEST. Of interest, 11 of the 13 patients with transient ventricular dysfunction identified by the VEST during mental stress testing had ischemic thallium-201 exercise responses.

In a follow-up report, Breisblatt et al. (1991) used the same provocative testing with the VEST combined with unprovoked monitoring to predict the prognosis of 52 patients after MI. Seventy-two episodes of left ventricular dysfunction occurred in 29 patients during an average of 200 ± 41 min of monitoring. Sixteen patients had subsequent cardiac events (defined as angioplasty or coronary artery bypass surgery, unstable angina, recurrent MI, or death). Twelve of the 14 patients with unprovoked left ventricular dysfunction had subsequent cardiac events, and 15 of the 16 patients with events had at least one episode of decrease in the ejection fraction at some time during the monitoring period. In this study, VEST responses that were predictive of an adverse outcome included a decrease in the ejection fraction that was greater than 0.10, an abnormal response during either mental stress testing or routine activity, and a decrease in the ejection fraction during the first 6 min of treadmill exercise.

Discussion

Although the number of patients who were evaluated with this new technique has been relatively small, ambulatory ventricular function monitoring may improve the detection of ischemic events (particularly in patients with silent myocardial ischemia) and may be important in determining risk stratification. In the published reports that used this technique, most episodes of left ventricular dysfunction were silent and occurred without ECG ST segment changes. Investigation during balloon occlusion of coronary angioplasty has demonstrated major ischemic left ventricular dysfunction, again frequently in the absence of pain and ECG ST segment changes.

Future Considerations

Mental stress may play a role in inducing episodes of myocardial ischemia in patients with coronary artery disease (e.g., Rozanski et al., 1988). Because mental stress is an essential feature of daily living, the sensitive assessment of the effects of mental stress on myocardial function both within and outside the laboratory could contribute to the improved prediction and treatment of myocardial ischemia for high-risk patients. Ventricular contractile measures during mental stress are much more sensitive than are ECG changes in detecting myocardial ischemia (e.g., LaVeau et al., 1989; Rozanski et al., 1988). In addition, ischemic episodes during laboratory mental stress testing determined by ECG methods poorly predict ischemic episodes outside the laboratory (Gottdiener et al., 1990; Linden & Davies, 1991). ECG methods thus have limited utility regarding the assessment of myocardial ischemia during mental stress.

Ambulatory ventricular function monitoring is a method of assessing ventricular contractile function that provides unique diagnostic and prognostic data. The observed decreases in the ejection fraction are most likely due to myocardial ischemia, possibly due to transient vasomotor changes or to transient thromboocclusive phenomena. Because most episodes during mental stress occur without significant increases in heart rate, a decrease in myocardial supply as opposed to an increase in demand has been proposed (e.g., Rozanski, Krantz, & Bairey, 1991).

Further research is necessary to delineate the multiple mechanisms that contribute to the occurrence of myocardial ischemia. More sophisticated on-line processing of ventricular function data during exercise and mental stress challenges may be required to provide real-time display and recording of the ejection fraction. With on-line processing, hemodynamic, biochemical, and metabolic measurements can be obtained simultaneously with the monitoring of the ejection fraction. Preliminary data with this type of device has indicated a good correlation with data processed off-line (Kayden, Suzuki et al., 1990).

More studies involving a larger number of patients in broader settings will be needed before the technique can be widely accepted, used, and appreciated clinically. To gain clinical acceptance, parametric studies may need to focus on the question of sensitivity versus specificity. Ambulatory ventricular function monitoring may provide potentially high sensitivity of detecting changes in the ejection fraction at the expense of potentially lower specificity. The clinical implications of such a trade-off in detecting ischemia will require clear definition.

References

Borer, J. S., Kent, K. M., Bacharach, S. L., Green, M. V., Rosing, D. R., Seides, S. F., Epstein, S. E., & Johnston, G. (1979). Sensitivity, specificity and predictive accuracy of radionuclide cineangiography during exercise in patients with coronary artery disease: Comparison with exercise electrocardiography. *Circulation, 60*, 572–580.

Breisblatt, W. M., Weiland, F. L., McLain, J. R., Tomlinson, G. C., Burns, M. J., & Spaccavento, L. J. (1988). Usefulness of ambulatory radionuclide monitoring of left ventricular function after myocardial infarction for predicting residual myocardial ischemia. *American Journal of Cardiology, 62,* 1005–1010.

Breisblatt, W. M., Wolfe, C., Follansbee, W. P., Burns, M. J., Weiland, F. L., & Spaccavento, L. J. (1991). Ambulatory radionuclide monitoring of left ejection fraction with the nuclear VEST: A useful predictor of prognosis in patients post myocardial infarction. *American Journal of Noninvasive Cardiology, 5,* 262–269.

Gottdiener, J. S., Krantz, D. S., Helmers, K., Lutz, H., Gabbay, F., Alikhan, M., & Rozanski, A. (1990). Silent ischemia induced by mental arousal is not predicted by ambulatory ST segment monitoring [Abstract]. *Journal of American College of Cardiology, 15,* 190A.

Gottlieb, S. O., Gottlieb, S. H., Achuff, S. C., Baumgardner, R., Mellits, E. D., Weisfeldt, M. L., & Gerstenblith, G. (1988). Silent ischemia on Holter monitoring predicts mortality in high-risk postinfarction patients. *Journal of American Medical Association, 259,* 1030–1035.

Gottlieb, S. O., Weisfeldt, M. L., Ouyang, P., Mellits, E. D., & Gerstenblith, G. (1986). Silent ischemia as a marker for unfavorable outcomes in patients with unstable angina. *New England Journal of Medicine, 314,* 1214–1219.

Grover-McKay, M., Matsuzaki, M., & Ross, J., Jr. (1987). Dissociation between regional myocardial dysfunction and subendocardial ST segment elevation during and after exercise-induced ischemia in dogs. *Journal of American College of Cardiology, 10,* 1105–1112.

Hung, G. J., Goris, M. L., Nash, E., Kraemer, H. C., & DeBusk, R. F. (1984). Comparative value of maximal treadmill testing, exercise thallium myocardial perfusion scintigraphy and exercise radionuclide ventriculography for distinguishing high and low risk patients soon after myocardial infarction. *American Journal of Cardiology, 53,* 1221–1227.

Kayden, D. S., Remetz, M. S., Deckelbaum, L. I., Cleman, M. W., Wackers, F. J., & Zaret, B. L. (1991). Continuous monitoring for silent left ventricular dysfunction: Validation with coronary balloon occlusion during angioplasty. *American Journal of Cardiology, 67,* 1339–1343.

Kayden, D. S., Suzuki, A., Remetz, M. S., Cleman, M. W., Cabin, H. S., & Zaret, B. L. (1990). A new technique for on-line continuous radionuclide measurement of left ventricular ejection fraction [Abstract]. *Journal of American College of Cardiology, 15*(Suppl. A), 171A.

Kayden, D. S., Wackers, F. J., & Zaret, B. L. (1990). Silent left ventricular dysfunction during routine activity following thrombolytic therapy for acute myocardial infarction. *Journal of American College of Cardiology, 15,* 1500–1507.

LaVeau, P., Rozanski, A., Krantz, D. S., Cornell, C. E., Cattanach, L., Zaret, B. L., & Wackers, F. (1989). Transient left ventricular dysfunction during provocative mental stress in patients with coronary artery disease. *American Heart Journal, 118*, 1–8.

Linden, W., & Davies, R. F. (1991). Laboratory psychological stress testing does not predict real life ischemic episodes [Abstract]. *Psychosomatic Medicine, 53*, 226.

Nademanbee, K., Intarachot, V., Josephson, M. A., Rieders, D., Vaghaiwalla, M. F., & Singh, B. N. (1987). Prognostic significance of silent myocardial ischemia in patients with unstable angina. *Journal of American College of Cardiology, 10*, 1–9.

Newman, G. E., Rerych, S. K., Upton, M. T., Sabiston, D. C., & Jones, R. H. (1980). Comparison of electrocardiography and left ventricular functional changes during exercise. *Circulation, 62*, 1204–1211.

Rozanski, A., Bairey, C. N., Krantz, D. S., Friedman, J., Resser, K. J., Morrell, M., Hilton-Chalfen, S., Hestrin, L., Bietendorf, J., & Berman, D. S. (1988). Mental stress and the induction of silent myocardial ischemia in patients with coronary artery disease. *New England Journal of Medicine, 318*, 1005–1012.

Rozanski, A., Krantz, D. S., & Bairey, C. N. (1991). Ventricular responses to mental stress testing in patients with coronary artery disease. *Circulation, 83*(Suppl. II), II-137–II-144.

Serruys, P. W., Wigns, W., van der Brand, M., Meij, S., Slager, C., Schuurbiers, J. C. H., Hugenholtz, P. G., & Brower, R. W. (1984). Left ventricular performance, regional blood flow, wall motion and lactate metabolism during transluminal angioplasty. *Circulation, 70*, 25–36.

Shah, P. K., Pichler, M., Berman, D. S., Singh, B. N., & Swan, H. J. C. (1980). Left ventricular ejection fraction determined by radionuclide ventriculography in early stages of first transmural myocardial infarction: Relation to short-term prognosis. *American Journal of Cardiology, 45*, 542–546.

Tamaki, N., Gill, J. B., Moore, R. H., Yasuda, T., Boucher, C. A., & Strauss, H. W. (1987). Cardiac response to daily activities and exercise in normal subjects assessed by an ambulatory ventricular function monitor. *American Journal of Cardiology, 59*, 1164–1169.

Tamaki, N., Yasuda, T., Moore, R. H., Gill, J. B., Boucher, C. A., Hutter, A. M., & Gold, H. K. (1988). Continuous monitoring of left ventricular function by an ambulatory radionuclide detector in patients with coronary artery disease. *Journal of American College of Cardiology, 12*, 669–679.

Wilson, R. A., Sullivan, P. J., Moore, R. H., Zielonka, J. S., Alpert, N. M., Boucher, C. A., McKusic, K. A., & Strauss, H. W. (1983). An ambulatory ventricular function monitor: Validation and preliminary clinical results. *American Journal of Cardiology, 52*, 601–606.

Wohlgelernter, D., Clemen, M., Highman, H. A., Fetterman, R. C., Duncan, J. S., Zaret, B. L., & Jaffee, C. C. (1986). Regional myocardial dysfunction during coronary angioplasty: Evaluation by two dimensional echocardiography and 12 lead electrocardiography. *Journal of American College of Cardiology, 7,* 1245–1254.

Yang, L., Bairey, C. N., Berman, D. S., Nichols, K. J., & Odom-Mayron, T. (1991). Accuracy and reproducibility of left ventricular ejection fraction measurements using an ambulatory radionuclide left ventricular function monitor. *Journal of Nuclear Medicine, 32,* 796–802.

CHAPTER 9

A Low-Tech Approach to Cardiac Reactivity: Psychophysiological Differentiation Using Heart Rate, T-Wave Amplitude, and Skin Conductance Level

John J. Furedy

As I have previously argued in detail (Furedy, 1983, 1984) in opposition to Stern (1964, 1984), psychophysiology is best conceived as the study and differentiation of psychological processes through the use of unobtrusive measures of relatively small changes in physiological functions, changes that are typically unavailable to consciousness. The significance of this last aspect is not metaphysical or even philosophical but rather practical. The practical import is that the measured physiological changes are not subject to confounding from bias that can affect both behavioral and introspective measures of psychological processes.

Another aspect of this sort of psychophysiological differentiation is that, depending on the psychological processes that are of interest, it is not always necessary or even desirable to use physiological measures that require a high level of electronic complexity both for recording and analyzing data. So in the case of this book's central topic, cardiac reactivity and disease, if the interest is in psychological factors (which undoubtedly play a role in reactivity), then functions like heart rate (HR), which are relatively simple to record and do not require computerization for mea-surement, may be appropriate. If, on the other hand, one is concerned with a physiological issue like the pumping action of the heart, then it is necessary to move to a more technical (i.e., "high-tech") measure like cardiac output, which requires complex instrumentation for pickup and computerization for measurement. Moreover, if the concern is psycho-physiological differentiation, then distinctions that are too crude for phys-iological purposes may be adequate for psychophysiological purposes. For example, as I elaborate, for differentiating between the processes involved in listening to a pair of numbers (encoding) and those involved in the arithmetic task of iteratively subtracting numbers, the (physiolog-ically crude) distinction between the parasympathetic nervous system (PNS) and the sympathetic nervous system (SNS) is sufficient. On the other hand, when attempting to provide a physiological account of cardiac function, the further distinction between β- and α-adrenergic SNS influ-ences must be made because myocardial SNS influences are predomi-nantly β-adrenergic, whereas vascular SNS influences (e.g., on peripheral vasoconstriction) are predominantly α-adrenergic.

The purpose of this brief chapter, as suggested by the title, is to indicate how psychophysiological differentiation can be applied to ques-tions concerning the effects of psychological factors on cardiac reactivity. In particular, I want to focus on the distinction between SNS activation and PNS withdrawal, a distinction that is not clear when one assesses only a single measure like HR because HR, being supraventricular in origin, can be significantly influenced by both branches of the autonomic nervous system. So an HR acceleration induced by some psychological challenge may reflect only PNS withdrawal or may also reflect SNS ac-tivation, with the latter factor being of greater potential relevance to the development of cardiovascular pathology. The PNS–autonomic nervous system distinction can be more clearly made if one uses, in addition to the "mixed" HR measure, another index that is a "purer" measure of predominantly SNS influences.

There is general agreement that such candidate SNS cardiac per-formance measures should be ventricular in origin because the neural PNS connections to the myocardium are minimal. Most psychophysiologists, however, have followed Obrist's (1981) recommendation of attempting to develop contractility-based β-adrenergic SNS candidate indices like the change in carotid pressure over time, pulse transit time, and preejection period. The alternative path is to focus on electrophysiological and cardiographic aspects. Of these, T-wave amplitude (TWA), first proposed for psychophysiology by Matyas and King (1976), has been the candidate SNS index that has received the most attention (e.g., Furedy, 1987). The question of the relative validity of contractility-based measures and cardiographic measures is one that is complex and controversial (e.g., Contrada, 1992; Furedy & Heslegrave, 1983; Furedy, Heselgrave, & Scher, 1992; Furedy & Scher, 1985; Heslegrave & Furedy, 1980, 1983; Obrist, 1981; Schwartz & Weiss, 1983), and I do not elaborate on this question here. What is clear, however, is that, compared with the contractile measures, TWA is more convenient or "low tech" because no additional electrodes to those used for picking up HR are needed and because computerization of record reading, though desirable, is not necessary. The most important scientific aspect of such convenience is that it allows more independent laboratories to check on the replicability of findings, and in any psychophysiological enterprise, the maximization of such cross validation is a consideration of some relevance.

In what follows, I summarize some previously published findings from the University of Toronto laboratory that appear to indicate that joint use of HR and TWA allows psychophysiological differentiation of processes relevant to cardiac reactivity to psychological stress. Then I report on a more recent study that used even less technical methods to assess a form of stress that is becoming increasingly relevant—that which results from user-hostile software in everyday computer applications.

Joint Use of HR and TWA With the Iterative Subtraction Task

The psychological challenge that we have found to be the most useful is an iterative subtraction task in which one number (e.g., 17) has to be repeatedly subtracted from another (e.g., 3,822) for short (usually 20-s) periods or trials at a slow (every 5 s, "easy") or fast (every 2 s, "hard") rate (for details see Heslegrave & Furedy, 1979). This task produces HR accelerations of between approximately 5 and 10 beats per minute and TWA attenuations of between approximately 30–50 mV, with some but not total habituation over trials and more habituation in HR acceleration than in TWA attenuation. Both indices are sensitive to the difficulty manipulation, with HR being more sensitive than TWA. There is also indirect evidence that the difficulty effect is not due to the higher rate of respiration under the hard condition in relation to the easy condition (Furedy & Shulhan, 1986) and that, contrary to one suggestion (Schwartz & Weiss, 1983), electrode placement does not affect the direction of TWA change in this experimental preparation (Furedy, Shulhan, & Scher, 1986). Finally, although the use of TWA in psychophysiological experiments has been rare outside the University of Toronto laboratory, especially in North America (an exception is Cacioppo, Petty, & Morris, 1985), a German laboratory (Rau, 1991) recently used the Toronto iterative subtraction task and has both replicated the main findings (see Rau, 1991, Experiment 3) and provided blockade-based evidence for TWA's validity as an SNS index in this sort of psychophysiological context.

The simplest form of psychophysiological differentiation involves *reactive sensitivity*, for which the candidate index yields a significant difference as a function of some psychological factor or factors. The reactive sensitivity of TWA has been shown to be superior to that of HR when, in terms of reaction to the arithmetic task, the TWA (attenuation) response was significantly ($p < .001$) greater in type A subjects than in type B subjects, whereas the HR (acceleration) response yielded only a nonsignificant trend in the expected direction (Scher, Hartman, Furedy, & Heslegrave, 1986). I agree with Sapira and Oken (1986), who concluded that, compared with cardiological studies that used the full complement of electrode leads and those that produced large-magnitude TWA changes, the Scher et al. (1986) study was indeed merely (low-tech) "scalar microelectrocardiography" and was unsuitable for such cardiological purposes as the assessment of myocardial function. Nevertheless, as Sapira and Oken's editorial conceded, "whatever the mechanism (or mechanisms) involved, the differences found between the two groups of men remain" (p. 157). In psychophysiological terms, given that each group contained only 15 individuals, the between-groups significance level of $p < .001$ reported by Scher et al. is an impressive testimonial to TWA's reactive sensitivity.

Another instance of TWA's greater reactive sensitivity to individual differences than that of HR is the finding by Shulhan, Scher, and Furedy (1986) that the TWA (attenuation) response to the difficult version of the iterative subtraction task was uniquely augmented in low-aerobic-fitness-level subjects. Both these instances of TWA's reactive sensitivity are independent of questions of TWA's status as an SNS index, but it is obvious that the SNS-index interpretation makes good sense of the results, which are consistent with the view that type A and unfit individuals overreact sympathetically when presented with a challenge that is psychological rather than metabolic or physiological. Furthermore, the HR index, being mixed, does not pick up these individual SNS-reactivity differences. It should also be noted that, although the TWA (and HR) changes involved are small and metabolically insignificant, they appear to be related in an orderly way to such physiological differences that underlie the type A versus type B distinction and those that distinguish physiologically fit and unfit.

More important, in my view, for psychophysiological differentiation is *specific sensitivity.* As has been detailed previously (Furedy & Heslegrave, 1984), an index shows specific sensitivity when it reacts to one process but not to a similar but different process. The specific sensitivity concept is contrary to the view, based on the prejudice against negative results (see Furedy, 1978), that an index's sensitivity is determined by the number of significant differences it yields. In this view, because HR produces significant accelerations both during the period of listening to the two numbers to be operated on and during the period of the arithmetic task itself, whereas TWA attenuates only to the task (e.g., Heslegrave & Furedy, 1979), HR would be considered to be more sensitive than TWA. In terms of specific sensitivity, however, such a pattern of results, which have been repeatedly found in subsequent studies (Scher et al., 1986; Shulhan et al., 1986), it is TWA that is the superior measure because it alone differentiates between the two similar but different psychological processes of encoding and then manipulating the arithmetic symbols during the task itself.

So far it may seem as if I have been denigrating the HR measure at the expense of TWA, but I suggest that the most useful information to be gained is from the joint measurement of these two cardiac performance functions. One striking example of such complementary utility is a pattern of results that yields HR acceleration without any TWA change, as occurs when the two numbers are presented during the listening period of the iterative subtraction trial. If one assumes that TWA is a relatively pure SNS index, then one can infer that the listening phase produces predominantly PNS withdrawal effects (vegetative withdrawal?) with little or no SNS excitation (fight-or-flight response?). The joint use of HR with an SNS index, then, can also yield patterns of results in which an inference to parasympathetic effects is possible. Moreover, with such short-duration, phasic responses (e.g., the listening period is only 5 s), use of more tonically oriented parasympathetic indices such as vagal tone is limited. And as Obrist (1981) noted, it is of considerable interest to be able to distinguish between those psychological challenges that result only in PNS withdrawal and those that result in SNS activation as well.

Joint Use of HR and Skin Conductance Level With a User-Hostile Computer Task

In this more recent research program, even less technical methods were used by gathering only minute-by-minute scored HR (obtained from a portable blood pressure arm cuff) and skin conductance level (SCL) in an arrangement that has been published only in abstract form (Vincent, Pelcowitz, Muter, & Furedy, 1990). Twenty-five subjects were presented with two simulated bank-transaction tasks (6-min duration), one user-friendly and the other user-hostile. The friendly–hostile contrast was based on some 16 different polarities. Two such contrasts were that between menu-driven versus command-driven software, and minimal, clear, and polite error messages versus rude and unhelpful error messages. To check whether any differences were due simply to sheer difficulty, easy (forward digit span) and hard (backward digit span) memory tasks were also presented to all subjects.

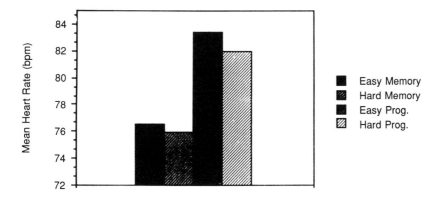

FIGURE 1.   Mean heart rate (beats per minute [bpm]) during the two memory and two computer tasks. (Prog. = progression.)

Figure 1 shows the mean HR data. The only significant effect was one due to task type, $F(1, 24) = 7.05$, $p < .05$. The computer tasks produced an acceleration in relation to the memory tasks, but task difficulty had no effect on HR. We interpret the HR difference between the computer tasks (which require the solving of problems through symbol manipulation) and the memory tasks as reflecting greater PNS (vegetative) withdrawal for the computer tasks. The fact that there were no differences within types of tasks as a function of difficulty suggests that this vegetative withdrawal is an all-or-none effect that occurs when the organism is called on to solve problems.

Figure 2 shows the mean SCL data. Because the SCL distribution (in contrast to the HR distribution) revealed a significant skewness (toward the low-scores end of the distribution), nonparametric (sign and rank tests) were applied to the SCL scores. As suggested by the trends in Figure 2, the hard-computer-task condition was unique in elevating SCL. Thus, a sign test between the hard- and easy-computer-task conditions yielded one tie and a 19/5 split ($p < .05$). In addition, a Friedman nonparametric one-way analysis of variance with four levels of the task factor yielded a significant result, $\chi^2(3, N = 25) = 9.05$, $p < .05$.

Although the underlying physiological mechanism of SCL changes is not fully understood, there is agreement that, at least peripherally, the

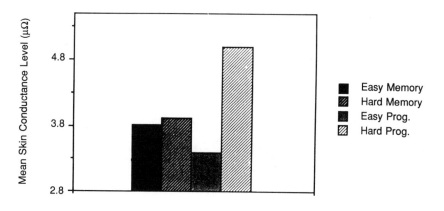

FIGURE 2. Mean skin conductance level during the two memory and two computer tasks. (Prog. = progression.)

dominant neural substrates are SNS related rather than PNS related. Accordingly, the results suggest that interfacing with user-hostile systems produced the increased SNS excitation that typically accompanies human fight-or-flight responses. A more theoretical question raised by the results is the psychological basis of the user-hostile SNS-excitation effect. The two most obvious alternatives are fear and anger. Anecdotal observations suggested that, at least in some subjects, anger rather than fear was operating. A number of subjects showed facial expressions that indicated anger during the user-hostile condition. In addition, 1 subject stated, after one try, that the user-hostile program was impossible and simply stared at the screen for the remainder of the 6-min period. Determining the psychological basis of the obtained effect will require systematic studies that correlate physiological changes with questionnaire-based assessments of emotions like anger and fear. It seems clear that the demonstration of psychophysiological differentiation in this study is only the beginning of the quest for a full account of the influence of psychological factors on reactivity.

References

Cacioppo, J. T., Petty, R. E., & Morris, K. J. (1985). Semantic, evaluative and self-referent processing: Memory, cognitive effort, and somatovisceral activity. *Psychophysiology*, *4*, 371–384.

Contrada, R. J. (1992). On T-wave amplitude utility: Reply to Furedy, Heslegrave, & Scher. *Biological Psychology, 33*, 249–258.

Furedy, J. J. (1978). "Negative results": Abolish the name, but honour the same. In J. P. Sutcliffe (Ed.), *Conceptual analysis and method in psychology* (pp. 169–180). Sydney: Sydney University Press.

Furedy, J. J. (1983). Operational, analogical, and genuine definitions of psychophysiology. *International Journal of Psychophysiology, 1*, 13–19.

Furedy, J. J. (1984). Generalities and specifics in defining psychophysiology: Reply to Stern (1964) and Stern (1984). *International Journal of Psychophysiology, 2*, 2–4.

Furedy, J. J. (1987). Beyond heart-rate in the cardiac psychophysiological assessment of mental effort: The T-wave amplitude component of the electrocardiogram. *Human Factors, 29*, 183–194.

Furedy, J. J., & Heslegrave, R. J. (1983). A consideration of recent criticism of the T-wave amplitude index of myocardial sympathetic activity. *Psychophysiology, 20*, 204–211.

Furedy, J. J., & Heslegrave, R. J. (1984). The relative sensitivities of heart rate and T-wave amplitude to stress: Comments on, and some alternative interpretations of, Pensien et al.'s results. *Biological Psychology, 19*, 55–61.

Furedy, J. J., Heslegrave, R. J., & Scher, H. (1992). T-wave amplitude revisited: Some physiological and psychophysiological considerations. *Biological Psychology, 33*, 241–248.

Furedy, J. J., & Scher, H. (1985). Intuitive and factual approaches in the comparison of contractility vs. repolarization measures of sympathetic myocardial activity. *International Journal of Psychophysiology, 2*, 235–237.

Furedy, J. J., & Shulhan, D. (1986). Effects of respiratory depth and rate on HR and TWA: An indirect assessment of the respiratory confound in cognitive task difficulty manipulations. *Physiology and Behavior, 37*, 515–517.

Furedy, J. J., Shulhan, D., & Scher, H. (1986). Effects of electrode placement on direction of T-wave amplitude changes in psychophysiology studies. *Physiology and Behavior, 36*, 983–986.

Heslegrave, R. J., & Furedy, J. J. (1979). Anticipatory HR deceleration as a function of perceived control and probability of aversive loud noise: A deployment of attention account. *Biological Psychology, 7*, 147–166.

Heslegrave, R. J., & Furedy, J. J. (1980). Carotid dp/dt as a psychophysiological index of sympathetic myocardial effects: Some considerations. *Psychophysiology, 17*, 482–484.

Heslegrave, R. J., & Furedy, J. J. (1983). On the utility of T-wave amplitude: A reply to Schwartz and Weiss (1983). *Psychophysiology, 20*, 702–708.

Matyas, T. A., & King, M. G. (1976). Stable T-wave effects during improvements in heart rate control with biofeedback. *Physiology and Behavior, 16*, 15–20.

Obrist, P. A. (1981). *Cardiovascular psychophysiology: A perspective.* New York: Plenum.

Rau, H. (1991). Responses of T-wave amplitude as a function of activity and passivity tasks and beta adrenergic blockage. *Psychophysiology, 28*, 231–239.

Sapira, J. D., & Oken, D. (1986). The psychobiology of the T-wave as seen by scalar microelectrocardiography. *Psychosomatic Medicine, 48*, 157–158.

Scher, H., Hartman, L., Furedy, J. J., & Heslegrave, R. J. (1986). Electrocardiographic T-wave changes are more pronounced in type A than in type B men during mental work. *Psychosomatic Medicine, 48*, 159–166.

Schwartz, P. J., & Weiss, T. (1983). T-wave amplitude as an index of cardiac sympathetic activity: A misleading concept. *Psychophysiology, 20*, 696–701.

Shulhan, D., Scher, H., & Furedy, J. J. (1986). Phasic cardiac reactivity to psychological stress as a function of aerobic fitness level. *Psychophysiology, 23*, 562–566.

Stern, J. A. (1964). Toward a definition of psychophysiology. *Psychophysiology, 1*, 90–91.

Stern, J. A. (1984). On "unobtrusive psychophysiology"—Fact or fiction? A rejoinder to Furedy (1983). *International Journal of Psychophysiology, 2*, 1–2.

Vincent, A., Pelcowitz, T., Muter, P., & Furedy, J. J. (1990). Psychophysiological measures suggest user-friendly programs produce sympathetic excitation [Abstract]. *Psychophysiology, 27*, S72.

PART FIVE

Assessment of the Research

Cardiovascular Reactivity to Psychological Stress and Disease: Conclusions

Jim Blascovich and Edward S. Katkin

Given a centuries-old backdrop of anecdotal information, the conclusion suggested by the chapters in this book, that psychological stress is related to cardiovascular disease, is hardly surprising. Given the inherent skepticism of modern science and modern medicine, however, this book's confirmation of cardiovascular reactivity as a mediating link between stress and cardiovascular disease is a milestone. Yet, there is much research remaining if not only the multiplicity of psychological influences on cardiovascular reactivity itself but also the likely multiple etiological factors connecting cardiovascular reactivity to cardiovascular disease are to be understood.

In this summary chapter, we highlight the evidence upon which the stress–reactivity–disease model is based. We also go beyond these highlights to several of the key issues raised by the stress–reactivity–disease connection that need further empirical exploration.

Evidence on Stress–Reactivity–Disease Models

To date, many cardiovascular reactivity researchers continue to explore only the stress–reactivity component of stress–reactivity–disease models. These researchers are basically seeking to understand how cardiovascular responses to environmental stressors are mediated and moderated by psychological factors. To their credit, many of these researchers have moved beyond examination of dispositional or personality variables (e.g., type A, hostility) to cognitive (e.g., attitudes, appraisals) and social psychological variables (e.g., social support). The value of stress–reactivity research, however, seems to be based more on loose implications for cardiovascular health than on tests of psychological theory regarding the stress–reactivity link per se. That is, the value of much stress–reactivity research is predicated on an implicit or explicit assumption that cardiovascular reactivity to psychological stress is a cause of cardiovascular disease. Unfortunately, the reactivity–disease link is comparatively much less researched. This is not surprising given considerations of expense, medical expertise, ethics, theoretical sophistication, and methodological obstacles. Nevertheless, there is evidence emerging, at least within the context of the major cardiovascular diseases, that cardiovascular reactivity to psychological stress is a causal factor.

Coronary Heart Disease

Within the context of atherosclerotic disease of the coronary arteries, several investigators have attempted to examine more-or-less directly the reactivity–disease link. Two such direct approaches for testing the validity of the reactivity–disease link are represented in this book: One focuses on the experimental manipulation of psychological stress and the progression of atherosclerotic disease in animals, and the other focuses on the clinical predictive validity of cardiovascular reactivity to psychological stress for coronary heart disease in humans.

Animal Models

The research of Kaplan and colleagues (see Chapter 1) is perhaps the most definitive and direct experimental research extant linking stress, cardiovascular reactivity, and disease. In an impressive series of longitudinal experiments using monkeys (cynomologus macaques), Kaplan and colleagues first demonstrated that manipulation of psychosocial stress was related to the extent of atherosclerosis. Their subsequent experiments demonstrated that frequent sympathoadrenal activation in response to behavioral stimulation is central to the pathophysiological relationship between psychosocial stress and cardiovascular disease.

In Chapter 1, Kaplan makes a case for the relevance of findings obtained from a primate model of cardiovascular disease to such disease in humans. He even suggests that the animal model may be conservative because the number and types of potential psychosocial stressors within the primate environment may actually be much less than those in the human environment. In our judgment, Kaplan's case is a strong one, and his research is pioneering.

Psychophysiological Stress Testing in Humans

If, as Kaplan and colleagues suggest, repeated sympathoadrenally driven cardiovascular reactivity to psychological stress is causally related to coronary heart disease over time and if there are persistent or stable individual differences in the extent of such sympathoadrenal activation, then individual differences in cardiovascular reactivity to psychological stress ought to predict such disease. It would be expected that reactive young adults would be more likely to develop coronary heart disease later, perhaps decades later, than nonreactive young adults. Although many researchers have undoubtedly gathered sophisticated reactivity data from young adults to determine whether such data are predictive of disease longitudinally, the results of most of these studies will not be available until these young adults mature.

Based on the same rationale, however, we would expect reactivity in older adults to be a marker for coronary heart disease because the normal progression of the disease process would have had time to run its pathophysiological course.

As Blascovich and Katkin report (see Chapter 2), over the past 2 decades a handful of researchers have investigated, with mixed but somewhat promising results, the clinical utility of psychological or psychophysiological stress testing for diagnosing coronary artery disease in humans. In a more recent study, Blascovich, Schiffert, and Katkin (1989) compared the relative predictive validity of psychological and exercise stress testing in a diagnostic hospital setting. Measures of cardiovascular reactivity during psychological stress statistically outperformed traditional cardiological measures (e.g., ST segment depression, premature ventricular contractions, pain) as predictors of coronary occlusion as determined by cineangiography performed within a few days of the stress tests. Indeed, these data were strikingly similar to the data reported in Chapter 1, in which a simple threatening stressor evoked individual differences in reactivity that was predictive of the extent of atherosclerotic coronary lesions upon autopsy in Kaplan's macaques (Manuck, Kaplan, & Clarkson, 1983).

Hypertension

The reactivity–disease link has also been investigated within the context of hemodynamic mechanisms. Cardiovascular reactivity has been identified not only as a mediator of the link between psychological stress and coronary heart disease, but it is also significant in the development of hypertension. Like the evidence supporting the etiological role of reactivity in coronary heart disease, support for the etiological role of reactivity in hypertension comes from both animal and human studies.

Animal Models

Again, as is the case with coronary heart disease, the clearest evidence linking stress, reactivity, and hypertension has been obtained using animal models. Saab and Schneiderman (see Chapter 3) review reactivity studies that used rodent models of hypertension. Particularly compelling are the research programs of Henry (e.g., Henry, Stephens, Axelrod, & Santisteban, 1975) and Hallbäck (1975). For example, Hallbäck (1975) has shown that even in the spontaneously hypertensive rat, in which individual animals show cardiovascular reactivity and typically develop essential hypertension by the age of 6 months, the normal cardiovascular pathophysiology can be eliminated by isolating them from social confrontation. The results of these and other studies prompted Saab and Schneiderman to conclude that development of hypertension in rats is facilitated by the interaction of stressful stimulation and cardiovascular reactivity. Furthermore, the cardiovascular reactivity of these animals is apparently central in origin and mediated sympathetically.

Psychophysiological Stress Testing in Humans
Compared with the research on the predictive utility of psychological stress testing for coronary heart disease, the predictive utility of laboratory stress testing for ambulatory blood pressure, including hypertension, has shown less promise despite the existence of sensitive noninvasive measurement techniques and well-defined laboratory stressors. There are a number of reasons, both theoretical and artifactual, for the lack of conclusive evidence to support the predictive utility of laboratory-induced hemodynamic reactivity as a predictor of hypertension. Laboratory researchers are still working to sort out the mixed set of laboratory results, with a particular focus on the ambulatory monitoring of hemodynamic responses, to ascertain the relationship of in vivo reactivity to the pathogenesis of hypertension.

Key Issues

Reactivity–Disease Mechanisms

It is becoming increasingly likely that there are multiple pathophysiological pathways by which cardiovascular reactivity to psychological stress can lead to cardiovascular diseases. Of course, there are causal links among the cardiovascular diseases. For instance, hypertension is a risk factor for coronary heart disease. Furthermore, although it seems clear that cardiovascular reactivity may directly cause certain forms of cardiovascular disease independently of other risk factors, it is less clear whether cardiovascular reactivity to psychological stress necessarily potentiates other risk factors such as hyperlipidemia or sodium retention.

There seems to be agreement among the authors in this book (see especially Chapters 1, 3, 4, and 6) that cardiovascular hyperreactivity can operate via arterial changes—both functional and morphological—to cause pathology. As Kaplan, Manuck, Williams, and Strawn (see Chapter 1) point out, functional arterial problems include vasospasm in the coronary arteries that can trigger ischemic coronary events independent of coronary atherosclerosis. Reactivity has been morphologically related to the narrowing of the arterial lumen in both coronary and peripheral arteries, albeit via different mechanisms. Furthermore, frequent sympathoadrenal responses to stress are hypothesized to increase hemodynamic turbulence, which in turn promotes endothelial injury in the coronary arteries, particularly at points of susceptibility to such turbulence such as arterial branches. Animal data (see Chapter 1) confirm this hypothesis.

As Saab and Schneiderman discuss (see Chapter 3), several proposed mechanisms, most of which converge on the increased vascular resistance, link cardiovascular reactivity to chronic hypertension. For example, Folkow (1978) maintains that frequent peripheral vasoconstriction in response to psychological stress leads to arterial muscle hypertrophy, which thereby decreases the arterial lumen and increases peripheral resistance. This leads to chronic elevations in blood pressure and increased hemodynamic turbulence during reactive episodes, which thereby promotes atherosclerotic lesions. Obrist (1981) suggested that recurrently activated autoregulatory mechanisms that are elicited by metabolically unwarranted overperfusion of tissues with oxygen eventually leads to chronically increased vascular resistance, whereas Julius (1987) emphasized the contribution of central neural factors to such a chronic increase in vascular resistance.

In sum, both functional and morphological mechanisms appear to mediate the influence of cardiovascular reactivity to psychological stress and disease. Interestingly, arterial malfunctions and malformations appear to be implicated in both atherosclerotic and hypertensive problems. The extent of any demonstrated direct causal relationships between cardiovascular reactivity and other cardiovascular diseases such as stroke, peripheral vascular disease, or valve problems for the most part remain to be specified. However, it is likely that such extensions will be made as causal issues regarding coronary artery disease and hypertension become resolved.

Patterns of Reactivity

Complicating the etiological picture still further is the fact that the label *cardiovascular reactivity* itself is superordinate to several basic forms or categories. Several contributors to this book have distinguished two major integrated reactivity patterns: myocardial and vascular. For example, Saab and Schneiderman (see Chapter 3) distinguish between an integrated pattern that is marked by peripheral vasodilation, increases in cardiac output, tachycardia, increased β-adrenergic activity, and decreased vagal tone and a pattern that is marked by peripheral vasoconstriction, bradycardia, increased α-adrenergic activity, and increased vagal tone. Kelsey (see Chapter 6) makes a similar distinction. Anderson, McNeilly, and Myers (see Chapter 4) as well as Manuck, Kamarck, Kasprowicz, and Waldstein (see Chapter 5) suggest that there are specific individual and group associations with myocardial and vascular reactivity. For example, Anderson and colleagues suggest that vascular reactivity is more prominent among African Americans than among European Americans.

It is clear that either a myocardial or a vascular reactivity pattern can create a common hemodynamic environment in which elevated blood pressure occurs. What is less clear, however, are the distinctive implications for cardiovascular disease of each pattern. Exploration of these implications represents a fertile area for research and may extend the pathological domain of cardiovascular reactivity to stress beyond coronary heart disease and hypertension, especially to the domain of peripheral vascular diseases.

Patterns Over Time

Taking into account reactivity changes over the time course of acutely stressful episodes adds another dimension to cardiovascular reactivity pattern identification and may provide a key to defining "benign" versus "malignant" patterns. In addition to directional fractionation of the various responses that make up myocardial and vascular reactivity patterns, these patterns may change in terms of intensity during even a relatively short stressful experience. Kelsey (see Chapter 6) demonstrates that during stressful tasks myocardial reactivity peaks quickly and habituates relatively rapidly, whereas vascular reactivity actually increases. These differences in patterns over time are consistent with the view that vascular reactivity may well be more pathological than myocardial reactivity. For instance, in our laboratory (Tomaka, Blascovich, Kelsey, & Leitten, in press), we found that, although increased myocardial reactivity is associated with greater challenge and less perceived stress, increased vascular reactivity is associated with greater threat and more perceived stress. These data suggest that high myocardial reactivity in the absence of vascular reactivity during active coping may be benign pathophysiologically, whereas the reverse pattern may be malignant.

We can also consider an intriguing possibility regarding changes in cardiovascular reactivity to psychological stress over several decades or even a lifetime. Morphological and functional changes that are associated with cardiovascular disease may invert the usual myocardial or vascular hyperreactivity pattern so that hyporeactivity occurs. For example, cardiac ischemia, hypertrophy, or myopathy may actually reduce myocardial reactivity below some adaptive level during psychological stress. This possibility is discussed by Blascovich and Katkin in Chapter 2, especially as it relates to psychological stress testing for coronary heart disease among older adults.

Dispositional Versus Situational Influences

Throughout the relatively short history of cardiovascular reactivity research, many if not most reactivity investigators have at least implicitly assumed a trait model of cardiovascular reactivity. That is, individual levels of reactivity are seen as robust and stable over time, which thereby allows investigators to assess dispositional levels of reactivity accurately at any point in time using a single laboratory task. Manuck and colleagues (see Chapter 5) question this assumption and argue that stable dispositional levels of reactivity must be assessed via multiple stressors across multiple points in time to eliminate systematic situational and artifactual influences. Applying this strategy, they do indeed demonstrate that there is dispositional stability regarding both the pattern and magnitude of cardiovascular reactivity. Manuck and colleagues, however, also demonstrate situational influences on these patterns and suggest that an interactive model of individual response propensities and evocative situational characteristics is most appropriate for understanding the generation of cardiovascular disease via cardiovascular reactivity to psychological stress. Kaplan and colleagues (see Chapter 1) also suggest that an interactive or dualistic dispositional–situational model may be most appropriate. On the basis of their animal model data, they suggest that environmental characteristics or demands may evoke pathophysiological cardiovascular reactivity even in individuals who are otherwise dispositionally nonreactive.

Heritability

Are the antecedents of the dispositional component of cardiovascular reactivity inherited or acquired? On the nativist side (see discussion in Chapter 3) are those who draw supporting data from the existence of nonhuman hyperreactive species and greater similarities in reactivity in monozygotic twins than in dyzygotic twins. Family history data, although not conclusive, also are consistent with the nativist view.

On the environmentalist side are those who draw support from data on shared situational effects. For example, Anderson and colleagues (see Chapter 4) convincingly argue that apparent racial effects in hypertension are most likely due to relatively high exposure to chronic or recurring social and environmental stressors among African Americans rather than to genetic factors. A similar rationale can be applied to interfamilial differences in cardiovascular reactivity. As is often the case with nativist–empiricist controversies, unnecessarily polarized positions emerge from the controversy. Regarding individual differences in cardiovascular reactivity to psychological stress, it is likely that some combination or interaction of biological–genetic and contextual influences is necessary for a full explanation of the variability among individuals.

Assessment of Cardiovascular Reactivity

It is quite clear from the contributions to this book that further advances in understanding stress–reactivity–disease models, especially those based putatively on morphological changes such as coronary artery disease and hypertension, are dependent on the ability of investigators to assess patterns of cardiovascular reactivity to psychological stress over time. As just discussed, there appear to be critical differences in the implications of myocardial and vascular reactivity for disease. Assessment using multiple measures is especially important if we are to distinguish and disentangle myocardial reactivity, which peaks relatively quickly and habituates relatively rapidly, from vascular reactivity, which peaks relatively slowly and may actually increase rather than habituate within the time frame of most laboratory stress tasks (see Chapter 6). Furthermore, it is not clear that distinguishing between patterns of myocardial and vascular patterns of reactivity is sufficient to understand the stress–reactivity–disease relationship if the pathology is due to stress-driven functional changes such as vasospasm or abnormal ventricular wall fluctuations.

Although it is probably true that sufficient information can be gleaned about sympathetically driven cardiac reactivity due to psychological stress from a minimal set of "low-tech" measures such as heart rate and T-wave amplitude as Furedy describes (see Chapter 9), the utility of this approach is limited primarily to understanding the psychological stress–cardiac reactivity component of the stress–reactivity–disease model. This is not to understate the considerable improvement and increases in cost efficiency such a strategy would represent for much stress–reactivity research (Blascovich & Kelsey, 1990); however, low-tech approaches are unlikely to provide the sophisticated pattern assessment demanded for an understanding of the necessary and sufficient conditions under which cardiovascular reactivity to psychological stress results in disease.

Fortunately, sophisticated cardiovascular assessment techniques have been developed and used more widely over the past decade or so. These technologies allow researchers to discern more complicated cardiovascular reactivity patterns that are associated with psychological stress on the one hand and to test hypotheses regarding various disease mechanisms linking cardiovascular reactivity with disease on the other hand. As Sherwood describes (see Chapter 7), impedance cardiography has become the state-of-the-art assessment technique among psychophysiologists for noninvasively determining both inotropic and chronotropic indices of myocardial reactivity. Furthermore, the marriage of impedance cardiographic technology with sophisticated continuous on-line blood pressure assessment technology makes possible concurrent assessment of important vascular reactivity measures such as total peripheral resistance. Miniaturizing impedance and blood pressure equipment will also allow for cardiovascular reactivity measurements in the field.

As Kayden and Burns point out (see Chapter 8), left ventricular dysfunction can be related to myocardial ischemia in the absence of coronary artery disease. They and others (see Kamarck & Jennings, 1991) suggest that left ventricular dysfunction may be causally related to episodes of psychological stress even in the absence of heightened myocardial or vascular reactivity. Thus, even state-of-the-art technology for assessing patterns of reactivity such as impedance cardiography and continuous on-line blood pressure measurement does not necessarily provide all the tools to evaluate stress–reactivity–disease models, particularly if the pathological role of reactivity is transient and functional. Kayden and Burns demonstrate (see Chapter 8) that an ambulatory left ventricular function monitoring device based on principles of radionuclide ventriculography can provide assessment of ventricular function via several continuous measures during psychological stress. Furthermore, although the necessary equipment is obtrusive, it is noninvasive and can be used in both laboratory and field settings.

It is likely that application of other as yet unspecified physiological assessment technologies will become part of the reactivity researcher's toolbox as the need for particular technologies are described and justified theoretically. It would not be surprising to see increased use of such techniques as oxygen consumption, echocardiographic, and positron emission tomography technologies for cardiovascular reactivity research as the need arises and as investigators become proficient in their use.

Summary

In the preface to this book, we posed a number of questions regarding cardiovascular reactivity to psychological stress and cardiovascular disease. The first set of questions concerned the concept of cardiovascular reactivity itself. It is now clear that this concept is best viewed as a superordinate one referring to multiple distinguishable patterns of physiological responses during the experience of psychological stress, including not only hyperreactive patterns but hyporeactive patterns as well.

Furthermore, some but not all of these patterns seem clearly predictive of or related to the pathophysiology of cardiovascular disease.

We also questioned the ecological validity of laboratory assessments of cardiovascular reactivity and inquired whether there was adequate technological sophistication to allow reliable measurement of reactivity in the field. The question of ecological validity remains, particularly with regard to hemodynamic reactivity measurements. However, we can also say that the technology for in vivo field studies is developing quickly, and within a few years, there should be some answers to the ecological validity question.

Questions about pathophysiological mechanisms mediating the reactivity–disease component of stress–reactivity–disease models were also raised. The contributions to this book suggest multiple pathophysiological vectors by which cardiovascular reactivity to psychological stress can operate to induce disease. Primary among these appears to be vascularly mediated hemodynamic responses facilitating the development of both hypertension and coronary artery disease independent of other traditional risk factors. In addition, functional abnormalities may also account for the relationship between cardiovascular reactivity to psychological stress and ischemia-related pathologies. We must point out, however, that the domain of cardiovascular diseases is large and the role of psychological stress and reactivity in regard to the major cardiovascular diseases of hypertension and coronary heart disease may represent only the tip of the iceberg.

We also asked about the trait–reactivity–disease relationship. Although it is clear that there is a degree of individual stability in cardiovascular reactivity to psychological stress both situationally and temporally, this stability by no means suggests that only "hyperreactive" individuals are at risk for disease. Indeed, it is also clear that situational influences can create hyperreactivity independently of any dispositional tendency. Not surprisingly, both nature and nurture can contribute to malignant cardiovascular reactivity.

In conclusion, we must note that this book, like similar books that have preceded it, is really a progress report. The issue of the relationships among cardiovascular reactivity, psychological stress, and disease has grown in importance as seminal findings grew into initial and then more focused theories and as these theories and technologies opened new opportunities for research. Cardiovascular reactivity to psychological stress cannot be ignored if we want to improve our fundamental understanding of the etiology of cardiovascular disease. On the other hand, until we can explain more fully the conditions under which reactivity is malignant and until we can delineate more fully the pathophysiological mechanisms linking it to disease, this area of research will not convince clinicians that we may be able to provide them with significant diagnostic and treatment applications.

References

Blascovich, J., & Kelsey, R. M. (1990). Using cardiovascular and electrodermal measures of arousal in social psychological research. *Review of Personality and Social Psychology, 11*, 45–73.

Blascovich, J., Schiffert, J. H., & Katkin, E. H. (1989). A comparison of exercise and psychophysiological stress testing for coronary disease [Abstract]. *Psychophysiology, 26*, 57.

Folkow, B. (1978). Cardiovascular structural adaptation: Its role in the initiation and maintenance of primary hypertension. *Clinical Science and Molecular Medicine, 55*, 3s–22s.

Hallbäck, M. (1975). Consequence of social isolation on blood pressure, cardiovascular reactivity and design in spontaneously hypertensive rats. *Acta Physiological Scandinavica, 90*, 455–465.

Henry, J. P., Stephens, P. M., Axelrod, J., & Santisteban, G. A. (1975). A model of psychosocial hypertension showing reversibility and progression of cardiovascular complications. *Circulation Research, 36*, 156–164.

Julius, S. (1987). Hemodynamic, pharmacologic and epidemiologic evidence for behavioral factors in human hypertension. In S. Julius & D. R. Bassett (Eds.), *Handbook of hypertension: Vol. 9. Behavioral factors in hypertension* (pp. 59–74). Amsterdam: Elsevier Science.

Kamarck, T. W., & Jennings, J. R. (1991). Biobehavioral factors in sudden cardiac death. *Psychological Bulletin, 109*, 42–75.

Manuck, S. B., Kaplan, J. R., & Clarkson, T. B. (1983). Behaviorally-induced heart rate reactivity and atherosclerosis in cynomolgus monkeys. *Psychosomatic Medicine, 45*, 95–108.

Obrist, P. A. (1981). *Cardiovascular psychophysiology: A perspective*. New York: Plenum.

Tomaka, J., Blascovich, J., Kelsey, R. M., & Leitten, C. (in press). Subjective, physiological and behavioral effects of threat and challenge appraisals. *Journal of Personality and Social Psychology.*

Index

About the Editors

Jim Blascovich is a former director of the Center for the Study of Behavioral and Social Aspects of Health at the State University of New York at Buffalo and an associate professor of psychology there. He received his PhD in social psychology from the University of Nevada, Reno, in 1972. His research interests focus on the social psychophysiology of arousal and its regulation. He has been active in professional affairs, having served on the committee that drafted *The Human Capital Initiative*. He is currently executive officer of the Society for Personality and Social Psychology (Division 8 of the American Psychological Association).

Edward S. Katkin is a professor of psychology at the State University of New York at Stony Brook. He received his PhD in clinical psychology from Duke University in 1963. His research interests focus on the psychophysiology of emotion and on psychological factors in physical disorders. He has published extensively in the areas of psychophysiology and behavioral medicine. Dr. Katkin is a past president of the Society for Psychophysiological Research, a fellow of the American Psychological Association, and a charter fellow of the American Psychological Society.